Geography of Discrimination

About the Author

Dr. Pragya Tiwari Gupta has earned her M. Phil and Ph.D. from the Centre of Regional Development Studies, Jawaharlal Nehru University, New Delhi. Currently she is working as Associate Professor in the Sharda University, Greater NOIDA. Before joining the university, she was in Ethiopia and taught in Ethiopian Civil Services University, Addis Ababa. She also taught in the International Institute of Health Management Research, Delhi (IIHMR), Delhi L.R. Institute, Solan and Lovely Professional University, Jullandhar.

Besides teaching she has also accumulated rich experience in the research organisations. To briefly specify, she worked at different capacities in the National University of Education Planning and Administration (NUEPA), New Delhi, National Institute of Urban Affairs (NIUA), New Delhi and several international organisations (UNDP, MII, World bank etc).

She has published several quality papers on public health, urbanization, labour issues and other development aspects in indexed journals and has executed some important project works.

Her main areas of research interest are development concerns, gender research and equity, environment and health, urban health, urbanisation.

She has been invited speaker at famous institutes and universities and a member of International Economic Health Association, Health Systems Global, Indian Association of Health and social Sciences and National Geographers Association of India.

Geography of Discrimination

Caste in the Urban Labour Market

Pragya Tiwari Gupta

CONCEPT PUBLISHING COMPANY PVT. LTD.
NEW DELHI-110059

ISBN-13: 978-93-5439-022-7

First Published 2021

Published and Printed by

Concept Publishing Company Pvt. Ltd.
A/15-16, Commercial Block, Mohan Garden,
New Delhi-110059 (INDIA)
T: 91 11 41101460, 91 11 25351460, 91 11 25351794
E: publishing@conceptpub.com, *W*: www.conceptpub.com

Cataloging in Publication Data--Courtesy: D.K. Agencies (P) Ltd. <docinfo@dkagencies.com>

Gupta, Pragya Tiwari, author.
Geography of discrimination : caste in the urban labour market / Pragya Tiwari Gupta.
pages cm
Includes bibliographical references and index.
ISBN 9789354390227

1. Labor market--India--Kānpur. 2. Labor market--India--Ghāziabād. 3. Occupational mobility--India--Kānpur. 4. Occupational mobility--India--Ghāziabād. 5. Discrimination in employment--India--Kānpur. 6. Discrimination in employment--India--Ghāziabād. 7. Caste-based discrimination--India--Kānpur. 8. Caste-based discrimination--India--Ghāziabād. I. Title.

LCC HD5820.K36G87 2021 | DDC 331.1209542 23

Preface

Development challenges in India are identified on the basis of socio-economic, spatial needs, however, behavioural challenges are hardly given adequate attention to make development as a mass movement. Society has become even more complex demographically and culturally due to the modern influencers like internet, modern methods of education, and globalization impact. Development which was defined by the Western parameters has been questioned for being too normative while no such standard exists which can explain development. This is what motivated me to search the problem behind the vertical development and felt that Indian social system needs to be once again researched, assessed for better transformative development efforts.

Initially, when finalising my doctoral dissertation topic, I was focusing on the aspects of inequity which later initiated me to the discrimination research work. The concept of discrimination became a principal research objective of my research work after comprehending how detrimental it could be for overall socio-economic upliftment. Discrimination is a very intrigue human behaviour which plays a major but covert role in deciding the choices of the people for miscellaneous network such as work engagement, social or political platforms. Caste system which over a time became exclusionary and discriminatory had also been a potent carrier of unequal development. Discrimination exists in every society in different forms like preferences, prejudice, selection etc. and each society had faced the phenomena of discrimination high or low. Caste as a social institution has acted as an impediment in holistic development and has led to disharmony, biases, and an unproductive competitiveness in the society. The research work hence along with the equity, considered discrimination as an explanatory tool for this unequal growth of Hindu social groups, even after several decades of positive discrimination and welfare policies.

Egalitarian ideals and equality of treatment is the major aim of a transformative developing society and Geography contributes to the spatial interpretation and it gives a unique dimension to understand the behavioural aspects as well. Geography promises from the theoretical order to pragmatic version of social justice. Social welfare functions and large scale attitudinal surveys can reveal the underlying design which needs to be examined for formative actions. So far development agenda ought to be explained at least to achieve more rational, acceptable, and equitable goals of the society. Rural India has been researched on various caste issues, but caste has not been weighed much for research theme in urban areas. Kanpur is one of the oldest industrial town, manufacturing and trade centre connecting with farther east region of India while Ghaziabad which has influence of Capital of India has very recently became a part of Megalopolis. This work, therefore, become an important contributor in Geographical studies which drew inspiration from behavioural, comparative temporal study in geography. This book has focused on discriminatory attitude of the people which is a huge burden and puts hinderance for the overall development of the society and how spatial differences can be reduced or removed for a welfare society and reduce caste-based discrimination. This book has systematically encapsulated geographical inferences if it was interspersed with the experience of inequity and discrimination and captures the journey of an individual from parental rearing to the world of work where he goes through several phases of finding work. Current discussion and debate on caste prejudices, atrocities against lower caste are sometimes fail to report the error of data and narratives of caste are been seen from the centric concept of lower *versus* upper, however, the turmoil and new rise of *rich* versus *poor* within the lower or upper layer of caste hierarchy are not given enough coverage. Though this is beyond the scope of this book, however, field experience told the tale of inner power struggle within the caste groups also. The welfare policy must target such sentiments to educate people from other social groups to be called a socially aware, just and developed nation.

This research work critically analyses various thoughts on equity and discrimination and delve on the various sources of discrimination. The book not only see the outcome of the urban market but also tries to seek the processual information related to the recruitment or employability of labour in the market. The research work deeply engages in the discussion on development while the politics also becomes one of the game changers in the caste identity. My Doctoral dissertation, which I carried out with a lot of passion and commitment became my academic pursuit to publish it to the social science researchers and other scholars.

New Delhi
October 2020

Pragya Tiwari Gupta

Acknowledgements

This book, which is the outcome of doctoral dissertation, is able to see the light of the day after creating some of the memorable milestones in my life. I begin with thanking my supervisor, Dr. Sachidanand Sinha, who exhibited uninhibited stamina with my nagging pursuance to work on the topic and formulate the whole concept of this thesis. No word can express my thankfulness to Prof. S.K. Thorat for giving me crucial support at every moment and evocative advices in the first phase of this study. I extend my thanks to Prof. Butola, Prof. Ravi Srivastava, Prof. Kulkarni, Prof. Atiya Habib Kidwai and Prof. R.K. Sharma for their constant words of support and suggestion for improvement.

My due thanks to the library staff at Ratan Tata Memorial Library, Delhi University and V.V. Giri National Labour Institute, the National Institute of Educational Planning and Administration, National Institute of Public Finance Policy and JNU, some of the very rich source of literature on my subject. The literature in these libraries was indeed inevitable for my work. My appreciation is reserved for Sheesh ma'am, Varghese ji for providing me very crucial help at the computer centre and letting me work independently for a few months.

I am also grateful to the Municipal Corporation of Kanpur and Ghaziabad and also to the Slum and Urban Development Authority of Kanpur and Ghaziabad for providing me essential knowledge about the city and allowing me to conduct survey in their knowledge.

My special thanks are reserved for the Dixit family who not only took utmost care, but also accepted me as one of the family members. I have exhaustive list of friends yet Preeti, Lokesh, Sohel, Kalyan, Partho, Ipshita, Waqar were my constant jovial and inspiring escorts.

My mother, whose strength and courage are unmatched, has been my sole guiding personality to bring this work to a larger readership. I am also very thankful to my sisters for cheering me up to get this work published, simultaneously sharing my thoughts, and giving stimulating ideas. I thank my mother-in-law who always supported and helped me. I cannot ably thank my husband for being so patient and supportive. My two angels made my time so enjoyable and I feel indebted to them for ignoring sometimes when they needed me the most. I profusely thank Mr. R.P. Upadhyaya, my benefactor for reassuring me to see that this work should be published.

I thank Concept Publishing Company Pvt. Ltd. also for accepting the book proposal and agreeing to publish this work without any delay.

October 2020 **Pragya Tiwari Gupta**

Contents

1
Introduction

The traditional social order based on the institution of caste has nurtured bias and discrimination against lower caste groups resulting in inequalities on socio-economic and political fronts. Each caste group has certain ascriptive roles to follow according to the caste system. These ascriptive roles combine commensality, endogamy and hereditary occupations as building blocks of caste order. Hereditary occupation is assumed as one of the main reasons behind the origin of the caste system[1]. The caste structure forced various functional rigidities in the past like means of livelihood, ritual performances and residential decisions etc. Caste as an institution is a select example of social exclusion leading to economic deprivation and social seclusion. Berrmann[2] says that the caste system is economically interdependent and occupationally specialized.

Since the caste system itself revolves around inequality and division of labour it not only exacerbates inequality amongst various social groups but also hinders mobility across the caste hierarchy and provides fertile ground for inequality and discrimination. On the premise of inequality in social system due to caste imposed sanctions this study plans to explore the caste discrimination as a barrier in fair treatment to the people and development. The point that the caste affiliations of a person affects opinion in the social and economic circle about his/her efficiency, education, occupation, life style and other day-to-day human behaviour can be the root cause of the paralyzed development efforts. This study tries to examine the relationship between caste background or identity and employment, occupation and earning differentials in the same order, drawing upon the field based information in urban setting.

1.2 Conceptual Framework

To explain discrimination Becker[3] says "One individual is said to discriminate against (or in favour of) another if his behaviour towards the latter is not motivated by an objective consideration of fact." The most important and noticeable in the given definition is objective consideration motivates a person to behave in certain way especially for non-pecuniary advantage in Western society. But the case of such discrimination may change Indian scenario.

Discrimination can be experienced where one group enjoys preference over the other group or an individual over that of another by virtue of his/her association with a particular social group. Therefore, one amongst many social malaises of the caste system is the discrimination in the day-to-day behaviour which has serious repercussions in the society. It becomes even more important while employing people in a society where people are already segregated on various socio-economic grounds. One of such factors is caste which this study has investigated.

Mal-development and unequal growth has baffled academia and policy-makers equally. It is when covering the aspects of inequity the concept of discrimination was discovered that human behaviour has a major role to play to bring equality or discard in equality to achieve a certain growth level. Discrimination as a concept has many *avatars* like prejudice, preference etc., these concepts differ in their *modus operandi* but show the same effect on society. This study hypothesizes that the caste affiliation of a person affects opinion in the social and economic circle about his efficiency, education, occupation, life style and other day-to-day human behaviour. Literature survey and the first phase (1999) of survey of this study indicates that there is caste discrimination not only in rural India but also in urban areas though the degree and typology[4] may vary from place to place.

And hence concept of discrimination has been framed on the one side by behavioural expressions and on the other the consequences of such attitudinal summation where 'lack of' (or good) accessibility to quality of life enhancement opportunities at the transition stage may give worse (or better) off outcome (Fig. 1.1).

This apparently simple behavioural attitude leads to serious repercussions in the market and thus workers in the lower segment of the market remain trapped in the vicious circle of poverty 'if not intervened' (positive discrimination). The process of education

Fig. 1.1: Conceptual framework of the study

(technical and general), recruitment and livelihood are the three main sub-sets of the enquiry of socio-cultural network in an urban labour market as depicted in Fig. 1.1 also. This study, therefore, attempts to understand how the rational thinking is eclipsed by the social prejudices and hinder the general functioning of a society and how it pushes back the overall development of a region.

1.3 Statement of the Problem

The caste system has played a role of socio-economic selector for occupations in the Indian society for centuries. Though the academia has also agreed on that the caste system is an inequitable system from several angles and has been studied exhaustively on all counts yet discrimination on the basis of caste background is one factor, which has remained away from the mainstream queries in caste studies.

The present study thus aims to explore this perspective which has affected not only the sociological outcome but also economic structure in the Indian urban labour market. Following dimensions are important to investigate discrimination in urban conditions.

1.3.1 Urbanization and Caste: a positive side—The assumption that urbanization has eliminated or reduced the barrier of caste, has led many academic enquiries in the field of urbanization and caste structure[5]. In cities people belonging to different caste hierarchies work together regardless of others social background. In an optimistic revelation Gupta[6] writes, "If there is a single factor that has contributed to the breakdown of the caste system, it is urbanization. Urbanization is developing at a fantastic rate in India." Thus, it can be assumed that after a gap of some years and accelerated rate of urbanization, caste may further lose its stronghold on Indian society.

1.3.2 A different story: negative side: The studies mentioned earlier[7] too indicated that there is still a long way to reach to a casteless society even in urban India. Two things emerge from the caste studies, first the influence of urbanization has made remarkable difference in the nature and type of discrimination experienced in urban areas from rural areas and second is that the caste system which has shown some notable shifts from the stringent rules to the flexible attitude in the recent past especially in urban India nevertheless the caste and caste relations in labour market could be interpreted in more than one way. Therefore, caste factors are no less significant in an Indian urban socio-economic structure than rural India[8].

It can be another reason why people (often lower caste people) migrate from rural areas to the urban places. Caste recycles and indirectly influences the urban India, where workers from rural India are generally absorbed in unorganised sector. Bhatt[9] finds in his study that government and non-government both face uphill task to break the nexus between the rural elite and landlords. Such nexus pushes marginalized people to migrate to urban area where they live in anonymity. These migrants are the people who constitute a major portion of the workers in informal sector of the urban India[10]. It is assumed that floating labour[11] (informal market) belonging to any caste identity gets position of advantage or disadvantage according to caste affiliation; for instance a potential worker because of his/her low caste background may not find a respectable job in market despite possessing required qualification[12].

Thus, this study focuses on both discrimination and inequality (cause and effect; as shown in the Fig. 1.1) which may have brought differences in occupations and cumulated earnings. After capturing the gist of discrimination as defined by Backer this study also considers discrimination as an aspect where same qualifications have given different output in terms of occupation and earning.

1.3.3 Stages of Discrimination: This study after reviewing the literature finds that discrimination can be identified in stages—(a) pre-market discrimination, (b) discrimination during hiatus between pre-market and labour market entry point, and (c) market discrimination.

- ***Pre-Market Discrimination*** can be measured by generating variables on parental education, land holding size in case of agriculturist, sources of income, size of the family, and education of the worker.

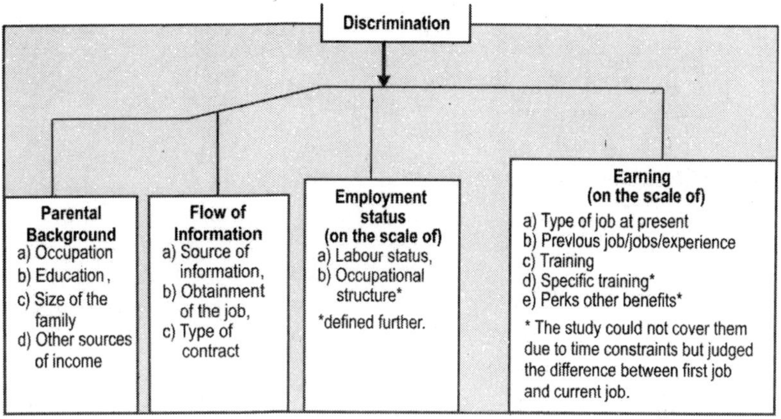

Fig. 1.2: Identified Stages of Discrimination in the study

- The variables during ***hiatus or waiting period*** are duration of unemployment and cost of sustainability (rental, loan from parents or relatives) and for the migrated respondent's age at migration, purpose of migration, occupation at migration, duration of waiting period, and their first job are the important variables to extract information on discrimination.
- ***Market Discrimination*** becomes crucial to interpret discrimination stages. Hence, recruitment process which means how a worker gets the information of the job, what are the skill requirements, exposure to on the job training, specific job training, information system, emotional and physical health[13]. Nature of job and scope of mobility are the central themes to find out discrimination.

1.4 Objectives

1.4.1 Main Objective

The main objective is to find out the discrimination and inequity in urban labour market in the context of Hindu social categories in two geographical spaces.

1.4.2 Sub-objectives

(i) On the basis of the main objective the study proposes to examine the nature of existing inequality in the structure of occupation and earning among various caste groups.

(ii) to examine whether such inequality is the result of discrimination.

1.4.3 Operational Steps to Achieve Objectives

To decide on the operational aspects of the first sub-objective the study examines primarily inequality in employment pattern. The employment pattern is studied in two ways—first by seeing occupational structure and second by the labour status. To reach to the next step of sub-objective the study digs into whether caste gets weightage or preference in the labour market.

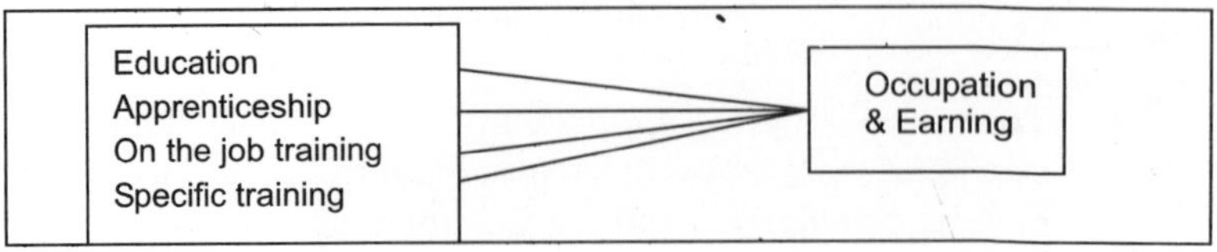

Fig. 1.3: Human Capital and Its Influence on Occupation and Earning

The study also wants to know the acquired Human capital[14] investment in a workers' job profile. Education, apprenticeship, on the job training, specific training, are the variables which are considered to be the main human capital investments and hence on one side this study separated equal attainment according to these variables and on the other side occupation, different earning.

This objective is difficult to judge operationally in the real life situation as not only the Indian labour market has changed drastically due to globalization but also due to changes in labour market policies and other developmental activities resulting in multifarious employment opportunities in the market at local level. Further variations in acquired human capital also add differences in the final outcome in the labour market. This again can complicate the situation when one considers personal nature, other physical endowment, environmental advantages and preference for jobs. All these acquired and personal components make it extremely difficult to arrange labour market in one symmetrical way.

(a) This study, therefore, further evaluates discrimination by seeing—
(i) waiting period, (ii) type of first job, (iii) job at present, (iv) on the job training, perks, and (v) any other benefits which a worker thinks important in his/her job. Besides these facets recruitment process (information of the job, obtainment of the job, type of contract and skill requirements) is very pertinent from the angle of discrimination in a workers' life. How a worker has come to know about the job; if he has attained job because of his qualifications or a selection procedure or simply by having acquaintance with the employer. Type of contract again covers vulnerability of a worker.

(b) Whether earning difference shows any correspondence with traditional caste occupation?
Earning is cross-examined by considering education level and type of job. Each caste group is further cross-examined by the level of education, occupation and earning differences.

(c) Lastly, the study proposes to analyse the parental occupation and the occupation of the respondents.

1.5 Research Questions

The present study has following research questions to achieve objectives:

1. What is the degree of association between the nature of job and caste identity.[15] (On the basis of working area, role of job, training, permanency, job duration, and accessibility to information)?
2. Does the occupational structure correspond to caste hierarchies? If yes, what is the degree of correspondence and what are the factors which govern lack of correspondence?
3. Do people enquire about caste background of potential employee before recruiting?
4. Do education helps in changing the values and attitude of the people?
5. How far the caste identity influences opinion about skill, efficiency and productivity?[16]
6. Do people belonging to lower caste feel if they were presented with better opportunity, they could have had better social standing?[17]

7. Do family background such as parents' working status, and their education affects one's present occupation. In other words do parental background influence or guide a person to follow more or less the same trade, which his/her parents pursued.

1.6 Study Area

This study tries to examine the relationship between caste backgrounds or identity and its economic outcome by analysing the field-based information from two different geographical spaces, i.e. Kanpur and Ghaziabad. Keeping in mind the objectives of the study it is decided to select cities where the caste factor is dominant since its historical past and also where caste may have diffused bearing in fast growing industries. These two cities can significantly show the difference in the caste factors in industrial economy because *Kanpur City*—

(1) is an old industrial town where social values are still traditional.
(2) has attracted short distance migrant population.[18]

On the other side *Ghaziabad*,

(1) where industrial development have been phenomenal in past three decades.
(2) has absorbed long distance migrant population.
(3) and being a satellite town of Delhi, it has shown change in respect of work culture and social values to a fairly good extent.

The study, therefore, has selected Kanpur an old industrial town and new modern industrial town Ghaziabad which is in the proximity of one thriving metropolis also. Selection of these two districts is, therefore, to know the geographical differences or similarities in the processes of discrimination and inequity if exist. To further emphasize the study intends to extract the factors which may be responsible to reinforce or reduce the impact on the discrimination and inequity.

1.6.1 Kanpur City[19]

Kanpur is the largest industrial town by its population strength, occupying the top position amongst the cities in the state since 1941.

The city claims to be one of the historical cities grown over a period of time. Its industrial legacy is from the British period and the present existence is an outcome of modern period (Table 1.1)

The district of Kanpur City lies in the Central region of Uttar Pradesh, within Allahabad Division. It is bounded on the north by the districts of Kanpur Dehat and Unnao, on the south by the districts of Fatehpur and Kanpur Dehat. The total area of this district is 1040 sq. kms.

Known as the 'Manchester of Northern India', is a city of mills and factories. The industrial development of Kanpur City started when East India Company used the infrastructure created by Subedar Almas Khan who camped there for security reasons for a very long stretch of time. With the stationing of first the army by Muslim rulers and then by East India Company led to the demand of merchandise and gave much boost to the prospect of trade in the town. In the early days of industries, country cloth, cotton print, and brass vessels were made. Later on cotton ginning, pressing, tanning, shoe making began with indigenous workmen taking up cotton, wool weaving and manufacturing cheap cutlery after the European style. The first cotton and woollen mill, which started production, was Elgin and Cawnpore Wool Mill (Lal Imli). Most of these factories have stopped production in late 1980s, with only a few mills like J.K. Jute Mill producing gunny bags and other ancillary products at a marginal scale.

Table 1.2 indicates that in all areas of Kanpur district sex ratio is negative. In workers category cultivators and agriculture labours are not present except Kanpur Municipal board area. Non-Household Manufacturing workers are found in satisfactory percentage in all areas except North Railway Colony and Chakeri C.T. Kanpur Municipal area and Kanpur Cantonment area have good percentage of workers in trade and commerce activities.

As per census of 2001, Kanpur total population is 2,551,337 as compared to the 1,874,409 people registered in 1991. It may be observed that the average annual growth in population has increased to 3.5 per cent during the period 1991-2001 from the average annual growth rate of 2.6 per cent in the previous decade (1981-91).

1.6.2 Ghaziabad

Ghaziabad is a satellite town of Delhi Metropolitan area and one of

Table 1.1: Population and Workers Distribution in Kanpur Urban Agglomeration: 1991

Indicator / Ward	Kanpur M.B.	Kanpur Cant.	Armapur Estate	N. Railway Colony	Chakeri C.T.	Kanpur City
Total pop.	1874409	95021	20598	25184	9666	2024878
Male % to to. Pop.	55.0	56.0	55.0	57.0	57.0	55.0
Female% to the to. Pop.	45.0	44.0	45.0	43.0	43.0	45.0
Scheduled Caste %	11.0	14.0	18.0	25.0	3.0	11.0
Literate to the to. Pop.	62.0	60.0	68.0	60.0	83.0	62.0
Main worker to the to. Pop.	26.0	29.0	25.0	28.0	34.0	26.0
Cultivator % to M.W.	2.0	1.0	-	-	-	2.0
Agri.lab. % to M.W.	2.0	.1	.06	-	-	1.0
Livestock, fishery etc. % to M.W.	1.06	1.04	.1	.07	-	1.0
Mining and Quarrying, % to M.W.	.02	.01	-	-	-	0.1
H.H. Manufacturing % to M.W.	.7	.03	.06	.04	-	1.0
Non H.H. Manufacturing % to M.W.	28.25	23.23	73.3	5.17	.31	28.0
Construction % to M.W.	2.02	2.4	1.6	.74	.03	2.0
Trade and Commerce % to M.W.	28.7	19.8	4.3	7.4	-	27.0
Transport, Storage and Communication % to M.W.	.07	6.8	1.4	73	-	7.0
Other Services % to M.W.	26.7	45.07	19.3	13.54	99.6	31.0

(Conted.)

(Conted.)

2001 No. of HH	Total Pop	Male	Female	Schedule Caste	P_LIT	M_LIT	F_LIT
439619	2551337	1374121	1177216	282368	1758807	997001	761806
%		53.85886	46.14114	11.06745		56.68621	43.31379
TOT_WORK All	Total. W. Male	Total W. Female	Main Workers	Main Culti	Main Ag.L	Household	Main Other
706361	637870	68491	639495	6556	4459	22962	605518
%	90.30	10.74	90.53	1.03	0.7	3.59	94.6869

Source: Census, 1991 and 2001. Kanpur Distt.

Table 1.2: Population Change in Kanpur City

Year	*Total Population*	*Decadal Change*	*Decadal Growth Rate (%)*
1951	638,734	—	—
1961	883,815	245,081	38.36
1971	1,158,321	274,506	31.05
1981	1,481,789	323,468	27.92
1991	1,874,409	392,620	26.49
2001	2,551,337	657,729	35.08

Source: Primary Census Abstract, Part II-B, Census of India, 1991, Primary Census Abstract, Series 10, Volume 1, Census of India, 2001.

the main small-scale industrial hubs. The district of Ghaziabad lies in the doab of two famous rivers Ganga and Yamuna. In the north and south, the district boundary extends to the boundaries of Meerut and Bulandshahar districts respectively.

Historically Ghaziabad is a part of the track of Vedic Aryan establishment. It was a first activity centre of Vedic culture. The district of Ghaziabad came into existence on 14th November, 1976. It was carved out of the old undivided districts of Meerut and Bulandshahr. The district at present comprises 5 tehsils and 10 Community Development Blocks with 24 towns and 744 villages (Table 1.3).

Close proximity to the Delhi Metropolitan Area has provided a solid foundation to the industrial development in Ghaziabad. The industrial establishments are concentrated in and around Ghaziabad town, which include the industrial areas of Meerut road, Bulandshahar road, Mohannagar, Sahibabad, and G.T. Road extending up to Delhi border. The industrial towns included in the belt are Modinagar, Pilakhua, Hapur and Narendra Nagar.

There are 14,160 small scale industries and 145 medium and heavy industries employing 73,130 and 31,200 people respectively. Some of the well known industrial names are Ajanta Tubes Ltd., Dewan Rubber Industries Ltd., Rathi Udyog Ltd., Rathi Ispat Ltd., Rathi Alloys and Steel Ltd., Swadeshi Polytex Ltd., The Tata Oil Mills Co. Ltd. are among main industries providing employment to the local and surrounding areas. Cement pipes, mustard oil, glassware, handloom cloth, railway signals, sewing machines, tyre tubes, soap, *gur* are the main commodities manufactured in the city while cement, cloth, iron, food grains, iron machinery, sugar, kerosene oil and cotton yarn are imported.

Table 1.3: Population and Workers Distribution in Ghaziabad Urban Agglomeration: 1991 and 2001

Ward *Indicator*	*Ghaziabad M.B.*	*Razapur Station*	*Ghaziabad Railway Colony*	*Ghaziabad*
Total.pop.	454156	46941	10662	511759
Male% to tot. Pop.	55	54	56	55.0
Female% to tot. Pop	45	46	44	45.0
Sch. Caste% to tot. Pop.	17	10	20	16.0
% of Literates to the tot. Pop.	54	65	65	55.0
T. Main wo. To the tot. Pop	28	27	28	28.0
Culti. % to M.W.	1.54	1.58	–	2.0
Ag. Lab. % to M.W.	1.3	1.58	–	1.0
Livestock, Fisheries% to M.W.	.42	.43	.14	0.001
Mining and Quarrying % to M.W.	.01	.47	.03	–
H.H. Manufacturing% to M.W.	1.38	.06	.17	1.0
Non. H.H. manufacturing % to M.W.	36.65	1.31	21.15	36.0
Construction% to M.W.	6.59	33.48	4.26	6.0
Trade and Commerce % to M.W.	20.39	5.03	6.2	19.0
Transport, Communication % to M.W.	9.37	7.69	43.8	10.0
Other workers % to M.W.	29.39	36.9	24.18	30.0

(Conted.)

(Conted.)

2001							
No_HH	*TOT_P*	*Male*	*Female*	*Schedule caste*	*Literate*	*male Lit*	*Fe.lit*
179947	968256	521026	447230	151484	657982	384366	273616
		53.81	46.19	15.65	67.96	58.42	41.58
Total workers	*Main Workers*	*Culti.*	*Agri.la*	*Household workers*	*Other workers*	*Marginal Workers total*	
266790	246827	4104	1448	7578	233697	19963	
	92.52	1.66	0.59	3.07	94.68	7.30	

Source: Census: 1991, 2001, Ghaziabad District.

Table 1.1 shows approximately same trends which previous table has given about Kanpur. Scheduled Caste distribution is quite significant in all areas. Since Ghaziabad is a satellite town of Delhi, it fulfils the demand of agriculture related products, therefore, and hence, it has a good number of people engaged in Agricultural activities. However, larger numbers of people fall under other workers category. For past few years Ghaziabad has experienced a rapid industrial growth also. Ghaziabad Municipal area and Ghaziabad Railway Colony have significant percentage of people engaged in Non-household Manufacturing units. Rajapur Station has very strength in construction workers. The study also encountered same phenomena when conducting field survey; the study found that Rajapur Station area has provided shelter in ghettos to many migrant labourers engaged in construction activities (Table 1.3).

1.7 Methodology

1.7.1 Survey Design and Sample Implementation

Initially the 2001 Census data of urban wards of both the cities, i.e. Kanpur and Ghaziabad, gave necessary frame for sample design. The wards thus have been arranged in ascending order according to the percentage of Scheduled Caste population. Wards which have higher percentage than the average Scheduled Caste population of the city has been segregated for the selection of first stage sample unit. Municipal Council Information on slums and voters list provided by the constituency office also offered a basic frame for final sampling along with the census ward level information.

The overall target of sample size for both survey areas, i.e. Ghaziabad and Kanpur was 320 households, i.e. 160 households in each city. The sample is designed in such a manner, which may give fair detail of both urban slums and non-slum areas which have people living from the lower economic strata of society (Fig. 1.4).

The required sampling fraction for urban slum and urban non-slum areas was determined by allocating the sample proportional to the population of the selected localities.

1.7.2. Sample Size and Reporting Domain

- Within each of the two sampling domains (slum and non-

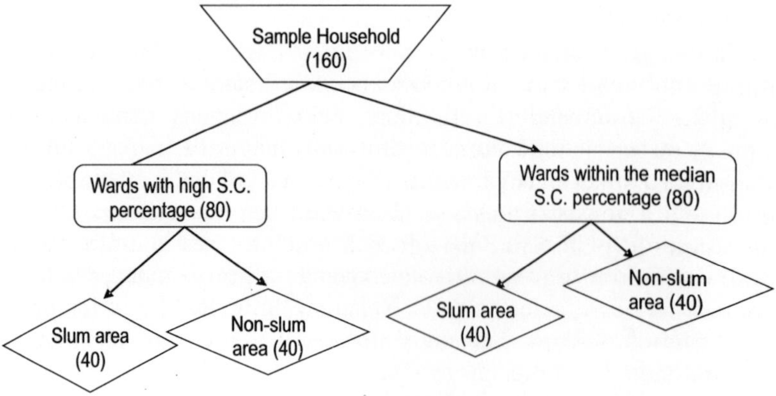

Fig. 1.4: Sample Domain and Size of the Study

slum) a systematic multi-stage stratified sampling design was planned. Amongst the wards having higher percentage of SC population and the wards which have mixed set of population of social categories were selected as First Sampling Unit (FSU).

- The Rationale behind selection of the wards which have mixed social category would give us the non-Scheduled Caste population also, further assuming that it will negate the possibility of getting high income group and give the sample which the study is aiming for, that is slightly higher than the low-income group or the persons residing in the slum areas.
- There are two factors which were looked into when visiting the field first whether the selected wards have slum areas or not and second whether the slum areas have such non-slum areas also where the study may find earning groups higher than the slum areas.
- The study saw the location of the slum and non-slum areas by simultaneously checking the population proportion of Scheduled Caste and non-Scheduled Caste population of Census Enumeration Block and the data made available by the Municipal Authorities at second stage in the selected ward.
- Though listing of the households was done at the third stage to derive final ultimate sampling units (USU) yet it was to know the overall existing mainstay of the people in that area. House listing also helped to select the ultimate sampling units in the following strata.

1.7.3. Criteria of Selection of Workers

Before going to the field this study proposed to select workers on the basis of their job experience. Rationale behind this criterion was to find the difference in the level of inequity and discrimination of a new worker in the market and of a worker who had accumulated experience of more than eight years thus a relatively new entrant *vis-à-vis* to the senior worker in experience and age both. But pilot survey in Kanpur City gave hints to change this selection criterion because while selecting final sample the study could not strictly demarcate junior workers and senior workers going by the definition of job experience and age as decided earlier. Even a young 25 years old male worker often had accumulated the experience of eight years or so. The study, therefore, restricted and selected sample by age group itself.

Also a job seeker (otherwise not studying) who is legally in the workers age group was also considered in the sample.

1.7.4.a Sample Wards of Kanpur

At the time of final collection of survey, it was encountered that the base of sample frame considerably got disturbed because of the ongoing Municipal Corporation Elections. A new schedule of delimitation came out which entirely reversed the selection of wards and hence after procuring the new delimited area data; once again the exercise of selection of wards was done. The data mentioned in Table 1.4 is given by Kanpur Municipal Corporation: Schedule of Delimitation 2005.

Table 1.4: Scheduled Caste and OBCs by Wards in Kanpur City

Sl. No.	*Ward No.*	*SC*	*OBC*	*Administrative Area within the Ward*
1	3	26.06	12.43	Govindnagar, Harizan Basti
2	93	2.6	6.59	Area of Govindnagar South
3	14	22.72	9.35	Ambedkarnagar, Kakadeo
4	87	5.45	16.9	Kakadeo
5	60	8.52	16.41	Barra
6	83	5.99	29.49	Naubasta West, Taj Nagar, Hanumat Vihar, Gadaria Purwa
7	25	15.64	15.07	Swadeshi Cotton Mill, Juhi Hamir Pur
8	34	16.57	15.3	Loharan ka Bhatta, NMP Mill, Double Pulia, Sarvodaya Nagar

Following the procedure as mentioned in the previous paragraph the present study selected six wards where S.C. population is more than 11.2 per cent (average S.C. population of Kanpur 2001 Census) and other four wards which have 11.2 per cent or nearest percentage to the average of the city S.C. population. Ward Nos. 3, 14, 25, 34, and have 26.06 per cent, 22.72 per cent, 15.64 per cent, and 16.57 per cent, of S.C. population respectively. Other wards, which fall below average S.C. population, are 93, 87, 60 and 83 (having S.C. population 2.6%, 5.45% and 8.52%, 5.99% respectively). Simultaneously these wards have high percentage of OBC population.

Table 1.4 shows the distribution of the households by the localities in Kanpur City. Kanpur has sizeable population living in slum area. According to the statistics provided by the Primary Census Abstract for Slum Areas of Million Plus Citites-2001 there are 64,486 households having a population of 367980 living in slum area. It has designated slums which are sometimes bigger than other residential colonies giving shelter to the retrenched labour of closed Cotton and Jute Mills and that is why location of some of the slums are within or adjacent to the cotton mills. Govindnagar has slum area which falls into three wards. Kakadeo was another area which has number of slums in this area and hence number of selected households is higher than other localities. These two localities satisfy one more condition of selection criterion, i.e. it has population which is slightly above the slum economy and more structured in economic terms.

Table 1.5: Number of Households by Ward in Kanpur City

Sl. No.	*Ward No.*	*Ward*	*No. of HH*
1	3 and 93	Govindnagar, Harizan Basti, Govindnagar South	62
2	14 and 87	Ambedkarnagar, Kakadeo	29
3	60	Barra	18
4	83	Naubasta, Gadaria Purwa	21
5	25	Swadeshi Cotton Mill, Juhi Hamirpur	24
6	34	Loharan ka Bhatta	7
	Total		161

1.7.5 Sample Wards of Ghaziabad

The story of Kanpur was repeated in Ghaziabad as well; while conducting final survey the time coincided with soon to be held Municipal Corporation Election. In view of the elections the Municipal

Corporation of Ghaziabad had also changed the boundaries of wards and hence the study had to change the selection of wards accordingly.

Ward Nos. 1, 2, 5 and 7 (45.09%, 49.26%, 49.46% and 36.3% respectively) have very high percentage of S.C. population and OBC as well. Ward Nos. 27, 31, 37, 39, 40 and 42 have lower percentage than average percentage of S.C. in Ghaziabad (Table 1.6).

Table 1.6: SC and OBC Distribution by Wards in Ghaziabad

Ward No.	*SC*	*OBC*	*Administrative Area within the ward*
1	45.09	10.32	Baalupura, Kalkagari, Prempuri, Hardeosahai, Kallupura, Jatwara, Kaazimal
2	49.26	8.70	Old Vijay Nagar
5	49.46	19.63	Maaliwada, Prangarhi, Deenagari, Meerut Railway line, East of Santosh M. College
7	36.31	20.81	Loharpura, Daulatpura, Jaiprakash North of Railway line and East of Kotgaon, Tejaab Mill
27	16.53	9.35	Sarainajarali, Nusratpura, North of railway line, Ganeshpura
31	14.30	13.76	North of railway line, Kotgaon East, Tejaab Mill till G.T. Road, Aaryanagar
37	15.86	21.65	Indus. Area and South of line, Hindon Pusta, Chitrakut Colony
39	15.36	40.27	Rakeshmarg, Girdharpur +
40	12.90	15.70	Rajendranagar Indus area, Bhatia Potteries

In Ghaziabad, slums were not limited to one locality. The spread of slums generally developed along the railway track and uninhabited sporadic location and hence the slums are smaller in size comparing Kanpur. These slums which fragmented and stretches to other ward's boundaries and therefore, number of households may look concentrated to one area, in reality the households might have been covered more than one ward. Adjacent parts of Kotgaon, Northern Railway line track, and Rakeshmarg remain major source of data collection (Table 1.7).

These two towns not only have different setting of industries but also have different industrial past, which has laid a typical requirement and production for industrial and domestic consumption. The social setting of these towns is also very separate from each other; Kanpur City having more of static population and Ghaziabad has been attracting more of long distance young migratory population. Slum size is bigger in Kanpur than Ghaziabad where small slums are scattered in the city. Another observation which this study would like to mention is that in Kanpur Slums are having quality of being special functional

Table 1.7: Number of Households Selected by Ward in Ghaziabad

Sl. No.	*Ward No.*	*Ward Area*	*No. of HH*
1	1	Kallupura and Jatwara	13
2	2	Old Vijay Nagar	10
3	5	Maaliwada and East of S M College	21
4	7	Loharpura Tejabmill, Kotgaon East	27
5	27	North of railway line, Ganeshpura	25
6	31	Kotgaon East and Aryanagar	23
7	37 and 40	Industrial area Chitrakut Colony, Bhatia Potteries	8
8	39	Rakeshmarg	31
		All	166

locations, i.e. slums have population of single caste people living as a clan (Kumahar Basti, Harizan Basti, Gadaria Purwa, people worked in Cotton and Jute mills at one place) while in Ghaziabad people from different castes live together without consideration of their caste occupations or caste background though one may find relatives living in neighbourhood.

1.7.6.a Type of Locality and Area in the Cities

In Kanpur we find that per cent of slum area is more than non-slum area. Within the slum area Govindnagar Harizan Basti have the largest share and in the category of non-slum area Govindnagar south, Kakadeo, Naubasta have higher percentage (Table 1.8).

Table 1.8: Households by Type of Locality and Area in Kanpur City

Area	*Slum*	*Non-slum*	*All*
Govindnagar, Harizan Basti	40.0	0.0	23.6(38)
Ambedkarnagar (Kakadeo)	10.5	0.0	6.2(10)
Swadeshi Cotton Mill	24.2	1.5	14.9(24)
Lohar ka Bhatta	4.2	4.5	4.3(7)
Barra	6.3	18.2	11.2(18)
Naubasta	7.4	21.2	13.0(21)
Kakadeo	2.1	25.8	11.8(19)
Area of Govindnagar South	5.3	28.8	14.9(24)
All	100.00(95)	100.00 (66)	100.00(161)

Note: Column Per cent, numbers in parentheses.

With very slight difference Barra, Gadaria Purwa, Kakadeo and Govindnagar South have Pakka Structures in the classification of Pakka Structure (Table 1.8).

Comparing per cent share of the type of residence in Ghaziabad is distinctly different from Kanpur. There is no significant difference in the spread of all types of residential structure of Slum area in Ghaziabad while authorized legal residential area presented in good strength (45.74%) in Ghaziabad whereas in Kanpur Pakka Structure Slum is a high in strength. Maaliwada, SM Medical College and Loharpura, Tejabmill Kotgaon are the main areas having the largest share of sample households in Ghaziabad. Non-slum area samples were mainly from Kotgaon (29.7%), Rakeshmarg (25.7%), Ganeshpura (24.3%) (Table 1.9).

Table 1.9: Households by the Type of Locality and Area in Ghaziabad

Area	*Slum*	*Non-slum*	*All*
Baalupura and Jaatwara	14.6	1.2	7.8(13)
Old Vijay Nagar	11.0	0.0	5.4(9)
Maaliwada and East of Santosh Medical College	22.0	3.6	12.7(21)
Loharpura, Tejabmill Kotgaon	35.4	1.2	18.1(30)
Ganeshpura	3.7	21.4	12.7(21)
Kotgaon East, Aryanagar	1.2	25.0	13.3(22)
Industrial area, Chitrakut Colony	2.4	7.1	4.8(8)
Rakeshmarg	9.8	29.8	19.9(33)
Bhatia Potteries	0.0	10.7	5.4(9)
All	49.4(82)	51.6(84)	100(166)

1.8 Classifications followed in the Present Study

1.8.1 Caste Classification

Caste classification is principally based on the caste studies conducted in the past and on the generally accepted classification in caste studies[19]. This study does not indulge in the procedures, debate and issues concerning caste classification but uses a functional classification of caste and also generally agreed principle of the pollution and purity to divide caste segments. While adopting the caste classification this study does not intend to injure the sentiments of any caste segment, therefore, the caste classification in this study is to measure the magnitude of the projected problem of the study. The caste classification also tries to capture the social terminologies addressing the social standing and not the government terms such as Other Backward Caste (OBC) or Scheduled Caste (SC) though they may match with the same classification.

The sample break-up of caste classification is as follows:

Upper Castes: Brahmin, Baniya, Rajput, Kayastha.

Intermediate Castes: Yadav, Jaiswal, Kurmi, Chaurasia, Bhurji, Teli, Mali, Tamoli, Lodhe Rajput, Kahar, Halwai, Nai, Badhai, Luhar, Kumhar, Sunar, Mallah.

Lower and Ex-Untouchables: Dhobi, Chamar, Kuril, Valmiki, Chikwa, Kori, Khatik.

The classification is strictly the first order division of castes[20], and does not include further division (sub-castes) within the main caste.

1.8.2 Urban Labour Market

It is pertinent to decide on the meaning of Informal and Formal sector in this study[21]. Researches on informal sector are divided on two concepts first applicable at the activity level and the other at the enterprise level. The activity level criterion used in the studies of the urban poor could disintegrate and integrate the formal and informal sector effectively[22]. ILO has suggested the criterion of activity level to distinguish informal sector. The other advantage of taking activity criterion is that it will include all sectors of industry, which employ both kinds of labour—formal and informal.

Therefore, the study has also adopted this criterion of activity to decide whether respondent belongs to the informal or formal sector. By this formula of activity level the possibility of locating informal employees can become easy in the manufacturing, construction, transport, trade and services sector which employ people formally and informally both[23].

Moreover deciding about the type of labour market in this study could not be restricted[24]—*first,* because the study primarily aims to know the discrimination and inequity as a whole in urban labour market and *second,* to meet the objectives of the study it is important to derive sample from mixed stock of workers, therefore, it was needed to target the heterogeneity of labour market rather than controlling the type of labour market.

1.9 Brief Profile of Households

1.9.1 Type of Locality and Caste Groups by Household

It was kept in the focus to have the representative sample from all caste groups while drawing sample from the selected wards. It was found that there also exists geographical segregation along caste lines in both the cities.

Table 1.10: Sample Household by Locality and caste

	Kanpur City			Ghaziabad		
	Slum	Non-slum	All	Slum	Non-slum	All
Upper Castes	7.40	40.9	21.1(34)	6.1	33.3	19.9*(33)
Intermediate castes	49.50	27.3	40.4(65)	75.6	56.0	65.7(109)
Low and ex-untouchables	43.2	31.8	38.5(62)	18.3	10.7	14.5(24)
All	59.0(95)	41.0(66)	100.0(161)	49.4(82)	51.6(84)	100(166)

*Column per cent, numbers in parentheses.

Due to past history of industrialization of Kanpur still has satisfactory combination of the people from higher caste groups and lower caste groups living in the slum areas whereas in Ghaziabad there is clear divide between the higher caste groups and lower caste groups by locality (Table 1.10).

Per cent share of intermediate caste groups is the highest in all caste groups in both the cities (Table 1.10) yet comparing this share with Ghaziabad it is significantly low. Representation of lower and ex-untouchables is considerably high (38.9%) in Kanpur while it is low (15%) in Ghaziabad. This study found that in Ghaziabad lot of migrants from Madhya Pradesh have settled around railway treks and on small land plots of the residential areas belonging to intermediate caste. Per cent share of upper caste (20.3% in Kanpur and 19.6% in Ghaziabad) same in both the cities in per cent terms.

1.9.2 Number of Respondents in Ghaziabad and Kanpur City

The upper caste representation in slum areas is low and hence the sample from upper caste was drawn from non-slum low income localities. In both the cities upper caste group has fair share from non-slum area while intermediate caste in Ghaziabad and Kanpur City has huge difference in slum and non-slum area. In Ghaziabad the representation of intermediate caste is noticeable (49.5% and 75.6% in slum and 27.3 % and 56 % in non-slum area respectively). In Kanpur households from lower caste and intermediate caste have very small difference but in Ghaziabad the difference in representation of these two castes is skewed in favour of the intermediate caste (Figs. 1.5 and 1.6).

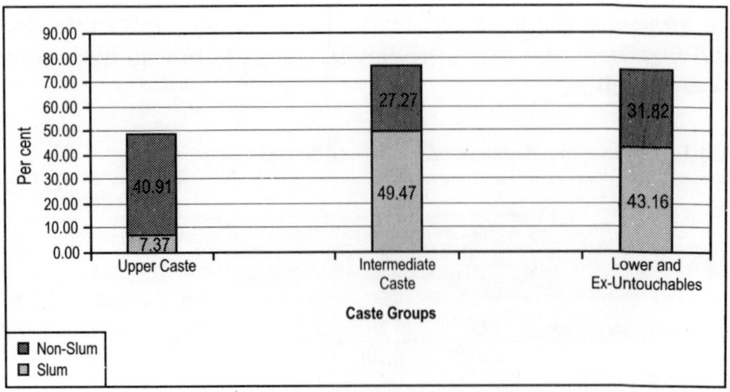

Fig 1.5: Caste Groups by type of Localities in Kanpur City

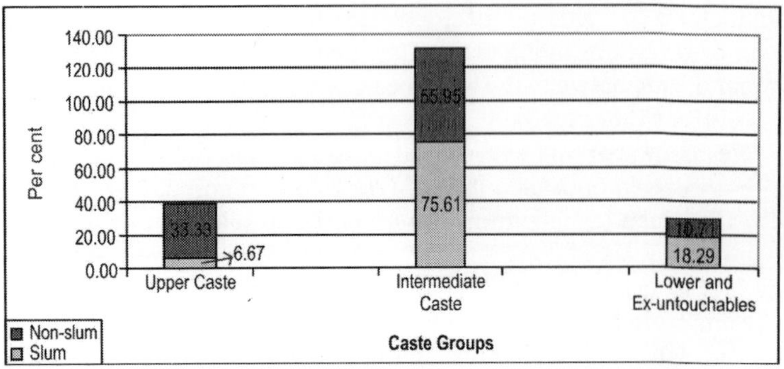

Fig. 1.6: Caste Groups by Type of Localities Ghaziabad

1.10 Socio-economic Profile of the Respondents

There were 256 respondents out of the total sampled households (166) in Ghaziabad and 266 people were found to be eligible respondents from the total sampled population in 161 households in Kanpur.

1.10.1 Caste of the Respondents

The percentage of intermediate caste is high in Ghaziabad because of the high migrants' population prevalence from Madhya Pradesh (districts of Madhya Pradesh) in Ghaziabad Slum area. Ahirwar though a Scheduled Caste population in Madhya Pradesh is considered Other

Backward Caste in Uttar Pradesh and hence considering the local administrative and ritual hierarchy of caste the present study also have considered them as Other Backward Caste (Table 1.11).

Table. 1.11: Caste of the Respondents in Kanpur and Ghaziabad

Caste Groups	*Kanpur*		*Ghaziabad*	
	Frequency	*Per cent*	*Frequency*	*Per cent*
Upper Caste	48	18.05	48	18.75
Intermediate Caste	111	41.73	167	65.23
Lower Caste and Ex-untouchables	107	40.22	41	16.02
All	266	100	256	100

In Kanpur lower caste and ex-untouchables (40.22%) have high presence than Ghaziabad where this caste group shares only 16.02 per cent to the total number of respondents[25].

1.10.2 Age Structure

The age structure distribution has been analysed across the caste groups. The aim of age structure analysis of the respondents was first to know the youthfulness of the sample respondents and also to know what is generally the common entry age of various caste groups in urban labour market. At this point the study also wanted to know what could be generally perceived age of retirement in casual/unorganized sector as well. People working at mature age are working willingly or forced to work.

There is no particular age group where it is concentrated yet 25-34 is the age group where comparatively high percentage (35.71%) of respondents is falling followed by 15-24 age group (26.32%) in Kanpur City. Across the caste group upper caste respondents are mainly in the age group of 25-34 (39.58%) even in the intermediate caste it is 25-34 (36.04%) age group which is highly represented[26]. In lower caste and ex-untouchables group there is a stark difference from other groups here 32.71 per cent of the respondents are from a very young group 15-24, they have joined work force either because of family problems, lack of education opportunity or perhaps because a large percentage of respondents who have migrated are in this age group[27] though highest percentage remains in 15-24 (33.64%) like other caste groups (Table 1.12).

Table 1.12: Age Structure by Caste Groups in Kanpur and Ghaziabad

Kanpur City				
Caste Groups	Upper Caste	Intermediate Caste	Lower and Ex-untouchables	All
15-24	10.42	27.03	32.71	26.32 (70)
25-34	39.58	36.04	33.64	35.71(95)
35-44	22.92	20.72	14.95	18.8(50)
45-54	14.58	9.91	12.15	11.65(31)
55 and above	12.5	6.31	6.54	7.52(20)
All	18.05(48)*	41.73(111)	40.22(107)	100.0(266)
Ghaziabad				
	Upper Caste	Intermediate Caste	Lower and Ex-untouchables	Total
15-24	18.75	32.93	36.59	30.86(79)
25-34	29.17	28.74	36.59	30.08(77)
35-44	29.17	24.55	14.63	23.83(61)
45-54	18.75	7.78	4.88	9.38(24)
55 and above	4.17	5.99	7.32	5.86(35)
All	18.75(48)	65.23(167)	16.02(41)	100.0(256)

In Ghaziabad total highest percentage share is in the 15-24 age group (30.86%) where ex-untouchables and intermediate caste respondents (36.59% and 32.93% respectively) have the highest respondents falling in this age group to the total respondents in their caste category. Somewhat equal distribution is noted in the Upper caste respondents (Table 1.12 and Fig. 1.7).

Though there is no striking difference in the age structure of Ghaziabad and Kanpur City yet interestingly respondents from Kanpur seems much older than their counterparts in Ghaziabad. The study puts forth three possible explanation regarding this observation first younger age group considered to be more mobile than other age groups; second, more plausible reason could be that there is out migration of the people from younger age group in recent past as the industrial stability has been greatly fluctuating in Kanpur City and in general people from younger age group migrate in higher proportion than other age groups, third could be that people from surrounding areas have stopped coming to Kanpur because of lack of good employment opportunity[28]. This could have affected the age structure in Kanpur where younger, more mobile age group is fleeing the city and not getting any replacement from other neighbourhood area.

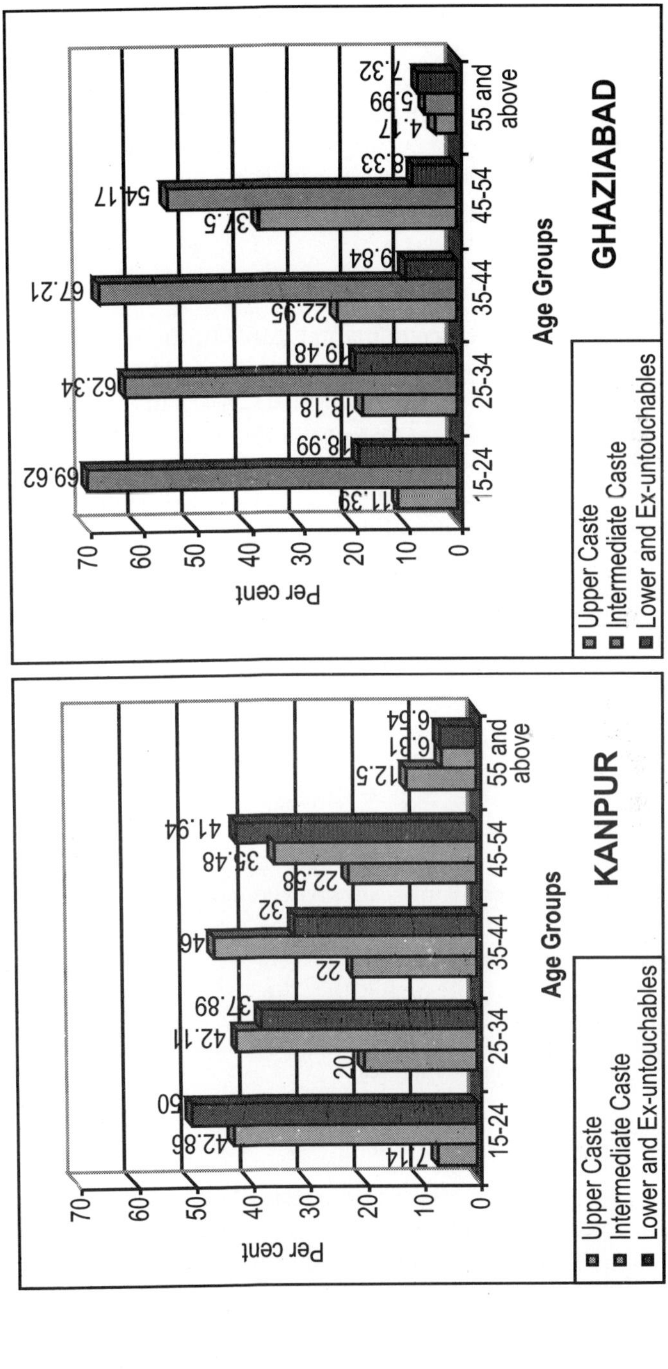

Fig. 1.7: Caste Groups by Age Groups in Kanpur and Ghaziabad

This is one stage where socially structured discrimination historically has put disadvantage on the lower caste groups. On one side they do not get opportunity[29] to study for various reasons consequently enter labour market at a fairly tender age and do miscellaneous jobs to keep alive. In the next chapter occupational structure and education is discussed to find out the relationship between human capital and occupation.

1.10.3 Marital Status

There is no significant difference in marital status of the respondents in Kanpur City and Ghaziabad. Approximately same percentage of the respondents was married (71%) and unmarried (24.8% in Kanpur and 26.2% in Ghaziabad). But while cross-examining marital status with age group one may say that Ghaziabad has higher percentage in 15-24 age group and possibly because of more respondents in younger age group influence the marital status (Table 1.13).

Table 1.13: Marital Status of the Respondents in Ghaziabad and Kanpur City

	Kanpur City			
	Upper Caste	Intermediate Caste	Low and Ex-untouchables	All
Married	77.1	73.9	65.4	71.1*(188)
Unmarried	14.6	24.3	29.9	24.8(66)
Widow	8.3	1.8	4.7	4.1(11)
All	100.0(48)	100.0(111)	100.0(107)	100.0(266)
	Ghaziabad			
	Upper Castes	Intermediate Castes	Low and Ex-Untouchables	All
Married	79.2	70.1	70.7	71.9*(184)
Unmarried	20.8	28.1	24.4	26.2(67)
Widow	0.0	1.8	4.9	2(5)
All	100.0(48)	100.0(167)	100.0(41)	100.0(256)

*Column per cent, numbers in parentheses.

1.10.4 Employment Status

There is a high share of casual workers and own account workers in Kanpur because people who were retrenched during industrial recession have been doing either petty business within the residential area or engaged in casual work. The respondents who are in the permanent category in Kanpur are those who are mainly working with Municipal Corporation as cleaner or in some government establishments while in Ghaziabad the permanent workers are mainly working with industries. Percentage of wage workers temporary is very high (43.36%) in case of Ghaziabad. These workers are working with the rolling mills, cycle assembly line and construction/infrastructure development companies (Table 1.14). Respondents which were in the unemployed category were very high in Kanpur City than in Ghaziabad. While talking with respondents informally it was found that the aspiration level was high in Kanpur and they easily do not like to pick up any sundry job for the sake of living and since they have sufficient backup they did not try hard to find job.

Table 1.14: Respondents by Employment Status

Sl. No.	*Employment Status*	*Kanpur*		*Ghaziabad*	
		Frequency	*Per cent*	*Frequency*	*Per cent*
1.	Casual worker (daily wage worker)	61	22.9	46	17.97
2.	Self-employed	16	6	22	8.59
3.	Own Account	76	28.6	44	17.19
4.	Wage worker (permanent)	20	7.5	19	7.42
5.	Wage work (temporary)	66	24.8	111	43.36
6.	Currently unemployed/Seeking job	27	10.2	14	5.47
	Total	**266**	**100**	**256**	**100**

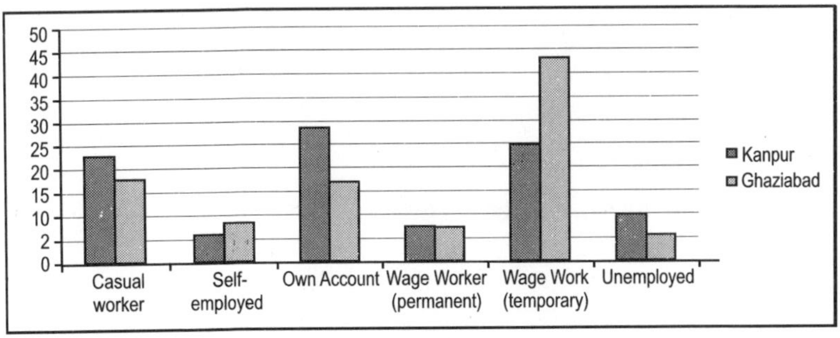

Fig. 1.8: Employment status of the workers

Caste configuration is entirely different; employment status, household size and age also correspond to the current scenario of the cities. Literature review on the current industrial scenario of these two cities confirms the field observations. In the next chapter education, employment and earning differentials have been analysed with the caste status.

1.11 Limitation of the Study

Studies on discrimination have used secondary data for inference; this could be one of the leading discrimination in studies to carry out an empirical work to understand the caste configuration and the pattern of recruitment in urban labour market. Though the study has taken utmost care to draw its sample yet there were various limitations while drawing sample such as heavily unbalanced representation of caste in slum and non-slum areas, differences in human capital investment, or lack of understanding of question of discrimination in people. Discrimination (*Bhedbhav* in Hindi) as a concept was not gullible to some of the respondents as there was hardly any interaction with other castes and therefore, interactive session with the respondents became important which was able to capture the views of the respondents.

This study initially became ambitious to take employers in its sample as well but field realities forced to limit this plan because employers are themselves heterogeneous and to study them will need another set of sample. The study nonetheless interviewed some of the employers belonging to the same strata in unstructured manner.

Discrimination is defined and identified when two persons from two different social groups having same qualifications get different treatment in the labour market. As already stated finding such samples was very difficult because of the variations in human capital, aspirations and other socio-economic factors in every field. It became all the more difficult where type of industry also influences the wage, occupation and occupational hierarchy in the labour market.

1.12 Structure of the Present Study

The study has been divided systematically keeping in the focal points on the predefined stages of pre-market and market discrimination. The introduction of this study presents background of the study and problem statement. Methodology is carefully planned to capture the discrimination and inequity and profile of the respondents. The second chapter is an exercise for theoretical explorations and develops understanding of the discrimination and other linking concepts which can be relevantly used in the present study. The chapter also presents theoretical and evidence-based studies on discrimination in India and other countries.

In the third chapter the study directly analyses the current employment status, labour status and earning in the backdrop of their social standing. Fourth chapter delves into the education level, recruitment processes and parental background to summarise the linkages if exist in the parental association and existing place of the labour. In the recruitment section the study elaborates on information and networking in recruitment in urban labour market; how do people gather information and pass on to other people and why do they select one particular occupation or even industry. Fifth chapter is on the qualitative findings where this study has used Likert scale on some of the key questions those were further probed if found contradictory in the given answers of scaled questions. The sixth chapter is evidence-based theoretical discussion on the studies of geographical spaces, discrimination and caste in India, while substantiating discrimination by the statistical models. The last and the seventh chapter is the concluding statement of the study with some important findings and policy suggestions.

NOTES

1. Beteille (1969). *Caste, Class and Power: Changing Patterns of Stratification in a Tanjor Village,* Oxford University Press, Bombay, p. 99; Pauline Kolenda (1984) p. 15, Venkatasubramanyam (1973), *Group Prejudice in India*; Shree Ram Centre for Industrial Relations and Human Resources, New Delhi, p. 2, discussed the origin of the caste and the role of caste in social order.
2. Berrmann (1979), *Caste and Other Inequalities*, Folklore Institute, Meerut, p. 74.
3. Becker, G. (1971) (II Ed.). *Economics of Discrimination,* Chicago University Press, Chicago. p. 7. 'Objective consideration of the facts' Becker means to say here that if a person is discriminating he/she would give up pecuniary advantage by hiring a person on a higher wage.
4. The types of discrimination which are discussed in literature overview are statistical discrimination, segregation and crowding etc. By virtue of birth, in caste system people are categorized and thus segregated. In rural India people do not take jobs which are the prerogative of other caste group because of the close knit social structure while in urban area people who take any available work or wait for the job related information from their relatives or friends.

This kind of situation leads them to stagnation in job opportunity or cyclic information of same kind of work.

5. Banerjee (Delhi), Kannan (Kerala), Deshpande (Bombay), Harriss *et al.*, (Coimbator) studied various aspects related to labour market in urban area, where this myth has been demolished that in urban areas caste has no role to play in economic life at all. Amongst many questions raised by Thorat is one how caste structure has influenced the economic outcome. He says that this question remained unanswered for quite some time that to what extent the historical legacy has restrained accessibility to resources of material and psychological benefit. Thorat (2001) "Caste and Economic Discrimination: Theory and Evidence on Rural Labour Market" in *Artha Vijnana*, Vol. XLIII, Nos. 1-2, March-June 2001.
6. Dipankar Gupta (2000), *Mistaken Modernity: India Between Worlds*, Harper Collins Publication, India. p. 113.
7. *Op. cit.,* Banerjee (Delhi), Kannan (Kerala), Deshpande (Bombay), Harriss *et al.,* (Coimbator).
8. Satish Saberwal (1990) (Sec. Rev. Ed.) *Mobile Men: Limits to Social Change in Urban Punjab,* Indian Institute of Advance Study, Shimla in Association with Manohar Publication, New Delhi, pp. 28, 32-33, 206-210.
9. Anil Bhatt (1989). *Development and Social Justice: Micro Action by Weaker Sections*, Sage Publication, New Delhi. pp. 18-22.
10. Jan Bremman (1976) "A Dualistic Labour System? A Critique of the Informal Sector-III", *Economic and Political Weekly*, Vol. XI, No. 50, December 11, p. 1940.
11. Floating Labour refers to the labourers shuttling between rural and urban areas or fringe area to the core area. Manjeet Singh (1990). *The Political Economy of Unorganised Sector*. Sage Publication, New Delhi, p. 15.
12. T.S. Papola (1981). *Urban Informal Sector in a Developing Economy,* Vikas Publishing House, New Delhi, in his study on the informal labour market in Ahmedabad. He concludes that percentage of Scheduled Tribe and Caste workers is comparatively higher to the non-Scheduled Caste.
13. G.S. Becker (1975). *Human Capital: A Theoretical and Empirical Analysis with Special Reference to Education*, National Bureau of Economic Research, New York, p. 97.
14. James J. Heckman "Policies to Foster Human Capital", *Research in Economics, 2000, No. 54.* The author is convinced with other economists that higher the investment in human capital lower will be the resulting inequalities.
15. World Labour Report 3, (1987). This report deals with labour and their vulnerable status. Report confirms the view that certain social groups are 'vulnerable' to instability, insecurity, low wages. Further says "Social stratification determines entry to particular labour statuses and sectors segmentation determines mobility between statuses and sectors." p. 124.
16. Banerjee and Knight (1982) "Caste Discrimination in the Indian Urban Labour Market", *Journal of Development Economics,* pp. 299-300, they say those

profit-maximizing employers in the absence of perfect information, may consider caste as an efficient indicator of one's productivity.

17. Berremann (1979). *Caste and other Inequalities*, Folklore Institute, Meerut, p. 127, says, "That people remain in an inferior position...does not mean that they do so willingly or that they believe it is justified, or they would not do anything in their power to change it, given the opportunity."
18. I.Z. Hussain, "Projection of Population and Labour Force for the Kanpur Region" in P.B. Desai (ed.) (1969) *Regional Perspective of Industrial and Urban Growth: The Case of Kanpur*, Macmillan & Company Ltd., Bombay. While Projecting the population for Kanpur City Husain says that nearly 50 per cent of the total persons enumerated in the city in 1961 were born outside the city—17 per cent of those born outside being migrants from within the district, 66 per cent from other districts of the state...., 11 per cent from other states ......maximum number of the migrants were contributed by Unnao, Fatehpur, Rae Barriely, Farrukhabad and Pratapgarh.
19. This Study found many creditable academic work on caste hierarchy criteria yet the present study has adopted caste classification based on the work of– 1. Shah and Desai (1988) *Division and Hierarchy*, Hindustan Publication House, Delhi. 2. K.S. Singh (1992) *Peoples of India*, Oxford University Press. Vols. I and II, New Delhi. 3. Brochure on reservation for Scheduled Castes and Scheduled Tribes (1987) (7th ed.), Government of India, Ministry of Personal and Public Grievances. Uttar Pradesh.
20. Shah and Desai (1988) *op. cit.*, p. 5.
21. Report of the Committee on the Unorganised Sector Statistics: National Statistical Commission, GoI, February 2012. While confirming between the strong linkages between the formal and informal sector the Committee suggested to constitute the task force to be constituted by NSO and may formulate methodological studies for strengthening data base on such aspects of linkages of the informal and formal sector, pp. 65-66.
22. Abdul Aziz (1984) *Urban Poor and Urban Informal Sector*, Ashish Publishing House, New Delhi, pp. 4-9.
23. Such absolute segregation of formal and informal labour is difficult in current situation of labour market in volatile global and local market. Several studies on labour market interlinkages show that these two sectors heavily depend on each other for sustenance. National Commission on Employment in Unorganised Sector recommends definition of informal sector with all possible combinations in three ways: first as Informal sector, second Informal worker/employment and third as Informal economy where variations of informal sector are reasonably covered under these three definitions. Report of the Committee on Unorganised Sector Statistics: National Statistical Commission, GoI, February 2012, pp. 11-12.
24. Studies have shown that it is difficult to separate the informal and formal market and both these types of labour market depend heavily on each other for various reasons and hence the present study also follow this principle and try to draw its sample from diverse labour market. R.S. Tiwari, "Formal

and Informal Linkages in the Development of Informal Sector: A Study of Kanpur Metropolis" in M.S. Ramanujam, I.C. Awasthi, Gayatri Pandey (1998) *Employment Promotion in the Urban Informal Sector,* New Age International, Delhi, pp. 249-267.

25. Caste representation has interesting difference between cities; Kanpur which is old industrial town has large share of lower caste and ex-untouchables and also have significant representation of Artisan Caste group as well. There are studies which have proved that people from artisan community was recruited in bulk in the woollen and cotton mills in Kanpur City.
26. Though the caste categories are not subdivided in the intermediate caste which has an important category as Artisan groups (it is not used for analysis purpose) and interestingly it was found the age group which they mainly belong to is 15-24 and later age group 61 and above. The study can assume that the artisan caste people start working early because of the three facts: (1) family assistance is there to train them, (2) due to low capital for on the job training, and (3) that by virtue of being at house they learn by default and therefore, there is no need to go to other place to learn the vocation. This fact is also reflected since they are able to work till they are physically strong or quite late in the age.
27. This study did not collect detailed data on migration because of lack of scope yet some of the migration related questions and migration data from other sources have been cited in this study wherever required and found to be relevant.
28. John Harris (1998) Vulnerable Workers in India in Caden and Holmstrom (1998) *Decentralized Production in India*, French Institute of Pondichery and Sage Publication, Delhi. Reported the industrial situation of Kanpur back 1984 when mill workers were sitting idle because of the closure of all cotton mills and crisis deepened due to sub-contraction by private mill owners.
29. Though opportunity itself does not ensure the positive outcome yet giving opportunity to the lesser fortunate group is the most important policy goal at present. Karla Hoff and Priyanka Pandey, 'Opportunity is not Everything', *Economic Transition*, Vol. 13(3) 2005, pp. 445-472, experimentally investigated village India how belief systems affect the groups' responses to economic opportunities. In this study the authors asked the students to solve puzzles without revealing the caste identity they interpreted that the students from deprived background outperformed privileged students though not significantly, while after revealing the caste identity to them reduced the average number of mazes solved by them but does not significantly change high caste performances. Social interaction and behavioural manipulation limits or give advantage to people belonging to different social background.

2
Discrimination in the Labour Market

This chapter gives an analytical overview of literature on the discrimination, similar concepts and caste factor in urban labour market. The chapter is divided into four broad sections. The first is on discrimination, types of discrimination and related concepts which propel discrimination or produce inequality, poverty, segregation and crowding. The second section deals on the agents of discrimination (or harbinger of discrimination) while the third section covers theories on the discrimination in the labour market. Fourth section exclusively throws light on the studies done on discrimination and caste discrimination in India. The literature which is relevant in the context of present studies is considered for review covering studies as early as 1933 till 2013.

2.1 Discrimination

Discrimination as defined by Backer when a minority group is treated differently (less favourably) from other majority group. Backer's model of discrimination was based on the 'taste of discrimination' where the employers hold a taste for discrimination and minority employee may work at higher or equal productivity for lower wages than the majority workers. This taste of discrimination was quantified and formulated as "coefficient of discrimination". Discussing the Backer's model David Autor[1] says that wage differential will arise if and only if the fraction of discriminating employers are sufficiently large. Charles and Guryan[2] in their critical analysis on the theory of discrimination by Backer and others say that racial wage gaps are determined by the prejudice of this marginal person and not by the average level of prejudice among employers. Therefore, the taste of discrimination as defined and analysed by Backer is discrimination on the margin and does not include discrimination on an average. Most analyses on discrimination are based on the statistical discrimination than on the taste of discrimination. Charles and Guryan[3] have shown that due to limited information firms depend on the most observable information such as race, gender, age, region etc. to infer the productivity of applicants. He also criticized Backer's model of discrimination on the ground that discriminating employers by sacrificing profits will be finally pushed out of the market in a long run in a competitive setting.

2.1.1 Manifestations of Discrimination

Evidences on racial prejudice opened many forms of debates on discrimination inequality inequity, prejudice, and segmentation. The debate started to analyse the economic outcome based on behavioural circumstances in society. Many thoughts developed and explained this interactive situation within the circumference of some particular schools. Some of the terms were considered synonymous like inequality, segmentation, crowding, prejudice to be the outcome of inequality and discrimination.

Inequality in society can be an attribute of discrimination. Discrimination is a functional attitude as Reynolds *et al.*[4] defines,

> "Discrimination occurs whenever someone's opportunities are not based on his or her individual capabilities but are limited because of membership in a group. Prejudice is an attitude. Usually, however, a prejudiced attitude will lead to acts of discrimination."

By giving even more clear difference between the two, Khan[5] in his study on the Harizan identity quotes Metta and Inpules that discrimination refers to overt behaviour.

> "It usually implies unfavourable conduct based on prejudice against some ascribed status group prejudice and discrimination is interrelated, however, there are occasions where prejudice may exist without discrimination against the other group. Similarly, it is also that there will be discrimination without

> any prejudice. Further, there may be occasions when discrimination and prejudice go together. Stereotypes are a type of national cartoons, which exaggerate the characterization of the typical member of the rival groups. Perceptions of some members of that group tend to be distorted by the expectations that each person will resemble the stereotype."

In this comment there are two very interesting derivations, first that prejudice enacted will lead to discrimination, without harming the target group. Second (perhaps) the established fact could be that these 'national cartoons' exaggerate the characteristics of the rival target group and support the stereotype. He also thinks about the distortions, which may occur in the absence of stereotype. (This study has tried to extract information on the opinion of the people where some people belonged to odd group and majority belonged to the stereotype group). Becker[6] says that prejudice can be reduced to a great extent by spreading knowledge. This type of situation can be explained as internalized discrimination where people follow the stereotyped notion about other group. Stereotype discrimination refers to existence of a negative stereotype about a group and blocks a rational thinking. In situations where the stereotype is applicable, affected member of group is at risk of confirming it. There are two studies[7] one where mathematical ability and gender was studied and another on African American, found that the mathematical aptitude was negatively affected when one was told to write the gender and ethnic background.

Segregation and crowding are the other linking concepts. Segregation exhibits the crowding of one particular community onto one type of activity. The method or process of segregation may be different. Crowding may happen naturally like citizens of some country may like to meet each other or commune together just because they all belong to the same country. On the other hand, some people will happen to crowd in a layer of society first due to convenience of time, money, and physical ability. Second could be a deliberate attempt of some people (e.g. the study indicates thus Valmikis are favoured for cleaning jobs only and eliminated from other jobs), third by way of preference females are 'preferred' for some jobs, saying they do it better than male counterparts (like plucking tea leaves, *bidi* rolling, Kindergarden teachers, nurses etc.). The reasons given behind these occupational crowding are always debatable, confusing and not convincing. Segregation may be due to discrimination, combining the result of both these two concepts of prejudice and discrimination, we find a cause and effect relationship.[8]

Venkata Subramanyam[9] quotes Bell (1961) who gives a different opinion on the subject of cause and effect relationship of caste prejudice and discrimination,

> "The system is considered to have contained only the practice of discrimination without prejudice as no section saw prejudice in discrimination."

This is a different outlook on caste prejudice and discrimination since we believed that without prejudice discrimination would not exist. Now going back to Reynolds (1987), Metta and Alex also verify that without an attitude for belief, prejudice or discrimination does not occur though prejudice may exist without discrimination. Giving a second thought on prejudice and discrimination and the origin of caste as a system we may agree with Bell's statement (which itself is an idea and may not be a fact), since the caste identity is attached with birth, and hierarchical order of society and hence we may infer that the evolution of the caste system inscribed the rules of caste behaviour. Prejudice may not have existed during that period but discrimination might have prevailed. After centuries, the caste system not only gave a direction to the social order in Hindu society but also has affected other religious social systems in India. This leads to the conclusion that there is a correlation between prejudice and discrimination.

Bradley[10] also thinks that discrimination may not give notion of injustice, which is very important if this study consider caste as a system on injustice and undemocratic way of dividing society. Poverty is another phenomenon, which may stem out of discrimination. Bradley's wrote at length on the subject of poverty and discrimination. He says that the inequality of the class inbred in capitalism, and poverty stemming out from discrimination, have the same process. He explained poverty borne out of discrimination, has been substantiated by two concepts. First 'flawed character' in which it is assumed people are poor because of their lack of motivation, initiative in school and in the job market, assuming that there are plenty of jobs and schooling skills are at par for every citizen and for other successful people in the job market. Second is 'restricted opportunity' where he says that poor are poor because they could not have access to good schools, jobs and income because they were discriminated on the basis of colour, sex or in any other identity background. The first concept is defined in the background of demographic forces, which define a person's human capital, in other words the difference in the number of people having abundance or lack of quality and quantity of education and skills and availability of jobs. Second concept is built on the notion of different demands for labour and the institution barrier erected by discrimination.

2.2. Actors of Discrimination

The present study would like to examine the issue of discrimination by using the typology[11] given by G. Becker. As the study discussed in the earlier section that there are many linked concept which have been perceived, empirically challenged and interpreted in more than one way by competent authors on the subject of discrimination.

2.2.1 Employer's Discrimination

Becker used employer discrimination to explain a situation when employer's subjective attitude or preferences get qualified by means of discrimination coefficient (DCs), and the intensity of desire to discriminate generally differs according to need and location and social variable.

Considering that there is wage productivity difference amongst the job applicant, the taste of discriminator can be identified if one applicant is giving preference over other. Reynolds[12] *et al.,* feel that discrimination is more vocal in the small firm or organization than the bigger one. Whether an organisation is big or small, it becomes different to track the discrimination by employer for several reasons: lack of negotiating power, opportunity crisis, above all lack of understanding of rational discrimination by employer.

2.2.2 Employee Discrimination

This is a very important level of discrimination. Becker[13] defines an employee as an individual selling labour under contractual arrangements specifying his return by time or output. He gives a lot of importance to minority and majority question in society to make employee discrimination being effectively seen. Employee discrimination is when one employee avoids working with other employees on the unknown ground, which indirectly can be sex, race, caste, region or religion. Two points are important to note that an employee, if he/she discriminates, will not lead to overall discrimination, and secondly, to avoid such a situation employers may recruit a larger number of the potential employees who do not discriminate thus resulting in employer discrimination.

2.2.3 Customer Discrimination

Becker called this type of discrimination as consumer discrimination. Customer discrimination is production oriented and quite expressive at the point of sale. Elaborating on consumer discrimination Becker[14] gave an example of a retail store, which faces select discrimination on the basis of sex, race, religion and personality of sales personnel. Thus, it may happen in the local market that a salesman would belong to the community, sex, race that is mutually accepted in the area, which that product covers as a saleable commodity. Even "question of exact buyer and seller relationship comes in different contexts, but in any case this aspect is irrelevant to the more normal situation in which those who make the goods do not meet buyers face to face."

2.3. Approaches to Discrimination

Theories developed on discrimination were explained on the basis of various prominent economic and social schools of thoughts. Each tried to give alternative policy formulation to combat discrimination, inequity in societies. The most prominent schools of thoughts are classical, neo-classical, dual-labour, institutional approaches. There are other theories also to explain the phenomenon of discrimination, developed under the tutelage of welfare economists lately.

2.3.1 Classical Approaches

The classical approach did not treat labour market separately but addressed the employment structure holistically in relation to the distribution of resources. In the short run, supply of labour is constant, thus demand for labour is only determinant for employment and wage structure. In the long run, factors substituting in response to demand available for labour. If labourers were in excess, even at lower wage rate, then there would be a shift to more labour intensive techniques of production. Perfect competition and homogeneity of labour was assumed in classical approach. But Adam Smith surmised existing wage differentials due to non-economic factors like easiness or hardship, cleanliness or dirtiness, honourable or dishonourable. These factors in the wage differentials, associated with occupation, are called *'compensating'* wage differences as a function of differences in the non-wage qualities of different jobs, *'real wage'* differences as a function of restriction on freedom of occupational choice.

One of the very first contributions was from Siddney Webb[15](1891). He surveyed four types of workers: (i) manual work, (ii) routine mental work, (iii) artistic work, and (iv) intellectual work. Webb ascribed differences in wage first to customs and public opinion; secondly to lower demand from women due to lower standard of living; and thirdly lower productivity by women caused by several factors including insufficient training, lack of strength and institutional restrictions. He did not limit his analysis to the labour market but extended to the institutional conditions of legislation, tradition, educational systems and family structure as well.

Eleanor Rathbone[16] said except productivity differences, other differences are found in wage for women, because of four other important factors: (i) women lack trade union, (ii) women's wages are only pocket money or to be considered as supplementary income of family, (iii) that women have a low standard of living, and (iv) ages are decided according to "individual subsistence requirement" (women are not normally the bread winner). Millicent Fawcett[17] felt that Rathbone has too greatly emphasised on productivity differences. He feels that it is due to the dominance of male segment in the trade unions, which in many cases, refuse to accept the presence of women. This typical attitude segregates them in certain type of jobs. Arthur Cicil Pigou[18] believed that certain type of jobs were closed for women and discussed the occurrence of what current terminology would label 'monopsonistic elements' in labour market. Francis Edgeworth[19] also stressed on the difference due to productivity and confirmed the views expressed by Rathbone in the context of the role of trade unions. Sargant Florence[20] criticised the advocates of the crowding theory and explained lower wages due to (i) the firms have monopsonistic position in the labour market, (ii) women are less mobile in the labour market, and (iii) certain type of indivisibility exists concerning decisions to employ female labour (men disapprove to work with female workers). Florence's model of discrimination includes both employer discrimination (monopsony) and discrimination by group of employees.

2.3.2 The Neo Classical Approach

The Neo Classical thoughts originated from the economic thinking of 1870s, which is famous as 'marginal revolution' in the annals of economic thought. Prominent contributions in this revolution were by Jevons, Menger and Walras (for micro-economic analysis), and while Marshall and Hicks spearheaded wage discussions. Marginal analysis rummaged for the optimal allocation of production services under specified conditions, which maximize production output and marginal productivity theory of input pricing. Cain[21] points out on Neo Classical Theory that first it is a theory of demand for labour contained in the marginal productivity theory and associated research on production function; secondly the theory of labour supply consists mainly models of labour choice/leisure and human capital investment. The Neo Classical Theory delves in marginal analysis on behavioural relations and gives many qualitative predictions and quantitative estimates. This may be the most famous and critically analyzed model to explain discrimination phenomena. Neo-classical model of discrimination is contributed largely by one of the most prominent writer like Gerry Becker[22]. Many authors have improvised and used this model in many ways. Gerry Becker himself has given a new turn to this model by branching out a new approach known as human capital approach in discrimination concept.

The main features of neo-classical theory are—

(i) One line of model 'competitive model' which predicts a long run disappearance of wage in market.
(ii) 'Non-competitive' is not given much respect while considering monopoly and monopsony is not a very important in empirical analysis.
(iii) 'Competitive statistical model' which stressed overwhelmingly on information unreliability to the extent of discrimination that we observe. Sometimes, he argues with neo classical pre-labour market sources of disadvantages, thus attempting to advance the burden of explaining market discrimination.

Becker's Theory of Discrimination is a deliberation on all earlier debates (mainly Classical School of Thoughts) covering almost all the aspects of discrimination but unable to frame up anything concretely under the socio-economic analysis. Becker developed the theory on two aspects by first dividing society into two parts and then fitting them into trade theory, and secondly, understanding this discriminatory phenomenon under the light of Nepotism. He used 'discrimination coefficient' to estimate the intensity of discrimination. Though, there are many practical difficulties in the application of his theory, which at times diverts it from the real life phenomena, yet it earns the credit of being the first socio-economic analysis of discrimination. His study showed that,

(i) In equilibrium both the groups discriminated and discriminatory lose. Where one group possesses excess of capital and one has excess of labour. In a condition where capital owners discriminate and export less capital to labour endowed group, further do not use easily accessible cheap labour. In such a condition labour excess group loose to the unemployment and capital-intensive group loose to the available cheap labour.
(ii) Different kinds of discrimination can have additive effects.
(iii) With perfect substitutability between the discriminated and non-discriminated labour, the market discrimination coefficient becomes equal to the discrimination coefficient regardless of the size of the discriminated group and the degree of competition in the commodity market.
(iv) There will be segregation, when there is a perfect substitution because each firm chooses to have a work force consisting of people from both the discriminated and discriminating group will have a higher cost than the firm which recruits employees from only one of the groups.
(v) There are forces which tend to reduce wage differences among employer, i.e. if preferences vary between different employers and commodity market are competitive monopolies transferable.

In practical terms, experience shows that discrimination does not disappear in the long run; rather it persists for a very long time. Secondly, he always assumed capital owners discriminating against labour group. He did not take up the issue at one labour group and other labour group level. However, he indirectly dealt with this point in his segregation analysis. This theory assumes full employment in equilibrium. That is the biggest folly of this theory because occasionally it is felt that the discriminated group have faced grave challenge of unemployment also and this condition would not lead to the full employment.

In his criticism on neo-classical theory, J. Petr[23] said that neo-classical theory is based on systematic behaviour in a market economy. This model is functional and equilibrium oriented rather than unstable and evolutionary. Neo-classists have assumed human behaviour as manifestations of universal human characteristics, and cultural patterns, which are time, and place specific and most often treated as constraints on behaviour but not as a main subject matter of economic study.

Measuring on the supply and demand side of market neo-classicists showed that the demand side took care of marginal productivity and other associated research of production function while the supply side consists of mainly involving labour leisure choice and human capital investment. Neo-classical theory resorts to behavioural explanation quite after this methodology. The theory adopted is income and price in relation with marginal analysis of behavioural relations. Jennings[24] compared institutional analysis with neo-classical and derived that neo-classicist bank on individualistic principles of personal choices and market rationality where social causation is generally not included.

2.3.3 Dual Labour

There were marathon discussions and debates to explain discrimination after the neo-classical approach failed to explain the never diminishing discrimination in the market. Dual labour approach arched subject of discrimination by visualizing market structure and nature of recruitment of labour in the market. The most prominent proponents of this theory were Piore and Doeringer[25] (1957). They say that there are set rules, which differentiate these two types of labour segments. In the words of Piore and Doeringer,

> "The internal labour market, governed by administrative rules, is to be distinguished from the external labour market of conventional economic theory where pricing, allocating and training decisions are controlled directly by economic variables. These two markets are inter-connected, however and movements between them occurs at certain job classifications which constitute ports of entry and exit to and from the internal market."

These external and internal markets are inter-connected but internal market has exclusive rights and privileges, which are not made available to the external labour force. Their rights may be like internal vacancy filling, protection from competition from external labour force etc. The phenomenon of internal labour market is thus closely akin to the problems, which other authors have identified as 'industrial feudalism', the 'balkanization of labour market', and 'property rights in a job'.

Succinctly saying dual labour market assumes that the labour market is divided into two parts. One part consists of primary job market and other secondary job market. In primary market certain "ports of entries" restrict labour from out side. This market provides job security, mobility chains, more automatic and people incidentally learn the job techniques while on the job. Secondary market consists of low security jobs, short training period and almost no mobility chain.

Kerr[26] distinguished between a structure less market and structured one. Structureless market has affinity with unorganized market where there is no other formal contract except the wage between the worker and the employer; no worker can have guarantee of job and the employer in return can have any hold on the employees. Kerr has the opinion that internal and external markets exist in the structured market. The internal market may be a plant or craft group. This part of market according to Kerr is based on prejudice or merit or equality of opportunity or seniority or some combination of these. The external market workers generally are available for new jobs within some meaningful strata. This whole definition of internal and external market leads to one segment of the labour market that is when the study talk of dual labour market, it indirectly focuses discussion on structured labour market only and unstructured market does not become a part of an external market (according to the dual labour market).

Dual labour market theory has captured the unresolved task left by the neo-classical theory. Neo-classical theory failed to explain the cause, behind persisting earning differentials. The psychological variables for measuring tasks, attitudes, and motivation for work are 'exogenous'. These psychological parameters may be the unexplored causal variables to explain employment, earnings and occupational differences. To answer this dual labour pointed that these psychological variables are endogenous and a result of labour market achievements.

Dual Labour explanations were not well accepted by other theorists and faced series of criticism from radical theorist, structuralist, and neo-classical economist. Cain[27] questions—

"On occupational structure a static snapshot reveal duality if so what matrix of occupational status produces this bimodality."

Nevertheless he praises dual labour market approach's contribution worth attention for: (a) idea of endogenous determination of attitudinal variables among workers, and (b) the institutional dimensions of internal labour market of the economics of bureaucratic organization.

2.3.4 Institutional Approach

The lack of explanation provided by marginal productivity within the framework of differential existing in market, gave headway to the rise of 'institutional approach', which explained wage differentials by forming theories on union bargain and other such institutions. Institutional approach surveyed for other than pure economic factors, bringing differences in wages. This approach further developed on political, social and psychological factors influencing decisions of workers regarding supply of labour. One approach that gained popularity in developing countries, and other parts of the world is the institutional approach. This approach could explain the residential phenomena, which other theories did not. Jerry Petr[28] advocated that this theory is holistic because change affects culture rather than just the economy and result in influencing the social institutions to evolving technology defined opportunities and constraints. "Institutional approach emphasizes on real rather than what is mythical and exhibits a concern with improvement of the human condition rather than merely intellectualizing it."

Institutionalism understands the present progress from the annals of past, starting from the scratch how this world progressed and what the progress ought to be. "Therefore work solidly grounded, from which broader understanding can be built, prized over deduced tautologies extruded from hypothesized premises and institutionalism accepts the humbling realization that both current objectives and constructive policies have a finite life. Evaluation, after all implies constant change and technology. Broadly defined, it mandates 'the habit of use', 'the institutions' that are the patterns of a culture."

Institutionalism also attacked the claim of neo-classical prediction of the disappearance of discrimination in longer term based on their faith in market rationality. Evolutionist or institutionalists believed that cultural symbolic processes do ensure that important social functions are carried out consistently and coherently but they also include hierarchical systems of invidious distinctions that are not necessary or desirable consequences of the processes of meeting social needs.

The concept of culture, though evolved independently, greatly influenced the institutionalists. The cultural definition of economic processes created institutional economics as an entirely separate, vibrating intellectual stream of thought. Institutionalist focuses on the 'habits of use', 'the institutions' that are the patterns of culture. Discrimination, which is believed to be an attitude in action, is deeply analyzed by the institutional techniques. Variables of culture are interlinked to find out the injustice, discrimination, inequality, choice, preference and their impact on the outcome in society. Veblen, John R. Commons, Wesley Mitchell are the major contributing founders of institutionalism.

2.3.5 Human Capital

Becker[29] also propounded human capital approach in the aftermath of the vehement opposition and criticism of the neo-classical approach. Within human capital approach he further suggests two approaches:

2.3.5.a The Egalitarian Approach

This approach sees demand conditions are the same for everyone and that the only cause of inequality is differences in supply conditions. Everyone more or less has the same capacity to benefit from investment in human capital. Investment and earnings differ because of differences in the environment, (family subsidies etc.), which give opportunity to some people to invest more than the others. Eliminating environment differences would eliminate these differences in opportunity and thereby eliminating the important differences in earnings and investments. The egalitarian approach implies that lower the marginal rate of return or cost, larger the invested in human capital.

2.3.5.b The Elite Approach

In this approach, conditions are identical and demand conditions vary among persons. Distribution of investment in human capital and earnings is more or less equal and approach thus assumes that everyone more or less has effectively equal opportunities. This approach assumes greater inequality in capacity.

In whatever circumstances, these two approaches explain little in the end of discrimination analysis. Thurow gave alternative approaches to interpret market discrimination; these two approaches were to explore basically pre-market discrimination.

Highlighting the importance and education in eradication of poverty and other social problem, Thurow stresses on the need of spreading education. Leftists, who argue the inferior education of the poor and minorities, reflects "a discriminatory effort to prevent them from competing with better educated groups and force them from competing with better educated groups to force them into menial, low income jobs. The right argues that the poor are poor because they have failed to work hard and get the education, which is open to them. Moderate generally refer to some mixture of these arguments, such as poor are poor because they have received bad education, partly, as a result of inadequately funded (and therefore inferior) school systems, partly as a result of sociological factors like disrupted families etc., that prevent poor children from absorbing the education that is available.

2.3.6. Social Capital

Social capital which has semblance of human capital and differs as it roots in the social/commune foundation whereas human capital involves human achievement through human skills acquired or inbuilt. Social capital concept has origin in the work of Robert Putnam[30] though there are several earlier similar concepts especially found in Coleman and Pierre Bourdieu[31] Structural Social capital[32] strictly involves various forms of social organization including roles, rules, precedents and procedures as well as variety of networks that contribute to co-operation. Cognitive social capital includes norms, values, attitudes and beliefs. They are complementary. Narayan and Pritchett[33] described five mechanisms which affect the outcomes; it improves social ability to monitor, increases possibility of cooperation in solving the problems, facilitate the diffusion of innovations, it reduces informal insurance. The concept of Social Capital becomes very important for the hind-sight of caste system as the caste groups provide the members social economic security and now even political security also lend them a powerful backup. Social capital may prove to be ideological weapon in the hand of the group which produces positive and negative ripples as well. The caste system if acts as social capital can be effective discriminator for other caste people easily while providing a safe base to their own members[34].

2.3.7 Wage Competition

This theory[35] assumes that people enter into the labour market with a definite, pre-existing set of skills (or lack of skills) and then they compete against one another on the basis of wages. In this theory education is crucial factor since it creates the skills with which people enter into the market. This approach shows three beneficial effects of the increase in the education level.

(a) An educational programme that transforms a low skill person into a high skill person raises his productivity and therefore, his earnings.
(b) It reduces the total supply of low skill workers, which leads in turn to an increase in their wages.
(c) It increases the supply of high skill workers and this lowers their wages.

The net result is that total output rises (because of the increase in productivity among formerly uneducated workers), the distribution of earnings becomes more equal and each individual is still rewarded according to merit. But this approach has raised serious doubts about the importance of the role of education in assigning right economic roles.

2.3.8 Job Competition Approach

Thurow[36] gave a more befitting reply to the above-mentioned approach by giving the example of the American labour market. He says that instead of people looking for jobs, there are jobs looking for people, exactly saying, for suitable people. According to the author in a labour market which is based on job competition, the function of education is not to give skill but to increase in productivity and higher wages on the workers. It is rather to certify 'trainability' and to enhance him by a certain status by virtue of his education level.

Thurow does not think that wage competition is compatible in its hypothesis. He argues that the usual explanation for the disparity of income is disproportionably affected by the combination of education and intelligence. Also while education has assumed greater equality in the post-war period the distinction of income has not. According to wage completion theory this should have led to a more equal distribution of earnings. In his words

> "Perhaps the most devastating problem with the simple wage completion is that it cannot explain the existence of employment. When the demand for labour falls; wages are supposed to fall until enough jobs have been generated to keep everyone fully employed at the lower wages. Yet the real world is full of unemployed workers whose presence does not seem to have led to falling wages for those who are employed."

Strongly favouring the job competition approach, he blames US Government's education and training policies for not having the predicted impact because they lacked job competition elements in the labour supplies of different job skills, but for matching trainable individuals with training ladders. Because most skills are acquired on the job, it is the demand for job skills, which creates the supply of job skills. But simultaneously he feels the permeability in the approach of picking and training the workers and for entry-level jobs; it is 'background characteristics' of the workers that forms the basis of selection. Those workers whose background promises the lowest training costs will be hired. These two approaches are placed at the centre stage and regarded in the contemporary approaches to find discrimination and alternative policy formations.

2.3.9 Other Approaches

2.3.9.a Cumulative Causation

This approach is an alternative to the 'equilibrium approach', which contain at the centre, the notion of instability. In "An American Dilemma" Myrdal[37] used circular cumulative causation and said it should and could be used instead of the neo-classical equilibrium concept. Myrdal distinguishes three components as being of strategic importance in the cause and effect relation that created a "Negro problem" in the U.S.A. (a) prejudices of whites and their discrimination towards blacks, (b) the standard of living of the blacks, and (c) black's intelligence, ambitions, health, education, mannerism, morals. This whole process of circulation becomes cumulative. Each state of equilibrium in the Myrdalian analysis thus becomes unstable and as soon as the system of equilibrium in the Myrdalian analysis is exposed to exogenous shock, which may have greater bearing on the next process thus influence the total outcome of discriminatory behaviour. He stressed the importance of gauging those other factors, which may have altered discriminatory practices for better or worse. In his words "a position, which in some sense can be described as a state of equilibrium between forces since a change does not call forth countervailing changes but, instead, supporting changes which move the system in the same direction as the first change but much further. Because of such circular causation a social process tends to become cumulative and often to gather at an accelerating rate." His work was wholly problem oriented and tools of analysis, which helps in shedding light on the "Negro problem" and its solution. Peter Skott, comparing neo-classical and cumulative causation, says that neo-classical approach saw discrimination in the market by first the preference and production possibilities while assuming all agents are perfectly rational. But cumulative causation kept preference and technical changes endogenous. Social factors thus interact with exogenous technical factors and the evolution of the economy depends on and is reflected in the social and institutional organization of the economy.

2.3.9.b Utility Approach

Arrow[38] hypothesized that initially all employees belong to one group and only later a new group enters in the labour market. The former group has a tendency to discriminate against the latter (this theory also lacks the compatibility in the sense it can not be applied in heterogeneous group, which already existed). At this point Becker had predicted segregation while Arrow says that there will be partial segregation and wage differences. The newly arrived group will be hired by certain firms, which would also retain employees from previous group. These members of the discriminating group who are employed in the integrated firms will receive higher wages and the employees from the new, discriminated group will receive lower wages than those paid by the firms that are still segregate. He finds 'utility function' as important as 'taste for discrimination'. He says there are two utility functions one is where the utility for the employer depends upon the profit and the numbers of persons in two groups employed U (b, w), in the second case where the utility depends on the profits and share of the employers who belong to one of the group U (b/w). In the latter case it is only the distribution between two groups and not the absolute number, which is decisive, and in this case employer tends to discriminate.

2.3.9.c Competitive Wage Theory

When all previous authors used models, judged in equilibrium, Lester Thurow[39] has shown how the economic gains of discrimination of the white society depend on the elasticity of the labour supply. The discrimination implies that the white employers' demand for labour from the discriminated black group decreases. He finds where there is discrimination; individual in the white society (the discriminator) maximizes a utility function that depends upon both income and physical distance from blacks. The changes in demand are assumed to be equal in all following three cases. In the first case, the labour supply is completely inelastic (Becker's case), in the second case infinite elasticity of wages and in the third case, the elasticity has a value somewhere in between these extremes. In the first case white society will gain, in the second case it loses as the supplied quantity of labour decreases with a given wage. The result in the third case is discrimination in a case where there is trade and at the same time, complete specialization in production. But this theory does not explain the continuity in earning gaps between these two societies. One explanation, which Thurow[40] provides is that discrimination, is held in place by white labourers and not by white employers (he meant to say that there are a few hidden trade secrets, which white employees refuse to reveal to black employees). The second explanation, which he gives, is very interesting, he begins with distinction made between "local and global optimum". Again in this phenomenon labour plays a very important role. He agrees that employer being a non-discriminaton will earn profit by shifting from all white to a mixed labour but he does not do so fearing the hostility generated amongst employees in short run. In his words "true if he continued to as blacks despite falling profits he would find that his profits would go up eventually, but to get from the local optimum to the global optimum he must go through a period of low profits." Assuming to be ignorant of such large profits he says that employers do not recruit a mixed labour.

2.3.9.d Social Custom Theory

Akerlof postulated the theory on social custom[41]. In which he had selected social customs and beliefs as a discriminatory factor. He explains discrimination with the help of economics and sociology. He proved people do discriminate because they consider consequences of their action first. He feels that people's utility depends not only on consumption but also on prestige in society. This prestige in turn, is assumed to depend on whether the persons follow the code of behaviour or not, in part on the percentage of the population which supports it.

Mancur Alson[42] does not find the ideas of preferences or prejudice or even consequences very convincing rather he emphasises on the economic gain made possible by the caste acquiring monopsony power. Some economists based their theory on incorrect information but Kenneth Arrow and Edmund Phelph perhaps were the first ones who hypothesized that employers generally want to possess correct expectations regarding the productivities of different groups but uncertainty concerning each separate individual leads them to misjudge the actual productivity of the potential recruit.

2.3.9.e Radical Labour

The basis of the market theory is profit maximizing firms with a monopsonistic position in the labour market. Radical theories are also similar to dual labour market theories in drawing upon sociological analysis of institutional change and power relations and also upon psychological analysis of determination of workers and employers' attitudes, preferences and motivations. Cain[43] states on behalf of radical segmented market theories that "class conflict and collusive behaviour by employer are emphasized." They assume that the workers' bargaining power is greatest when the labour force is ethnically homogenous.

2.3.9.f The Structuralist

High rate of unemployment in 1960s led think tank of leading labour economist—consisting of 'structuralists' who challenged orthodox theory of macro-economics of aggregative monetary policies, could rehabilitate full employment. "Structuralist claimed that the problems of poverty and employment were attributed to structural shocks and imbalances."[44] Structuralist argued that its principal patterns of industrial production, foreign competition and similar features which disrupted the matching of jobs and workers in the labour market.

2.3.9.g Social Structure of Accumulation (SSA)

Social Structure of Accumulation framework has brought new clarity to analysis of labour markets.[45] The integration of neo-Marxian class analysis with labour market segmentation models marks a major contribution of the SSA approach as developed in the late 1970s and early 1980s. The SSA theorists say that Institutionalist and Marxist labour market segmentation market analysis lacked a theoretical and historical basis. SSA theorists identify the development of labour markets and labour process as the central focus of the model. SSA theories offer a handle for social change while introspecting the labour contribution in economic development by identifying the role of race and gender.

Table 2.1: List of the Proponents of Discrimination Concepts and Causes

Author/Proponent	*Causes of discrimination*
Webb (1891)	Old customs and public opinion.
Fawcett (1917 and 1918)	Dominance of upper caste and rejection in the job market.
Sargant Florence (1931)	Monopsony (employer discrimination) and employee discrimination.
Myrdal (1944)	Three stages: (1) low standard of living due to socio-economic factors (Cumulative Causation), (2) Low esteemed and depressed, and (3) affects education, health, job and other mannerism.
Cicil Pigou (1952)[46]	Employment segregated or closed entry in some jobs.
Becker (1957)	An optimistic theory, which assumes discrimination, will disappear in long term. His opinion is well accepted that different kinds of discrimination will have additive effects.
Dual market (1957)	If employed in secondary job market then difficult to shift to primary job market.
Akerlof (1980)	Prestige in society and generally afraid of the consequences.
Rathbone (1977)	Lack of trade unions or unity (leadership).
Olson Mancur (1982)	Economic gains made by dominant caste for a long time.

2.3.9.h Welfarism, Social Choice and Social Justice

Discussion on approaches to understand discrimination cannot be concluded without any discussion on social choice, Welfarism[47] and social justice. Welfarism uses economic value to evaluate achievement of two objectives: efficiency and equity. Efficiency asks whether a proposed change produces more economic value than it consumes and whether it produces more net economic value than it consumes.

The welfare state is considered the highest desired achievement for policy makers. Welfarism further says that if the decision maker accepts certain value judgements, essentially that the good of society depends only on the welfare of individuals, as judged by those individuals and if certain technical assumptions are satisfied, then the decision makers judgements can be represented by a 'Bergson-Smauelson-Social Welfare-Function'. This approach is often called Welfarism, a term coined by Sen (1979).[48]

Welfarism has close connection with Utilitarianism and social justice. The word 'Utility', which originally signified the power of physical objects to give pleasure, has come to be used as a term for pleasure itself and so the utilitarian criterion can be expressed as the maximization of utility (this can conveniently be accepted as the most rational explanation of social justice). But society does not act on the principle of utilitarianism. We encounter at this point the concept of social choice. Rawls[49] in his famous theory of Social Justice explains, "So the principle of social choice is to realize the greatest good summed overall the members of society. We arrive at the principle of utility in a natural way, by this principle a society is rightly ordered and hence just, where its institutions are arranged so as to realize the greatest sum of satisfaction." Social choice theory has links with cooperative and non-cooperative game theory. The theory of social choice is concerned with deriving a social out come from individual preferences, with 'pareto-optimality' as one main constraint. The constitutional designer in social choice theory ask themselves what pareto-optimal outcome ought to be preferred, given what they know about individuals preferences and their notion of how the outcome ought to reflect or respect them.[50] The postulate of social choice theory has dealt at length how to relate the actual preferences of the actual individuals over the actual alternatives, on the one hand and the socially preferred outcome on the other[51]. They also impose consistency conditions on how the preferred outcome ought to change when we vary preferences of the individuals, the number of individuals or the set of feasible alternatives.

2.4. Discrimination and Caste

After having visited the theories and approaches to discrimination studies, we find that most of them have sought explanation in Western experience of gender inequality in wages and racial prejudice in various forms. Akerlof[52] tried to build theory based on social customs as a "means of discrimination" and experimented in behavioural traditions (believer and non-believer in traditions) in economic matrix to evaluate the outcome. Other theories have taken industrial societies, employment in public and private enterprises, wage structure etc. as main faculties of enquiry. Inasmuch as we cannot vaguely study discrimination pattern and behaviour, therefore, we need to look for areas, institutions, conditions where we can judge discrimination. By and large, all theories have similarities in principles yet they differ in methods adopted to scrutinize discrimination and interpreted discrimination according to individual perceptions. This study has concentrated on the common features that can be applied overall in the caste system to examine the discrimination and connected issues in the study areas.

Discrimination (social and ritual) can be traced in rural areas also but the kind of discrimination we find in labour market is entirely different, since caste categories dilute and people can easily hide their caste. What we observe in rural India is perennial existence of discrimination, which has perpetuated as inequality.

People live in harmony in villages without retaliating and questioning caste system. Seldom caste-conflicts have emerged in rural India as an outburst of economic deprivation (which have different dimensions). Banerjee and Knight[53] also comment "Economic discrimination against Scheduled Caste operates powerfully in the rural areas and it predominantly takes the form of discrimination 'prior to market', i.e. in access to land, property and education."

Since urban market is vast, opportunities are immense and there are numerous ways to operate even single job and hence their discrimination related experiences also vary and can be understood in plurality keeping socio-economic, psychological aslo political explanations in the job market. The subject of discrimination is complex which integrates hoard of other factors too. Kannan[54] comments succinctly on the caste and labour connections in urban sphere—

> "While a number of traditional institutions (such as the caste based division of labour among the upper and intermediate level of castes, patron client relationships, unpaid work and credit-labour linkages) have loosened their sway due to the pace of overall social transformation, the basic characteristics

> of social stratification and segmentation are still reflected in the status of labour and functioning of the labour market.... The 'obstructionist, image of the labour is a different kind of problem altogether and has to do with the psychic costs that entrepreneur are prone to attach to their investment decisions."

Psychic cost[55] is what Becker understood as 'taste for discrimination'; Papola and Rodgers[56] also acknowledge this fact stating:

> "It is also widely recognized that labour markets are segmented, that wage differentials unrelated to efficiency or productivity are the rule rather than exceptions and that quite often casual, unstable and low paid employment exists alongside high paid protected employment."

Jennings[57] finds four forms that may foretell the discriminated status of a labour (a) ranking of role, (b) accessibility to social resources necessary to develop personal capabilities, (c) activity associated with work, and (d) difference in the permission to develop particular capacities by a group.

Therefore, to understand urban market, distribution of labour according to social system like caste we need to follow a systematic, comprehensive approach. This study has primarily dealt with the approaches, which might lead to discrimination in any form on the basis of prejudice. Papola and Rodgers[58] choose to argue on this debate where the institutions such as economic, social and political, can affect economic outcomes. They refer about the instruments, which may influence end product, are contracts, property rights, system of priorities and patronage of hierarchies, further there are generally accepted values and purposes rules norms, which influence the rationality. They find it necessary to analyse all these institutions to judge all-round social and economic development.

Thus, this study intends to follow the theoretical frame of neo-classical studies to the rational approach of new labour status analysis of Harriss *et al.*[59] Inasmuch as there is no single approach, which can satisfy the need to understand institutions and labour market fluctuations significantly, this study blends all these four approaches to meet the objectives and name it "neo-institutional approach". These principles or notions can be the force behind discrimination and can be observed in caste discrimination too, in other way these principles can be kept under the headline of opinion, which can be proved or disapproved at the later stage of field survey. The literature survey has partially confirmed a few concepts behind discriminatory behaviour like prejudice, preference.

Deliberation on the discrimination got thrust when discriminatory attitude of whites increased towards black and coloured people. Evincing firm and irrational belief that whites are superior than black created a hiatus in society, which consequently generated racial conflict and oppression on blacks. Literature review on inequalities emanated due to the caste system is divided in two sections, first on caste and second on discrimination.

The literature on caste is reviewed to keep in mind the caste related inequality and resulting unequal distribution of power. Though most of the studies have examined the caste and resulting inequalities by the system, yet the dynamics of market forces and capital accumulation due to the caste system is given special reference in this study.

In the introduction of book Ahmed[60] (1993) projects that large portions of Scheduled Castes are employed as labourers, it may be high or low from place to place. He wonders,"whither money or development?" He judges and declares "thus the very nature of social and economic deprivation in rural India suggests that they are interwoven and the social structure operates as major constraints on the goal of equitable distribution of development gains." What this study has assumed as hypothetically, his statement more or less confirms it. In his words:

> "The traditional social structure in which hierarchical values command wide respect are likely to strife the cause of quality and distributive justice. The process of economic change, which was designated to generate impulses of overall growth, may succumb to the compulsions of the caste structure and thus fragments the effect of development in a few sectors of society."

Paper written by Kashi N. Singh[61] says about the caste and its various 'arms' which control the minutest subdivision of local rural settlement and illustrated over the residential part of caste society. Another paper deals with the relationship of landownership and caste. Mandhavdhare[62] studied rural parts of Marathwada region and concluded that there is a close linkage between historical economics, ritual supremacy and present distribution of land ownership. Atal[63] (1968) examined how caste consciousness is becoming important on the sphere of occupation and checked out the modern pattern of occupations, caste and psychological consequences of caste category. Along with change in caste occupations he explained the reservation policy and vested interest of privileged caste. He presented a full profile of the function of caste in Madhya Pradesh (Jaurasia, District Gwalior). He experienced the break off of the traditional *jajmani* system, economic indices have also changed in behaviour, mind as well.

Berreman (1979)[64] did a comparative study on the structural phenomena existing in India and America by selecting a north hill village called Sircanda in southern U.S.A. He says, "in U.S., colour is a conspicuous mark of caste, while in India, there are complex religious features which do not appear in America." He expresses view that caste as such was not often seriously questioned in the villages. Objections were characteristically directed not at caste but at my position in caste hierarchy. He dismisses the desire of low caste people who are suppressed under this system, on the same time never fail to abuse their subordinate group or fallows. It looks inevitable if author is discussing caste, to know the economic relations in caste. Berreman also underpinned the *jajmani* system, says it is an exploitative relation, and accounts following relations worth-mentioning in this aspect.

(i) When there is an important disparity between the economic power of *jajman* and worker, especially when latter is directly dependent upon the former for livelihood. This happens when (a) lack of essential services to offer the client; (b) lack of occupational monopoly; (c) lack of assured clientele; (d) lack of independent or alternative source of income; and (e) lack of organization which follows in a cohesive group.

(ii) Important disparity between the political power of the *jajman* and the worker.

(iii) When there is an important disparity in ritually prescribed status.

Thus, we can say Berreman tried to say that if any group economically, politically, ritually empowered becomes patron group who provides security to other castes. This high and low power status decides the local hierarchy of the caste groups.

Though the wedge amongst different caste people is not limited to the upper caste and lower caste label but it is sometimes very obvious within lower caste segment as well. Ghurye[65] said that the intra-caste restrictions and notions are also strictly followed where he mentioned very low castes themselves are quite strict about contact.

Though, there is a plethora of literature on village studies, yet Beteille (1974)[66] felt there is no substantial study conducted on the agrarian class structure. He warns those potential students who are interested in this field, which heavily bestowed on caste structure rather then class because of the acute paradoxes existing in caste and class structure even in a small place which can be entirely different from the neighbouring village. Two sample villages are structured in caste and class together and then taking discernible characters in the pattern of caste we have tried to study discrimination and caste.Beteille believes in village:

> "Hindu caste system which formed the basis of social divisions in traditional India may be viewed as the prototype of a hierarchical system. Caste has been particularly important in the social system centring around agricultural production, especially control and use of land."

Beteille has also mentioned that by the time government policies reach to the micro-level, they automatically are deliberated by the local dominant caste thus these policies actually are enjoyed by this privileged caste group. He tells how "the predominance of hierarchical values in the largest sector of a society has implications for the society as a whole. When new organizations are created they are frequently pervaded by these traditional values. Thus, in India it is remarkable how quickly Cooperatives, Block officials and even schools, boards become involved in hierarchical pattern." He observed that after the new era of development agriculture structure and bond between landlord and tenants has undergone a tremendous change. Therefore, he anticipated that personal bondage (*jajmani*) is gradually being replaced by commercial and political bond.

Frykensberg (1979)[67] has studied the landowner, and social structure in British India. He illustrated the influence of caste in *Ryotwari* administration in south. He says that caste system and customs exercised vast influence which no one could deny. There were administrators who tried to eliminate this kind of caste dominance and caste privilege but ultimately under the strong pressure of these landowners and then due to famous divide and rule policy of Britishers did not implement it. In other article he discovered though in *Ryotwari* system peasants were to pay directly to government deputed *zamindar* yet this rich peasantry was so influenced and blatantly manoeuvered at the time of renting a village for higher collection of revenues. If one has to infer from the book it becomes easy that all authors were at consensus, all landowner generally belong to the upper castes become rich in this whole process of selection of *Rayat.*

Jayaraman (1981)[68] studied incidence of class with caste structure and summarised that agriculture is the main source of livelihood in rural India. The upper castes own most of the land, while the agricultural labourers belong mostly to the middle and lower castes. Positions of caste hierarchy tend to coincide with positions of class structure of rural India.

Paranjape[69] (1970)first questioned the longevity of caste and attachment of people to the caste system. Then he studied caste and limitations faced by a particular caste in educational institutions in Pune. He did a psycho-economic analysis taking Bogardus' (1925) social distance scale. He defined the concept of social distance as the degree of and grades of understanding and feeling that a person experiences for other person. Based on this taste he felt the most common single type of complaint was that social status or prestige was denied to their caste. Almost all the Harizans complained and reported having actual experience of this type. He found discrimination in employment is a complaint fairly common to all three-caste groups. He also reported that upper caste students were anguished over non-availability of prize and scholarship but someone from lower caste won on the basis of his caste membership.

Srinivas[70](1987), one of the stalwarts in caste and caste related phenomena describes caste system as a harbinger of social inequality and harassment. It is a vicious circle of exploitation, he reaches to the conclusion from his various studies that dominant castes are generally non-Brahmin and owner of the land are among the worst practitioner of inequality and exploitation, their victims being local poor particularly the landless poor of Scheduled Castes. He infers in his studies that land owning is the means of going upward in hierarchy in villages. He gives various chances in which persons shift their calling by changing their residence, migrating to the urban places which may lead to a new formation of caste. He gave examples of ritual discrimination too.

Study done by Baljeet Singh[71] (1961) on the impact of land reforms in land holdings and agriculture structure says "Not only have the recent land reforms not touched the issue of land distribution but these have also failed in prevailing subletting and land renting." In such a pecuniary consequence he found that ratio of agriculture labourers is only 22 per cent and those who cultivate through hired labourers is 8 per cent only. He brings in the light the fact that consolidation itself is good but it is self-defeating if introduced prematurely without land redistribution and industrialisation to provide outlet for surplus agricultural labourers. He wonders at the highly coveted position of land in determining a status and power to a group on the same time this power acclamation deprives women and caste to a submissive position. In sensational revelations he tells almost 80 per cent of land is under possession of less than 40 per cent of upper and intermediate castes. He examined the impact of land reforms at the level of family, marriage, kinship and *jajmani* system share-cropping and labour system. He explains phenomenon of exploitation, because no legal system exists for agricultural labourers for wages. He proves that labour class is originated from lowest castes but then degree of exploitation has reduced a little bit. He reasons it that *majdoor* in rural setting have come under one umbrella and showed resentment whenever found denial of required wages in respect of some other labour class. Still the ultimate result favours landowners due to discriminatory institutions.

Delving into the literature on discrimination proceeded on how to handle discrimination keeping the caste system in view when whole body of academia is at consensus that the caste undoubtedly is highly discriminatory system in itself. The caste system has tried to capture international attention on the basis that it should be equated with race and a racial phenomenon as the caste system not only operates on the basic denial of equality but also it leads to the same results as the racial prejudice.[72] This study finds researches done on discrimination in race and gender sphere.

Ashenfelter's[73] (1973) edited book contains papers on discrimination by various economists with different perspectives. First paper by Finish Welch explored the possibility of discrimination in schooling and labour. Ashenfelter has hypothesized that unionism to a larger extent prevents wage discrimination. Ronald Oaxaca provides formulae for measuring discrimination against women. The last paper by Phyllis Wallace stirs the policy measures taken by government against black and female workers.

Backer[74] (1971) did his doctoral dissertation on discrimination in market, propounded different theories of discrimination, their mechanism and measurements. He gave first ever idea to measure discrimination providing term discrimination coefficient, typology of discrimination in thesis work.

Smith[75] (1979) investigated discrimination in 1966 among the residents from India, Pakistan, West Indies and white original population in United Kingdom. He analysed discrimination by choosing religion, language, academic qualification and these factors influencing the percentage of employment earning. To explain this he followed self-developed methodology of "The Actor Testing" in which two actors were taken, one white and other from any of the minority then they were sent for manufacturing unit first then housing application. In this controlled experiment his objective was how the actual level of discrimination can be supplemented by an account of how Asians and West Indians see discrimination and what the experience means to them. Also detailed studies of a particular plant and large organizations will show how discriminatory practices develop, why they are allowed to continue and how they can best be combated. In result, he says that the discrimination was stronger against applicants for non-skilled than for skilled jobs, that it is mainly based on colour prejudice against foreigners.

Freeman's[76] (1972) survey shows some positive changes in discriminatory phenomena. He finds there is a significant change in the number of trained black workers. He does not find utility theory of discrimination to find answer of occurring changes rather he thinks it should be supplemented by the education, training by non-competitive discrimination especially governments.

Akerlof[77] (1976) studied caste discrimination by applying economic model of equilibrium (as a set of the economy in which caste customs are obeyed). The difficulty in his study is that he uses caste phenomena in same way as race. He could not explain convincingly the compensation, which a person may earn by breaking down the custom or not. He said that the caste discrimination may persist due to the statistical discrimination.

Gannicott[78] (1985) has investigated earning differential if men and women are paid accordingly to the same wage structure, different endowments may account for the wage differences. He chose Human Capital Theory, and decomposed sex specific earnings into an endowment component and a discrimination component. His findings indicate that gender based wage discrimination though calculated by Discrimination, yet these results do not reflect the rational choice of men and women. He supplemented his statement by saying that women may rationally choose to invest more time in household and child rearing and less in labour market experience.

Lundahl and Wadenszo[79] (1987) evaluated neo-classical models of discrimination by deciding Becker's model as point of departure and finally developing alternative model of discrimination, evolving solutions based on these models. Knight and Sobot[80] (1982) evaluated labour market discrimination by sex and by race in poor urban economy, surveying manufacturing employers in Tanzania.

Ray[81] (1972) sketches various neo-classical model of discrimination. After discussing the pioneer work of Becker, he signifies the main differences between Becker and Krueger's approach. Giving special emphasis on Marcus Alexis's efforts to analyze discriminatory problem on the line of Krueger's idea of motivations of racial discrimination, he explains this question in *Envy Malice Model*. Here Marshall differs from Alexis's model, feeling that white capitalist should formulate this question in terms of benevolence towards white workers. Krueger and Alex both give equal importance to the class and group decisions. Praising Arrow's theory of utility function he concludes that his aim is to explain racial wage differentials not on productivity but uninformative category of imperfections without clashing with the social factors. He brings the case of maximising utility function. He discussed dual labour market theory also which came into the existence when scholars were studying ghetto labour market in 1960s. This theory deals with discrimination mainly as a factor in labour market segmentation in primary and secondary workers. In the end he disagrees with neo-classical economist that discrimination is more of a status phenomenon rather than a physical or superficial association of discriminator and discriminatee. Too much of emphasis on wages makes Marshall uneasy and he confesses "The neo-classical model fails to do this because it does not deal with bargaining between groups and assumes wages are workers only objectives and wage differentials change basic causal forces." A theory of discrimination should be able to explain the causes of discrimination and show how the economic variable in the model interacts with the central phenomenon to be explained. He ardently advocates for bargaining model, which takes the account of group decisions, a need to build public policy, stresses the need to explore the relationships between attitude, overt and institutional discrimination.

Stiglitze Joseph[82] (1972) followed the steps of conventional neo-classical theory for discrimination. He gave an in-depth analysis of theory. He stresses that economic point of view does not merely look for wage differential but education, on the job training, absenteeism, strength or IQ add to the last productivity of an individual yet "with conceptual approaches to the economic of discrimination, we can be satisfied by defining an economic characteristics as anything which affects the marginal productivity of an individual. In his efficiency wage model he described the efficiency to increase in developing countries due to nutrition and in developed countries due to psychological factors.

Marcus[83] (1972) has already been discussed in Marshall's paper. Here he is not in concordance with Becker's theory, however, he agrees that one has to take interpersonal comparisons of utility, in the long run, namely technology, personal comparison of utility he has quoted from Valvnis and says: (i) each man's (woman's) utility function is at least an ordered metric and (ii) one party manifests his utility to another and that manifestation increases with utility. He tried to explain the reasonableness of the "aversion doctrine" by assessing traditional view of employer and complementary factors of discrimination but he could find satisfactory answer. He seeks to explain rest of the questions based on envy malice model.

Solaun & Sidney[84] (1973) in their book aim to explain why racial discrimination has not been accompanied by substantial racial violence in Latin America. They found that the upper class consistently appeared as the discriminators and the lower class felt discriminated against. Further, the upper class strictly followed endogamy and maintained hierarchical race relations by blocking the access to its ranks of upwardly mobile Negroes. Though, writers accept that there is a crack in this kind of shield and even some of the upper caste people have started recognizing exogamy and non-hierarchical race relations.

Some of the recent addition in discrimination studies[85] examined relation between discrimination and psychological effects on people. The authors researched the effect of discrimination on the early childhood of Indian Americans. Perceived discrimination may interfere with establishing identities by introducing confusion regarding self worth (internalization of hatred and disrespect they see around them) or by contributing to angry, externalising reactions which may result in self-destructive behaviour such as delinquency and substance abuse.

The empirical research focused to find out the attitudinal shift and resulting change in the labour market post 9-11 episodes in America towards the minorities in Sweden. They concluded after the research that nothing could be as such interpreted as discrimination in labour market but it may be just due to their main concern often the change in the labour market situation rather than discrimination *per se* and also discrimination is not based on preferences that change quickly and employers and job searchers do not seem to react immediately to shift in public opinion or reports in the media[86].

Sarita Agrawal[87] (1993) reviewed literature on discrimination. She divided all these theories in three parts—first, neo-classical, second institutional and third being radical school. Agrawal thinks discrimination against women starts at the alter of home where she is not found worthy to go out and have work experience, and other productivity enhancement opportunities. She called this type of discrimination Pre-market discrimination, and second type is Post-market discrimination in which one group is ascertained some behaviour on the pre-conceived notion and thus thought fit to take in one area only. Extending analysis on all neo-classical economists, she explained the crowding model developed by this economist for instance Fawcett (1918) and Edgeworth (1922). She also discusses statistical discrimination, which in fact a kind of theory based on profit maximizing behaviour. She broached human capital theory inputting education as an important variable furthered by different educational programmes, price of education. These additional things add up to the final income of a worker. Dual market labour model which was discussed by Marshall in a huff, Agarwal sincerely appreciated the model which challenged earlier model because in mature market where she presumes market becomes segmented and non-competitive abandoning shifting of jobs thus halts the process of wage differences.

Bannerjee and Knight[88] (1985) published paper on discrimination and caste system. They surveyed in metropolitan city of Delhi, the "gross" differences between Scheduled Caste and non-Scheduled Caste workers. An interesting and highly motivating study on migrants from other parts of country, throwing light on their background, village or place of migration, type of job and salary have told a lot about this never fading shadow of caste category. Result displays highly variable conclusions. He found in the earning functions for production workers that urban experience for non-Scheduled Castes but not for Scheduled Castes.

Summing Up

- Overview of literature on theories, concepts and their implications explicably convey us that there is more than one explanation to discrimination in labour market both statistical and behavioural. Theories invariably overlap in describing psychogenetic and socially embedded phenomena such as discrimination, which could not find any hindsight by economic explanations. Theoretical models applied in empirical phenomena too lack principle of judging actors of discrimination through the perspective of one approach and took resort in all the theoretical approaches; sometimes behaviour conjectured endogenously and other time it may lie exogenously.
- The present study explains discrimination keeping institutional approach as centre model but also exercise neo-classical approach while judging discrimination.
- This study has found that though caste is a social system distinct from racial phenomena but can be studied under the wider umbrella of theories given on racial and gender labour market. Since these theories are based on the biological feature of individuals in labour market and hence are inefficient to capture caste discrimination, which is not a biological indicator but a social system, based on ascriptive roles (though can be explained).
- The caste system has historical origin and one of the theories behind the origin of the caste, is on the labour division of society thus it is very significant to see the nature of changes in market occupational dynamics and the caste hierarchy in the labour market.
- None of the study on discrimination has empirically judged caste as discriminatory factor and also these studies do not consider caste as processes and procedures, which may alienate one particular caste group in some distinct occupations in the market.
- The other aspect, which this study has taken care of, is the applicability of theories in the caste phenomena. The study takes care of these shortcomings, therefore, looked the caste system as processes in the labour market at the time of upbringing, recruitment, and finally, at the time of occupation and earning.

NOTES

1. David H. Autor (2003). http://economics.mit.edu/files/553, p. 4.
2. Charles and Guryan (2007) http://www.nber.org/papers/w13661.pdf, p. 1.
3. Charles and Guryan (2007). *Op. cit.*, p. 2.
4. Reynolds, Masters and Mosers (1987). *Economics of Labour,* Prentice Hall, New Jersey, pp. 355-356.
5. Metta Spences and Alex Inpules, "Foundation of Modern Sociology" in Mumtaz Ali Khan (1994). *Identity Formation and Self Identity Among Harizan Elite*, Uppal Publishing House, New Delhi. p. 207.
6. G.S. Becker (1971). *Economics of Discrimination*. Chicago University Press, Chicago, p. 22.
7. Steele and Aronson. (1995). Stereotype Threat and the Intellectual Test Performance of African Americans. *Journal of Pers Social Psychology*, 69(5):797-811 and Shih *et al.* (1999). *Psychological Science* 10(1):80-3.
8. Reynolds *et al.* (1987). *op. cit.,* considers segregation in the physical distance among the groups, and hence intensity of discrimination can be measured in respect of the physical distance emerged in the society. Going back on the caste discrimination we can say, if discrimination can be measured in race terms, then the caste hierarchy in contemporary society will make definition clear. The customs, opportunity and overall socio-economic profile may explain the hidden figures of preferences. p. 356.
9. Venkata Subramanyam (1973). *Group Prejudice in India*, Shree Ram Centre for Industrial Relations and Human Resources, New Delhi. p. 2.
10. Bradley R. Schiller (1980). *The Economics of Poverty and Discrimination*. Prentice Hall, New Jersey. p. 39.
11. Reynolds *et al.* (1987). *op. cit.* pp. 361-369, have divided the concept of discrimination in three main parts first which is 'Preference Discrimination', explained as employer, employee, customer and occupational crowding. 'Statistical Discrimination' is a situation where lack of information gives way to the stereotype decisions. In condition of scarcity of market players, few manoeuvre market supply and demand; this condition is called 'Monopoly Discrimination'.
12. Reynolds (1987), *op. cit.* p. 353.
13. Becker (1971). *op. cit.,* p. 55.
14. Becker (1971). *ibid.*, p. 77, p. 123.
15. Sidney and Webb (1891). *The Wages of Men and Women: Should They be Equal*, Fabian Society and Allen & Uhwin, London.
16. E. Rathbone, (1977). "The Remuneration of Women's Services", *Economic Journal,* Vol. 45, pp. 74-91.
17. Milicent Fawcet, (1918). "Equal Pay for Equal Work", *Economic Journal,* Vol. 28, pp. 1-6.
18. Pigou, C. (1952). *Essays in Economics*. Mcmillan, London, p. 7.

19. F. Edgeworth, (1922). "Equal Pay to Men and Women for Equal Work", *Economic Journal*, Vol. 32, pp. 431-457.
20. Sargant Florence (1931). "A statistical contribution to the theory Women's Wages", *Economic Journal,* Vol. 41, pp. 19-37.
21. G. Cain (1975). "The Challenge of Dual and Radical Theories of the Labour market to Orthodox Theory", *American Economic Association*, Vol. 65, No. 2., p. 17.
22. Becker (1971). *op. cit.*
23. Jerry Petre, *Comparative Economic Systems* in Hodgson, Samulson and Tool (1994). (ed) *Institution and Evolutionary Economics*, Edward Elgar Publishing Company, Vermont, p. 17.
24. Jennings, *Discrimination, Economic Policies to Counter* in Hodgson, Samuels and Tools (1994). *op. cit.,* p. 161.
25. Doeringer and Piore (1971). *Internal Market and Man Power Analysis*, Lexington Books, D.C. Heath; excerpts published in J.E. King (1980). *Readings in Labour Economics.* Oxford University Press, London. pp. 107-117.
26. Clark Kerr, "The Balkanization of Labour Market" in E. Wight Bakke (ed.) (1954). *Labour Mobility and Economic Opportunity*, Cambridge: MIT Press; excerpts of this article published in J.E. King (1980)(ed.) *op. cit.,* pp. 305-309.
27. Cain (1975), *op. cit.,* p. 20.
28. Jerry Petr (1994). *op. cit.,* pp. 69-75.
29. Gary S. Becker, *Human Capital and the Personal Distribution of Income,* Lecture excerpts republished in J.E. King (1994). *op. cit.* pp. 242-251.
30. Rober Putnam (1993), *Making Democracy Work: Civic Traditions in Modern Italy*, Princeton University Press, New Jersey.
31. James Coleman (1999). *Foundation of Social Theory,* Cambridge University Press and Pierre Bourdieu (1977). *Outline of Theory of Practice*, Cambridge University Press.
32. Uphoff (1999). in Graham Hobbs, *What is Social Capital? A Brief Literature Overview*, Economic and Research Foundation, June 2000. p. 3.
33. Narayan *et al.* (1997). *Voices of the Poor: Poverty and Social Capital in Tanzania*, World Bank, Washington DC, USA.
34. Dwaipayan *et al.* (ed.) (2004). *Interrogating Social Capital: The Indian Experience*, Sage Publication, New Delhi. This book explores social capital concept political assertion of Dalits, various development movements in hill area and even universal primary education have been analysed as tool for transformation. The study agrees with the authors that the social capital theory should be understood within the cultural setting.
35. Lester C. Thurow, *Education and Economic Equality*, republished in J.E. King (1994). *op. cit.* pp. 253-254.
36. Thurow (1975), *op. cit.*, p. 257.
37. Myrdal (1944). *The American Dilemma: The Negro Problem and Modern Democracy*. Harper and Row, New York p. 13.

38. K. Arrow, (1972). "Models of Job Discrimination", in Pascal (ed) *Racial Discrimination in Economic Life*. Lexington, Mass: D.C. pp. 83-102.
39. L. Thurow, (1969). *Poverty and Discrimination.* The Brooking, Washington D.C.
40. L. Thurow, (1975). *Generating Inequality*, Basic Books Inc. Publishing, New York, p. 161.
41. Akerlof, (1980). "A Theory of Social Customs, of Which Unemployment May be One Consequence", *Quarterly Journal of Economics*. Vol. 90, June, pp. 599-617.
42. Mancur Olson, (1982). *The Rise and Decline of Nations*. Yale University Press, New Haven. p. 21.
43. Glen G. Clain (1966). "The Challenges of Segmented Labour Market to the Orthodox Theory: A Survey", *Journal of Economic Literature*, p. 1226.
44. Glen G. Clain (1966). *op. cit.*, p. 1228.
45. Katze, McDonough, Reich (ed.) (1994). *Social Structure of Accumulation*, Cambridge University Press, Cambridge. p. 213.
46. The other way interpreting segregation hypothesis is done by Barbara Bergmann famous 'Crowding hypothesis', the difference in this hypothesis from segregation is that here certain jobs are identified as work of particular community. She used this hypothesis to distinguish women role in the market especially. In Elaine Sorensen (1990), "The Crowding Hypothesis and Comparable Worth", *Journal for Human Resource*, Vol 25, No. 1, p. 56.
47. Johnson and Johnson (ed.) (1990). *Economic Valuation of Natural Resources: Issues, Theory and Applications*, Westview Press, Boulder, USA, p. 13.
48. Shawn Hargreaves Heap *et al.* (1992). *The Theory of Choice: A Critical Guide*, Blackwell, Oxford, UK, p. 226.
49. Shawn Hargreaves Heap, *op. cit.*, pp. 270-271.
50. Elster and Hylland, (ed.) (1986). *Foundation of Social Choice Theory*, Cambridge University Press, Cambridge. p. 3.
51. Amartya Sen, "Foundation of Social Choice Theory: an Epilogue," in Elster and Hyland (1986), *Ibid.*, p. 214.
52. Akerlof (1980), *op. cit.*, p. 750.
53. Banerjee and Knight (1985). "Caste Discrimination in the Indian Urban Labour Market", *Journal of Development Economics*, Vol. 17, p. 281.
54. Kannan (1992). "Labour Institution and the Development Process in Kerala," pp. 49-52, in Papola and Rodgers (1992). *Labour Institutions and Economic Development in India*, ILO Research Series, 97.
55. It is a higher wage, which a person pays due to prejudice or discrimination. He favours his own social group while employing persons. Discriminator becomes irrational and that is how he is paying more as pecuniary cost (Marcus, 1973). Weber also wrote about irrational and rational attitude of a person. Discrimination emerges from this irrational behaviour of a person. He gave a concept of Wertrationalitat (where choice of means is oriented to the

rationalization of single absolute value). Zwerckrationalitat it is oriented to a plurality of values in such a way that devotion to anyone of them is limited by possibility of its entailing excessive cost in the form of sacrifice of others. In Harlomb and Parsons (1990). *op. cit.*, p. 14.

56. Papola and Rodgers (1992). *op. cit.* p. 2.
57. Jennings Ann, *Discrimination, Economic Policies to Counter,* p. 163, in Hodgeson and Tool (1994). *Institution and Evolutionary Economics* (ed.) (1994). Edward Elgar Publishing Company, Vilmont.
58. Papola and Rodgers, p. 2 *op. cit.*
59. Harriss, Kannan, Rodgers (1990). *Urban Labour Market Structure and Job Access in India*, ILO Research Series, 92.
60. A. Ahmed (1993). *Social Structure and Regional Development*, Rawat Publications, New Delhi, pp. 8-11.
61. Kashi N. Singh, "Caste and Clan in Indian Rural Settlment Syatem" in Ahmed (1993). *ibid.* p. 51.
62. Mandhavadhare "Caste and Land Relations: Evidences from Marathwada" in Ahmed (1993). *ibid.*
63. Yogesh Atal (1968). *The Changing Frontiers of Caste*, National Publication, New Delhi, pp. 205, 237-239.
64. Berreman (1979). *Caste and other Inequalities*, Folklore Institute, Meerut, pp. 5, 73, 83-85.
65. Ghurye (1979). *Caste and Race in India*, Popular Prakashan, Bombay. He says that the Bansphor and Basor themselves branches of the Dom caste will touch neither a Dom nor a Dhobi whilst the Basor with all the intolerance of the Parvenu extends his objections to the Musahar, Chamar, Dhakar and Bhangi. pp. 49-57.
66. A. Beteille (1974). *Agrarian Social Structure*, Oxford University Press, Delhi, p. 50.
67. Frykensberg (1979). *Land Control and Social Structure in Indian History*, Manohar Publications, New Delhi.
68. R. Jayaraman (1981). *Caste and Class*, Hindustan Publishing Corporation, Delhi, p. 10.
69. A. Paranjape (1970). *Caste and Social Change*, National Institute of Community Development, Hyderabad, pp. 2, 212.
70. M.N. Srinivas (1987). *The Dominant Caste and Other Essays*, Oxford University Press, Delhi, pp. 10, 47, 76.
71. Baljit Singh (1961). *Next Step in Village India*, Asia Publishing House, Bombay.
72. Narang (2001). "World Conference against Racism: Prospects and Challenges", *Economic and Political Weekly*, July 7th, Vol XXXVI, No. 27. p. 2495.
73. Ashenfelter and Rees (1973). *Discrimination in Labour Market,* Princeton University Press.
74. G. Becker (1971). *op. cit.*

75. Smith J. David (1979). *Racial Disadvantage in Britain*, Pelican Publications, U.K.
76. R.E. Freeman (1973). "Decline of Labour Market Discrimination and Economic Analysis", *American Economic Review,* Vol. 63, No. 2.
77. Akerlof (1976). "The Economics of Caste and of the Rat Race and Other Woeful Tales", *Quarterly Journal of Economics*. Vol. 90, November. pp. 599-617.
78. K. Gannicott (1985). "Women, Wages and Discrimination: Some Evidences from Taiwan", *Economic Development and Cultural Change,* Vol. 34, No. 4.
79. Lundahl and Wadensjo (1984). *Unequal Treatment: A Study in the Neo-Classical Theory of Discrimination*, New York University Press, New York.
80. Knight and Sobot (1982). "Labour Market Discrimination in a Poor Urban Economy", *Journal of Development Studies.* Vol. I, No. 19, pp. 65-87.
81. Ray Marshall (1972). "The Economics of Discrimination", *Journal of Economic Literature,* Vol. 12, pp. 849-71.
82. J.E. Stiglitz (1973). "Approaches to the Economics of Discrimination", *American Economic Review*, Vol. 63, No. 2.
83. Alexis Marcus (1973). "A Theory of Labour Market Discrimination with Independent Utilities", *American Economic Review,* Vol. 45, pp. 74-91.
84. Solaun and Krounus Sidney (1973). *Discrimination Without Violence*, Interscience Publications, Wiley.
85. Whitebeck, Hoyt *et al.* (2001). "Perceived Discrimination and Early Substance Abuse among American Indian Children", *Journal of Health and Social Behaviour*, Vol. 42, December, p. 405.
86. Olof Aslund and Dan Olof Rooth (2004). "Shifts in Attitudes and Labour Market Discrimination: Swedish Experiences after 9-11".
87. Sarita Agarwal (1993). "Gender Discrimination in Labour Market: A Review of Literature", *The Indian Journal of Economics,* Vol. 36, No. 2. pp. 152-168.
88. Bannerjee and Knight (1985). "Caste Discrimination in the Indian Labour Market", *Journal of Development Studies.* Vol. 17, pp. 277-305.

3
Occupation and Earning

Studies on discrimination based on race, religion gender or region specific can be put in two broad heads, one segregation and second access to skill enhancing capitals. This chapter largely tries to find out if occupations and earnings are aligned on caste lines. The chapter, therefore, first presents employment status, labour status after which occupation is examined on caste background. The second section delves on the nature of occupation as told by the respondents. Finally, analysis moves over to the earning section where the study has examined earning differences cross-sectional and also each caste group separately analysed on the basis of occupation, education and earning.

Studies on discrimination derived two methods to obtain occupational discrimination; first by finding out the distribution of occupation in the targeted groups, second by cross-examining education and occupation. The present study has also adopted the same method while simultaneously trying to segregate the degree of discrimination by knowing the nature of job also. However, the nature of occupation could not be easily established by just percentage distribution due to statistically small number of respondents in this category. The inference, therefore, has been taken out from the observation and some from the workers history of respondents.

3.1 Employment Status and Caste

Discrimination embarks at the time of selection of labour[1], therefore, to fathom the magnitude of discriminate. This chapter first divides workers according to the sectors they are working in. Employment status is different from the labour status in this study as employment status is defined employment in public, private, casual, self-employed workers, apprentice and unemployed workers. The scheme for employment status is as follows:

1. Casual workers (daily wage worker)
2. Own Account worker
3. Wage worker (temporary)
4. Wage worker (permanent)
5. Self-employed
6. Unemployed/Currently Seeking job

Employment status connotes the affiliation of respondents with the class of employment encompassing terms of employment, informality or formal bonding with the job they are working in.

Employment status fails to throw light on the aspects of the nature of job but for an overall picture of the employment structure in the labour market the present study has divided all respondents in such a structure which can give comprehensive overlay of the labour market. Employment status impinges upon the segmentation theory where the employment opportunities are regulated and circulated in the same types of jobs. This study also finds clear dimension and division in the labour market as supported by the dual market approach which divides labour market in two sections one progressive occupation and other dead end jobs. The vulnerability aspect[2] is given a very important thrust in the labour status studies and hence, it is but inevitable to bring in the concept of labour status to visualize and decode discrimination in labour market.

There is concentration of own account workers in all caste categories, yet intermediate caste, and upper caste workers have significant share in this category (34.2%, 27.1% in same order) in Kanpur City and this employment status also have the highest percentage (28.5%) share in all employment status groups. Second highest percentage (24.8%) is found to be in the temporary wage worker group to the total where the upper caste and lower ex-untouchables share highest percentage (25.0% each) while the intermediate caste workers are represented by an insignificant difference 24.3 per cent. In the self-employed category the upper caste respondents have the highest per cent share (18.8%) to the total percentage of upper caste workers. The casual work status is dominated by the intermediate caste and lower and ex-untouchables caste group where they have 23.4 per cent and 30.8 per cent to the total percentage of their respective caste groups. The occupation category stands third in the importance of employment provider (22.9% to the total). Unemployed situation is bad in Kanpur City because 10.2 per cent of the respondents said to be unemployed and willing to work, of which it is grim in the lower and ex-untouchables caste groups (15%) while second lowest in the upper caste group (8.3%) to the total workers in the caste categories (Table 3.1).

Table 3.1: Employment structure in Kanpur City

Employment Status	*Upper Castes*	*Intermediate Castes*	*Low and Ex-Untouchables*	*All*
Casual work	4.2	23.4	30.8	22.9*(61)
Self-employed	18.8	3.6	2.8	6(16)
Own account work	27.1	34.2	23.4	28.6(76)
Wage work (permanent)	16.7	8.1	2.8	7.5(20)
Wage work (temporary)	25	24.3	25.2	24.8(66)
Currently unemployed /seeking job	8.3	6.3	15	10.2(27)
All	100.0 (48)	100.0 (111)	100.0 (107)	100.0 (266)

*Column Per cent, Numbers in parentheses.

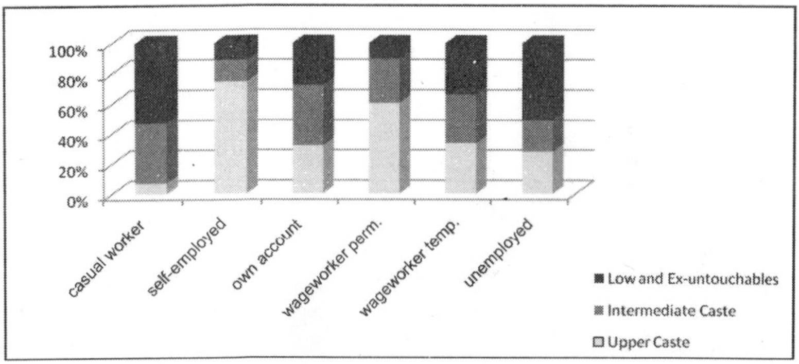

Fig. 3.1: Employment Status amongst Caste Groups in Kanpur City

The data (Fig. 3.1) suggest respondents from lower caste categories have high concentration in temporary wage work group though other caste as classified has different concentration point by employment status in Ghaziabad. The lower and ex-untouchables do not have significant representation in other employment status except temporary wage work and casual work (those who are employed in a construction industry).

There is a cyclic presentation of the Ex-untouchable migrants from eastern U.P. and Northern M.P., who are living in the shanties and working as unskilled, skilled casual labour). Some of them claim that they are contractors for construction workers, therefore, ask relatives, friends, neighbours in case of extra work available. The Intermediate caste respondents are found to be engaged in the highest percentage (46.1%) in temporary wage work group. If study interprets in terms of distribution spread in temporary wage work status in all caste segments then it can be inferred, this category has given employment to all caste (43.4%). Casual workers category again has heavy tilt in favour of the intermediate caste respondents. While observing the unemployment status the study finds that once again percent of respondents unemployed was highest (7.8%) in the intermediate caste. A very small per cent of people from the upper caste and the lower ex-untouchables have said to be unemployed (2.1% and 2.4%) (Table 3.2).

Table. 3.2: Employment Structure in Ghaziabad

Employment Status	Upper Castes	Intermediate Castes	Low and Ex-Untouchables	All
Casual work	4.2	20.4	24.4	18.0*(46)
Self-employed	22.9	3.6	9.8	8.2(21)
Own account work	14.6	16.2	22	16.8(43)
Wage work (permanent)	14.6	6	7.3	7.8(20)
Wage work (temporary)	41.7	46.1	34.1	43.4(111)
Currently unemployed/seeking job	2.1	7.8	2.4	5.9(15)
All	100*(48)	100(167)	100(41)	100(256)

*Column Percent, Numbers in parenthesis

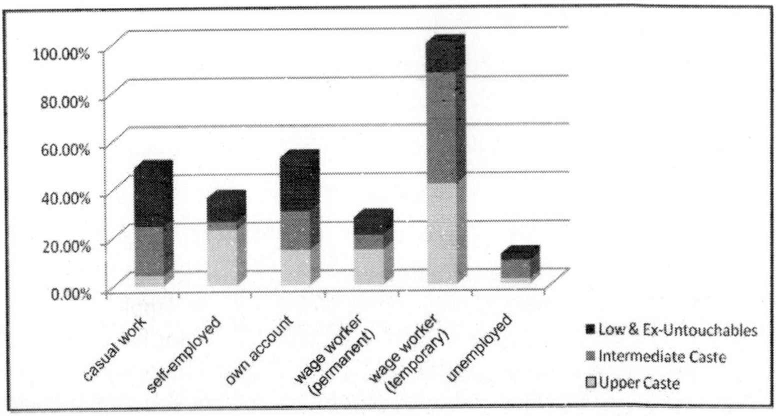

Fig. 3.2: Employment Status amongst Caste Groups in Ghaziabad

Chitra Joshi[3] in her study found the same writes—

> "Seeing the decline in the industrial economy of Kanpur, new industries have groomed up in the outskirts of Kanpur. Where wage cost is low and tradition of trade union movement was silent. Workers turned to other works; rickshaw pulling, pan, vegetable and fruit vending etc."

The legacy of industrial town of Kanpur City may have changed yet not altered entirely is evident in Fig. 3.1 temporary wage workers (consisting mainly factory employment and small establishments) still employs 25.2 per cent of all respondents, where all castes are represented almost equally with very slight difference.

Academicians in the West gave more attention to the earning differentials and occupational segmentation. Becker gave two conditions; first hypothesizing individuals have differences in human capital inputs resulting in the variation of available opportunity. Second approach says inputs are same in all individuals in the market but demand (or opportunity search and obtainment of the job) changes from person to person and place to place. Like Becker, Thurow has also given explanation for occupational discrimination on two premises first he theorized that people compete with each other for wage on the basis of qualifications, and second approach says that actually education is screening a person's productivity and trainability in the market. While Becker's approach determines pre-market discrimination (human resource approach), and also market discrimination (*taste of discrimination*) then Thurow assesses his theory in post-market discrimination.[4]

3.2 Classification of Labour and Labour Status

There are not only one but several classifications devised by experts in labour studies encompassing different magnitudes. In India the Census started defining 'Worker' as early as 1872. Over a period the term 'work' and 'worker' as defined by Census of India have undergone several amendments to suit the changing dimensions of work[5]. Work is defined as participation in any economically productive activity with or without compensation, wages or profit. Such participation may be physical and/or mental in nature. Work involves not only actual work but also includes:

(a) Supervision and direction of work;
(b) Part time help or unpaid work on farm, family enterprise or in any other economic activity; and
(c) Cultivation or milk production even solely for domestic consumption.

Accordingly, as per Census of India, all persons engaged in 'work' defined as participation in any economically productive activity with or without compensation, wages or profit are workers.

Following are some of the best-known classifications given by experts on Labour issues.

(1) World Labour Report[6]

(a) Permanent labour in Progressive jobs.
(b) Casual employment:
    (i) short term wage work in large scale enterprise,
    (ii) wage work in a small enterprise, and
    (iii) dependent self-employed.
(c) Apprentices.
(d) Domestic workers.

(2) Bromley and Gerry (1979)

(a) Stable wage work
(b) Short term wage work
(c) Disguised wage work
(d) Dependent work
(e) True self-employment.

(3) Harris and Rodgers (1986)

(a) Protected wage work
(b) Competitive regular wage work
(c) Unprotected wage labour
(d) Self-employed and family labour in 'productive' small-scale activities
(e) Marginal activities.

The present study has borrowed the labour status classification by Harris, Kannan and Rodgers[7]. They studied labour status in Coimbatore, Tamil Nadu. The labour status as studied by them basically aims to capture the 'vulnerability' of a worker in the labour market. This classification also takes care of employment status, distinction between employer and self-employed, unpaid family worker and wage worker. Hence, the present study examines inequality in occupation and labour status as mentioned in the given schema and felt it appropriate to apply in this study. This typology also subsumes the organizational difference and captures other personal details also.

(a) Formal:
    (i) job security
    (ii) regularity of work
    (iii) levels of stability of income
    (iv) training facility and promotion.
(b) Casual:
    (i) hired for short term basis by large scale private or public enterprises
    (ii) by small scale enterprises.
(c) Dependent self-employed or autonomous wageworkers: who work on contract basis or in labour gangs.,
(d) Capital owning self-employed.

Table 3.3: Classifications of Workers by Harris and Rodgers

Labour Category and its components
1: Formal (i) job security, (ii) regularity of work, (iii) levels of stability of income, (iv) training facility and promotion prospects
2. *Casual* *(i) hired for a long term in private sector (unprotected, regular)* *(ii) hired for short term in private enterprise (unprotected, irregular)*
3. *Dependent self-employed* *(or autonomous workers, who work on contract basis or in labour gangs.)*
4. Capital owning self-employed

They have developed this typology basically to rule out the minute neglected aspects, which are not incorporated in general classification of workers where employment status, distinction between employer and self-employed, unpaid family worker and wageworker is not clearly spelled out and hence it could not reflect different labour processes or modes of insertion into labour market. This classification of workers has one more merit which engulfs every part of the labour market in a very precise manner, giving proper attention to regularity, autonomy, protection, these points which are more 'vulnerable' elements (italics in Table 3.3.) to discrimination and in reverse enhances one's living standard.

The discussion on workers classification leads this study to adopt the classification given by Kannan and Rodgers where vulnerability includes aspects of security, compensation on the work floor and regularity of job as the most important or variables to consider discrimination. Going into more details of respondents work, their labour status is promoted on the basis of legal protection, regularity, duration of job and type of contract, as developed by Kannan and Rodgers[8] in their study on Coimbatore. The scheme is as follows:

(1) Protected Regular Wage Work
(2) Unprotected Regular Long Term Wage Work
(3) Unprotected Regular Short Term Wage Work
(4) Unprotected Irregular Wage Work
(5) Independent Wage Work
(6) Capital Owning Self-Employed (Fixed Capital more than Rs. 500)
(7) Marginal Self-Employed (Fixed Capital less than Rs. 500)

This scheme fetches more attention as it includes parameters like protection provided by the employers and job tenure. Regularity in occupations is a very important aspect especially as it reduces the chances of vulnerability and enhances the chances of partial stability in the market. The study also favours this scheme since many casual labours once clubbed together can be distinguished according to duration (short or long) of the availability of jobs. The other significant category is independent wage work. The workers who were earlier fall into self-employed category (e.g. cart pullers, gardeners, contractors, labour, loading-unloading workers), be extracted out from self-employed category as Harriss, Kannan and Rodgers define "This is work for wage where the wage relationship with a single employer is less clear than other categories."

Harriss and Kannan[9] have differentiated between labour status and employment status, using legal guarantees or protection for a permanent labour status and without such protection as temporary workers. Authors do not get guided by the protection and non-protection for labour status but includes 'regularity of employment' within the purview of labour status, regarding this authors believe that workers in temporary unprotected jobs also get jobs regularly and hence they include regularity as the second element in labour status. The concept of regularity and irregularity presumed to be varied in private and casual workers. Casual workers (construction, contract workers etc.) face not only irregularity of work but also work tenure is highly seasonal.

3.2.1 Labour Status

Labour status evinces details on regularity and permanency factors, which earlier table on employment status did not explain. The upper caste apparently has the highest percentage (35.4%) in protected regular work classification and the lowest falls in low and ex-untouchables category in Kanpur City. It is necessary to mention here that workers not only working in public enterprise but also in private organizations possesses written contract in case of protected regular work.

Table 3.4: Labour Status by Caste Groups in Kanpur City

Labour Status	Upper Castes	Interme-diate Castes	Low and Ex-Untouch-ables	All
Protected Regular Wage Worker PR	35.4	21.6	10.3	19.5(52)
Unprotected Regular Long Term Wage Worker (UR)	8.3	22.5	19.6	18.8(50)
Unprotected Regular Short Term Wage Worker (URST)	4.2	7.2	8.4	7.1(19)
Unprotected Irregular Short Term Wage Worker (UI)	0	9	16.8	10.5(28)
Capital Owning Self-Employed	39.6	11.7	12.1	16.9(45)
Marginal Self-Employed	0	16.2	15	12.8(34)
Independent Wage Worker	4.2	6.3	3.7	4.9(13)
Unemployed	8.3	5.4	14	9.4(25)
All	100 (48)	100 (111)	100 (107)	100 (266)

*Column Per cent, Numbers in parentheses.

The second highest percentage (18.8%) to the total percentage of labour status can be found in unprotected regular short term wage work. In category, the low and ex-untouchables once again have higher percentage (8.4%) to the total respondent of this caste. Seemingly the lower and ex-untouchables caste respondents have rather high representation in the more vulnerable labour status such as unprotected irregular short term[10], marginal self-employed (16.8% and 15%

respectively). Unprotected regular long-term (UR) segment shows that intermediate caste (22.5%) has the highest number of respondents in this labour status group and also the low and ex-untouchables have the highest percentage (19.6%) of the respondents falling in this labour status. The low and ex-untouchables group have presence in other classes as well, i.e. protected regular wage worker (10.3%), unprotected regular wage worker (19.6%), capital owning self-employed category (12.1%) to the total respondents in their caste group. One reason behind such observation can be that overall lower and ex-untouchables dominate the sample size and on the other side this conclusion enforces the overall inferior position of ex-untouchables in the market also. It is not so surprising that the upper caste shares the highest percentage (39.6%) in the capital owning self-employed group and second with marginal difference in regular protected jobs (35.4%). Overall protected regular wage workers have convincingly good percentage (19.5%) share in all types of labour status while other two groups with marginal difference are unprotected regular long term wage workers (18.8%) and capital owning self-employed group (16.9%). The high per cent in unprotected regular wage workers amongst all types of labour status categories also indicate that people are still able to fetch regular jobs and also specifically this category included the organizations which are registered and where labour union is also present such as municipal corporation occupations and hence have respectable figure in this labour status category in Kanpur City (Table 3.4).

Table 3.5 shows that the upper caste respondents have the highest percentage (41.7%) to the total upper caste respondents in protected regular wage work segment in Ghaziabad also while the unprotected regular long-term wage work is dominated in the intermediate caste respondents (29.3%). Even in the unprotected regular short-term wage work section too the study finds that the intermediate caste[11] and lower ex-untouchables have been leading (17.4% and 12.2%) to the total percentage of their caste groups.

The study would like to recall here that in Ghaziabad also the intermediate caste respondents were higher in proportion than other caste categories. Independent wage worker in the labour status is different from other labour status levels which is approximately includes all own account workers. The upper caste respondents have the higher share (12.5% to the total) while all other caste categories have only 6.6 per cent in intermediate caste and 2.4 per cent in ex-untouchable category.

Table. 3.5: Labour Status by Caste Groups in Ghaziabad

Labour Status	*Upper Castes*	*Intermediate Castes*	*Low and Ex-Untouchables*	*All*
Protected Regular Wage Worker PR	41.7	13.2	17.1	19.1*(49)
Unprotected Regular Long Term Wage Worker UR	16.7	29.3	26.8	26.6(68)
Unprotected Regular Short Term Wage Worker URST	2.1	17.4	12.2	13.7(35)
Unprotected Irregular Short Term Wage Worker UI	0	13.2	24.4	12.5(32)
Capital Owning Self-Employed	25	8.4	7.3	11.3(29)
Marginal Self-Employed	0	4.2	7.3	3.9(10)
Independent Wage Worker	12.5	6.6	2.4	7(18)
Unemployed	2.1	7.8	2.4	5.9(15)
All	100(48)	100(167)	100(41)	100(256)

*Column Per cent, Numbers in parentheses.

It could be because the upper caste respondents have longer stay in Ghaziabad and the respondents reported to be working as liaison, contractor which falls under the labour status classification as independent wage worker. In the capital owning self-employed section percentage share progressively declines from the upper caste respondents to the lower ex-untouchables caste group and the upper caste respondents reported to have large percentage share (25.0%) (Table 3.5). Unemployment situation though can be considered better to Kanpur City yet unemployment is high in intermediate caste categories (7.8%).

Ghaziabad differs from Kanpur City if the study evaluates marginal self-employed and independent wage work categories. Marginal self-employed section in Kanpur City has significant 12.8 per cent workers in this category, while Ghaziabad shows negligible representation (3.9%). In independent wage work category Ghaziabad has better representation (7.0%) than Kanpur City (4.9%). In both the cities the study finds that protected regular wage workers and unprotected regular long term wage workers have the highest percentage share among all labour status categories especially in Ghaziabad. The ex-untouchables representing mainly unprotected irregular wage work, unprotected regular short-term wage work. The low castes have highest percentage in self-employed category.

3.3 Caste and Occupation Structure[12]

There is huge literature available on the classification of occupation, however, there seems to be no consensus amongst the academicians and learned people on the subject. The study has a small sample size thus occupations as told could not be incorporated due to fragmentation and therefore, grouped for analysis.

3.3.1 Occupational Classification

Occupational structure is worked out to find out the demarcation of high end jobs, middle jobs and low or dead end jobs while keeping the functional importance of the occupation also in the job structure (attached dignity).

Thus, the job structure is classified as managerial other professionals (teachers, managers, clerical) skilled, menial/unskilled and agriculture (Table 3.6). The occupational structure is further cross-examined by observing the change in the occupation of the respondents and parental occupation. It was even more intriguing to find out how respondents work in the industrial economy and successfully integrate their traditional mode of earning[13].

Table 3.6: Classifications as Adopted in the Study

Sl. No.	*Occupation*
1.	Professional/Managerial
2.	Skilled
3.	Semi-skilled
4.	Menial/Unskilled

Once again this classification of occupation is to keep the skill and prestige both (professional/managerial, skilled, semi-skilled, and unskilled, second classification is earning focused worked under the head of employment status and third is labour status which covers vulnerability and insecurity of a labour. Under professional jobs managers, clerks, teachers and supervisors with diploma are included. All the teachers who are imparting education in any field have included under this head even if they are taking coaching classes. Supervisors, welders, machine tool operator, carpenter's (who are not self-employed) kind of jobs are included skilled other type of jobs. Skilled transport workers are drivers, mechanics, while construction skilled jobs are those, which need some level of specialization like *Rajmistry* (mason), mistry, contractor, and painter. Respondents involved in trading, business activity at least worth of Rs. 500— fixed capital asset. The other semi-skilled categories have workers who are vendors, small shops, tailors (doing only altering), small sweet shop and whole seller etc. Self-employed in agriculture is also included in the semi-skill category. Menial unskilled activities are those, which are largely unskilled like load-unloader, rickshaw puller (not owners), servant, agriculture labourers, watchman, washer man, cleaner, shoe shiner, waiter etc.

Table 3.7: Occupational Structure by Caste Groups in Kanpur City

	Upper Caste	*Intermediate Caste*	*Low and ex-untouchables*	*All*
Professional	20.8	8.1	2.8	8.3*(22)
Skilled	54.2	39.6	18.7	33.8(90)
Semi-skilled	16.7	27.9	36.4	29.3(78)
Unskilled	0	18	27.1	18.4(49)
Unemployed	8.3	6.3	15	10.2(27)
All	100.0*(48)	100.0(111)	100.0(107)	100.0(266)

*Column per cent, numbers in parentheses.

Like Kanpur, upper caste respondents are concentrated in professional group of works in Ghaziabad (Table 3.8) also. There is variation in workers found in the types of jobs in both the places, for instance there is larger number of workers found in construction industry in Ghaziabad, which shows the demand for workers in construction industry in and nearby areas of Ghaziabad (influence of Delhi in this matter cannot be ignored). Kanpur respondents, who were vendors, reported that they were once mill workers and still drawing pensions from the closed mills. The figure on occupation indirectly depicts the industrial condition in both areas. Share of skilled (machine operator and also helper) workers in Ghaziabad connotes the healthy status of industries, whereas Kanpur does not have so robust industrial situation considering the percentage of skilled workers. People engaged in semi-skilled (mostly own account workers, or petty shop owners) workers are higher in Kanpur City than Ghaziabad. In Kanpur intermediate and low ex-untouchables caste respondents have highest percentage in semi-skilled category amongst all occupation groups, on the same time upper caste respondents show highest percentage in skilled category.

Both the study areas show a different type of graph of occupations of respondents according to caste categories. The data in Table 3.7 show though there is large number of workers employed in unskilled activities especially share of low and ex-untouchables caste respondents is comparatively high in both the study areas[14]. The figure displays a glaring account of the occupational segregation along the caste categories. Upper caste respondents dominate white-collar jobs. The upper caste and ex-untouchables respondents are (upper cast workers were at the post of clerk, supervisor in Court 'Munsifi' while ex-untouchable workers were in sweepers, Supervisor 'cleaner', '*Khallasi*' in Municipal Corporation, Railways) employed in public sector; upper intermediate caste is conspicuous by its absence in Kanpur City. Other jobs though show different share by each caste group yet sweeper, shoemakers/shoe-mending are the jobs, which are done by ex-untouchable caste invariably, and upper caste and other intermediate caste share jobs considered clean and prestigious while other jobs distributed with marginal difference amongst other caste categories for example occupations, which do not show such biasness for example salesman, tailors, machine tool operator, machine fitter, and construction worker. Though these occupations can be done by anybody yet nature of job is the basis to derive discrimination in the jobs.

Table 3.8: Occupational Structure by Caste Groups in Ghaziabad

	Upper Caste	*Intermediate Caste*	*Low and Ex-Untouchables*	*All*
Professional	14.6	1.2	0	3.5*(9)
Skilled	64.6	51.5	43.9	52.7(135)
Semi-skilled	14.6	19.8	22	19.1(49)
Unskilled	4.2	19.8	31.7	18.8(48)
Unemployed	2.1	7.8	2.4	5.9(15)
All	100.0 (48)	100.0 (167)	100.0 (41)	100.0(256)

*Column per cent, numbers in parentheses.

People are absorbed in petty jobs in public, private enterprises, and self-employed with very low investments starting as from as low as Rs. 100. The self-employed workers were from the industries, which were closed down under the declaration of the sick industries. These workers saved some capital to invest in any paltry business and did not try to join any other type of work. The cause told by some of the respondents is that they could not join casual workforce for the simple reason they do not want to and are still drawing salary from the closed mills. Some of them could not sustain the uncertainty of casual workforce, however, managed to open small shops tea stall etc. The respondents were found to be concentrated in business activities though the caste representation is varied in both types of business categories. Besides giving good account of field experience the study has developed classification where skill and earning are clubbed to see the profile of occupation by caste groups. The upper caste respondents (20.8%) were able to show up in the professional occupation group while intermediate caste and ex-untouchables (8.1% and 2.8% respectively) were not able to leave influential trace in this group. Unskilled jobs were mainly done by the lower ex-untouchables (27.1%) caste groups in Kanpur City (Table 3.7) but it is interesting to find that in Ghaziabad such obvious segregation disappears and respondents (Table 3.8) from the intermediate caste (19.8%) also show the highest presence in this occupational group, the study found a large number of people engaged as *Baildar* (load and unload) in construction and factories.

Coming back to the division of occupations by caste in Kanpur City and Ghaziabad there is a clear-cut polarization of jobs by caste.[15] The intermediate caste falls between the poles of upper caste and ex-untouchables. Jobs of high professions like manager, teacher, and clerks are invariably pitched for higher castes. Jobs like cobbler, cleaner, washer man, and carpenter were carried as designated by the caste system. Ghaziabad has good percentage of (51.5%) of intermediate castes representing skilled group of occupation as machine tool operator, welder, driver etc. though the ex-untouchables also have significant (43.9%) person working in the skilled category. The jobs, which are unskilled like rickshaw puller (menial activities), vendors (self-employed) are largely taken up by the lower castes and ex-untouchables. Looking at the unemployed percentage by caste groups the study finds that low and ex-untouchables respondents were highly concentrated (15.0%) in Kanpur City and in Ghaziabad the share of intermediate caste respondents have higher presence (7.8%).

One of the theories of emergence of caste system is given to the occupation theory. Occupations decide caste hierarchy and the resulting stratification order in the past. Deepak Lal[16] thinks that mobility among all occupation was acceptable irrespective of one's caste or *Varna*. He sees close cooperation amongst all castes, in his words:

> "In its practical aspects, the basis of the caste as it evolved was not so much the four *varnas* or great classes (or castes) but the interrelationships and adjustments of numerous sub-castes (*jatis*). These sub-castes were based on occupational specialization, but mobility was possible and did occur within the inter- or intra-caste status hierarchy."

Beteille[17] also comments on the mutual dependency within caste hierarchy on economic spheres, though exclusive when kinship and marriage ties assumed to be within layer. This study especially tries to cement the broken links in caste system and occupation hierarchy in urban areas. The caste studies so far have shown the segmentation and not inter-linkages among caste and occupations while administering the idea of dualism in urban market.[18]

3.4. Nature of Job in Occupations

Jennings suggested one of the factors to differentiate discrimination in the market was to know the differences in nature of jobs in relation to the groups. Even in the same kind of jobs, which are considered, to be inferior in nature than others; like packing and labelling may be smaller jobs but just using machine for shoe cutting will not put shoe cutting higher than the packing and labelling job, though latter job may be better paid than the previous one. Again this is conjectural to rank occupations by nature of jobs since social groups rank jobs differently depending on their way of evaluation[19]. Workers at the bottom of labour market have their own opinion and ranking of jobs. Caste Hindu prefers some jobs even if they earn less than their counterpart lower caste Hindu. A.U.P. Ranga Rao's[20] study in Andhra Pradesh on Madiga and Manda two Scheduled Caste communities showed that workers belonging to different occupations. Semi-skilled manual occupations (such as helper, heavy load carrier, lineman, driver contractor, and businessman) are rated higher in comparison to non-Scheduled Caste respondents. Author gives reason that they have greater exposure to such occupational categories either at work place or at the community level.

Though this study has done nature of job analysis on the three-digit level occupation classification within the national occupation classification yet due to small sample size reliability of the analysis cannot be ensured. Nevertheless this section on the nature of job could be considered as a statement on the factual fieldwork experience[21] only.

The statements are to find the vertical placement of the respondents industry-wise.

3.4.1 Agriculture

The respondents were many times flummoxed because they still consider agriculture their mainstay and working in urban area (if the job is not permanent) does not provide them a sense of security and hence they often reported their main occupation what they were at the survey time doing yet when asked about their usual status of work many of them said working in the field and they necessarily did not tell the earning from the agriculture produce most of the time it for self-consumption or only meant to the sustainable extent.

The lower and ex-untouchable caste respondents invariably told to be working as agriculture labourer in their native places. In case if they owned land the size of land was miserably low which was not sufficient enough to support the entire family as a result they said that they worked in others' field.

3.4.2 Manufacturing Industry

The intermediate caste and low caste respondents in manufacturing industry were engaged as spinner, wrapping activity, packer and labeller, material handling equipment helper. The lower and ex-untouchable respondents occupied packer and labellers' level.

The ex-untouchables workers working as supervisor (Jute textile), shoe cutter lasters in manufacturing of leather were discernible. The upper caste respondents occupied supervisor, clerk and manager, however observation dictates that upper caste in manufacturing of leather worked put as sales supervisor and selling agent.

Ghaziabad gives a slightly different picture and occupants of white-collar jobs were upper caste respondents, though also engaged as machine operator, metal melting handler, tailor and watchman. Metal heating, casting, rolling kind of jobs were done by ex-untouchables. Other Intermediate caste workers had significant presence in manufacturing industry and worked at all levels, except at supervisor and clerk level.

3.4.3 Construction Industry

The ex-untouchable workers were the largest in number engaged in all sorts of work relating to the construction. The upper caste respondents were small in strength, working as supervisor in construction activity and painting. The artisan caste respondents did white washing and well boring at construction sites in Kanpur City.

In Ghaziabad too majority of workers were from ex-untouchable caste group, doing variety of jobs at different layers in construction industry. But most of them were supervisors of construction work (contractor, mistry or Rajmistry) construction workers like loading, unloading and bricklayer. In the upper caste group there were very few respondents work as bricklayer, terrago worker and construction worker. Intermediate caste respondents were doing sporadic jobs at construction sites. Van der Loop[22] stressed on the kinship ties in construction industry where workers come in circular migration citing example of Vellor and Salem in Tamil Nadu. He says "half or more of the entrepreneurs and labourers belong to one caste and another one-fifth of the labourers belong to the Scheduled Castes."

The above written statement rather confirms the deluge of lower castes and ex-untouchable respondents in the construction industry[23].

3.4.4 Trade and Commerce Industry

After construction industry, ex-untouchables found refuge in trade and commerce industry since closing down of many tanneries and cotton spinning mills in Kanpur City. Many ex-untouchables showed their inability to do their 'caste occupations' like shoe making (in their own way of understanding) because of the high initial investment of cost in the leather raw material. Most of the respondents had taken up activity like vending several types of items ranging from vegetables, cloths, scrap iron, waste materials etc. The other Intermediate caste respondents reported to have some hard cash to invest in small shops of fixed capital asset starting from Rs. 1000-7000, thus these respondents actually engaged in vending various articles of household utility. Also waiter and cook occupations are executed by upper and other Intermediate castes. The upper caste respondents evidently are only shopkeepers.

In Ghaziabad the upper caste group was not as well represented as in comparison to the neighbourhood caste groups as in Kanpur City. Few workers reported to be at the status of shopkeepers, other respondents in this caste category are shop assistant or demonstrators. Other Intermediate castes and the ex-untouchables too worked as demonstrator and shop assistant. Overall there is under representation of all caste people in trade and commerce activities in the trading sample of this city.

3.4.5 Transport Industry

Upper caste has no representation in transport industry in Kanpur City. The local transport was mostly dependent on manual rickshaw with limited use of three wheelers as city transport. The Intermediate caste respondents were clustered as rickshaw puller in largest number. Ex-untouchables are found in good number employed as rickshaw puller again. The artisan caste respondents also work as rickshaw pullers.

In Ghaziabad automobile transport is more operational because close to the other connecting towns than Kanpur City, resulting workers are found working as driver, transport equipment operator, machine fitter (Upper Intermediate caste, lower Intermediate caste, Ex-untouchables). Upper caste workers are engaged as manager in various connected fields of transport industry. Rickshaw pullers were represented by lower castes only.

3.3.6 Service Industry

Amongst all occupations tailoring, rickshaw pulling are some activities, which can be considered the most democratic occupation along caste lines in Kanpur City. The ex-untouchable group like Valmiki executed sanitation services and shoe repair was again done by the leather workers (*Chamars*). More specifically saying leather workers (*Chamars*) have adopted this traditional job. Housemaids were from other intermediate caste workers. The upper caste respondents were in education services.

Comparing the two cities, Ghaziabad does not have as many workers in service industry as in Kanpur City. It has been observed that the jobs like tailoring, helper ('*helperi*' as they usually refer to job specifications), vendors and mechanics are still adopted jobs by all caste people and do not find crowding of certain castes in these jobs in both the cities. The study considers these occupations caste secular. Yet just finding occupation division secular may risk the generalization of overall phenomena of discrimination if study detaches wage and earning analysis in occupations.

It becomes explicit in both study areas that less dangerous or accident-prone jobs are occupied either by upper caste or Intermediate castes. Manufacturing industries workers like packing, labelling, spinning, shoe cutter, crusher and pressers, metal cutting, metal reheating, machine jobs were represented by other Intermediate castes, lower castes and the ex-untouchables. On the other side, the upper caste workers dominated machine operators, supervisor level of jobs and seldom other caste categories were also found. The study would like to distinguish here is that in the manufacturing of leather, sales supervision and selling agents were high caste respondents but shoe cutter and workers on lathe machine were ex-untouchables (*Chamars*).

The respondents in trade and restaurant industry were petty traders mainly who have generally inherited property, business. These respondents were from upper caste. The respondents who were shop assistants, demonstrators, and hawkers (according to the main occupation category vendors) belong to lower caste categories. Striking thing was the presence of upper caste respondents as cook. Kanpur demonstrates that the ex-untouchables had occupations like vendors (most of them were vegetable vendors) and did not report to have been facing any problem in job market, and people do not discriminate in purchase but on the same time vendors from Ghaziabad showed disenchantment. They faced resistance from co-workers in obtaining a licence and visit market place (incidence of employee discrimination).

In Kanpur two Valmiki respondents, one waitor and the other worked as cook in marriage seasons told that they did not reveal their true caste identity and remain unscrupulous.[24] Ghaziabad had good number of Gujjars having transport business now, who earlier get into this business as conductor, driver, *khallasi* etc.; hence transport business is generally controlled by the other intermediate caste. Kanpur City respondents from lower caste group are rickshaw pullers. Construction work has primarily three types of workers first load lift (*Baildar*), Mason (*Rajmistry*), Contractor for the labourers. In this hierarchy people get promoted though it is not necessary people follow this hierarchy strictly. Most of the young energetic people reported to become mason very soon in true sense skip the middle level strata. The upper caste people rarely enter into this industry as labourer or as contractors.

Personal and community services are a very important segment to interpret as *shudras* are designated as the service caste for higher caste society. High profession like teaching has the cartel of high caste people whereas ex-untouchable caste people generally do sanitary services, domestic servant, tailor etc. No denying the fact that situation which perpetuated long back still not able to brake away the old casting; for the reason of old domination of upper caste and lack of awareness in lower caste respondents.

3.5 Earning Differences

The occupation structure and concomitant earning has given constant research challenge to isolate the discrimination. Virtually every respondent felt that earning is the sole motive to do anything irrespective of danger involved in work, long hours or odd hours. They all intended to get more money in any form such as accommodation, food, clothing etc. causes may allow them to save money indirectly. Mode of payment and duration of payment are other variables, which leads to excessive uncertainty and vulnerability. Piece rate, daily wage are the types of payment, which respondents express, do not leave any extra money to invest in the welfare of the family.

3.5.1 Earning and Caste Groups

The highest percentage (44.6%) falls in 'below 2000' group. The respondents of Intermediate caste (37.9%) in Ghaziabad compete with upper caste respondents (55.2%) in higher earning group yet have second lowest earning share (2.4% can be seen earning between 'Rs. 5000-6500') to the total respondents of intermediate caste. They have highest percentage (44.9%) in 'below Rs. 2000' earning group. The ex-untouchables group finds its place in the lower earning groups reaching to the, Rs. 5000-6500 class. Within the caste group the lower ex-untouchables have highest percentage in the 'below Rs. 2000' earning group.

Table 3.9: Distribution of the Respondents by Monthly Earning and Caste Groups in Ghaziabad

(In persentage)

Caste / Earning in Rs.	Upper Castes	Intermediate Castes	Low and Ex-Untouchables	All
<2000	10.4	44.9	46.3	44.60*(99)
2000-3500	22.9	28.1	39	28.9(74)
3500-5000	16.7	10.8	7.3	11.3(29)
5000-6500	12.5	2.4	0	3.9(10)
6500>	33.3	6.6	4.9	11.3(29)
All	100.0 (47)	100.0(154)	100.0(40)	100.0(241)

*Column per cent, numbers in parentheses.

The upper caste respondents can be located in every earning group almost homogeneously in Kanpur City (Table. 3.10). As it has been observed that they are found in the most coveted and higher occupational groups, the upper caste respondents also occupy the higher earning slabs. Earning category of Rs. <2000 emerges to be dominated by first intermediate castes and second by the lower and ex-untouchables. After this earning category, (Rs. 2000-3500) category is the domain of the intermediate caste respondents. This study finds that most (61.1% to the total percentage) of the respondents fall in Rs. <2000 earning slab of which the lower and ex-untouchables have the highest percentage share (67.3%).

Table 3.10: Distribution of the Respondents by Monthly Earning and Caste Groups in Kanpur

(In persentage)

Earning in Rs. / *Caste*	*Upper Castes*	*Intermediate Castes*	*Low and Ex-Untouch-ables*	*All*
<2000	12.5	59.5	67.3	61.09*(146)
2000-3500	18.8	25.2	12.1	20.9(50)
3500-5000	31.2	7.2	1.9	10.5(25)
5000-6500	18.8	0.0	1.9	4.60(11)
6500>	10.4	0.9	0.9	2.92(7)
All	100(44)	100(104)	100(91)	100(239)

*Column per cent, numbers in parentheses.

The significant observation can be stated that in Kanpur the respondents start declining from low to higher income group but in Ghaziabad the presence of the respondents though tapers from low income group to high income group yet it picks up in the last high income group, i.e. >6500 group.

Debate on wage, earning and in the end consumption pattern shifts focus from caste to class means that the study indulges in a discussion both if earning of a particular caste coincides with the class (divided into strata of earnings) they may belong. Inequality in earning has been discussed both on theoretical and empirical models.[25]

Consumption pattern, saving, investment, life style, size of household are interlinking concepts with earning and resulting into difference in the structure of earning or caste too. The study would like to cite work of Shitla Prasad Saxena[26]on Kanpur dated back 1937.

In his work he reported different consumption patterns, where low-caste worker may not spend on furniture, chattels, and food items so much, on the other hand a Brahmin worker may be also elaborative on these expenditures. It was also observed during field work that caste background defined a set pattern of living and often delineated according to the caste ideologies. William[27] *et al.* studied the recruitment phases in academics in British Universities wrote on the essentials of job search in professional labour and manual labour. The economics of education has, through that of Becker and his successor, shown how profession of different amounts and different types of human can help to account for differences in earnings that economic theory otherwise finds difficult in accounting for. The authors say while studying the life time earning profile of the workers that the most manual workers who constitute the bulk of the subject matter of traditional labour economics reach their peak earning capacity early in life and on the evidences of cross-sectional data at least their relative earnings remain more or less constant untill after middle age when declining physical powers tend to reduce their income somewhat. Another important difference between the operation of professional labour markets and those for unskilled labour is the extent of non-pecuniary advantages. People do not choose between jobs solely in terms of expected financial remuneration especially professional occupations have wider range of such non-pecuniary benefits than manual jobs.

3.6 Occupation, Earning Difference and Caste Groups

Though the earning variation in occupation is accepted unanimously in the intellectual circle as indication of discrimination in market, yet this deduction have several factors which leads to variation in earning also for more than one apparent reason like duration in job market, level of education, quality of education, training period or on the job training, job experience, affiliation with institutions and other innate personality traits etc. However, economist and sociologist are in unison with this postulate of earning difference in the same occupation could be due to discrimination, assuming if certain groups after achieving certain qualifications do not get access to desired job.[28] Here the study though with all limitations has tried to see only two sides of the discrimination theory by analysing earning difference one in occupations and other by age (Figs. 3.3 & 3.4).

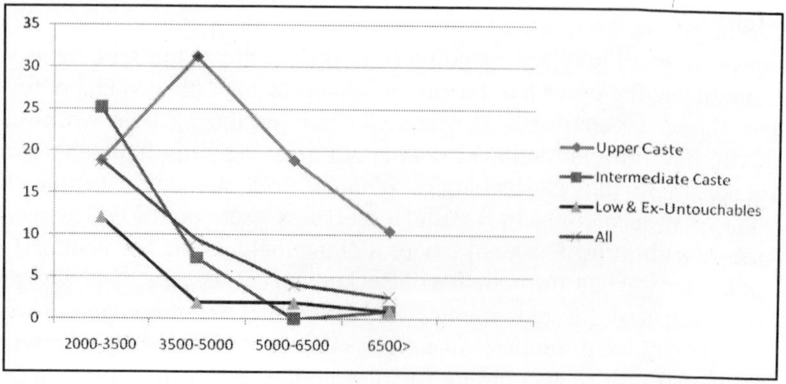

Fig. 3.3: Monthly Earning of Respondents in Kanpur City

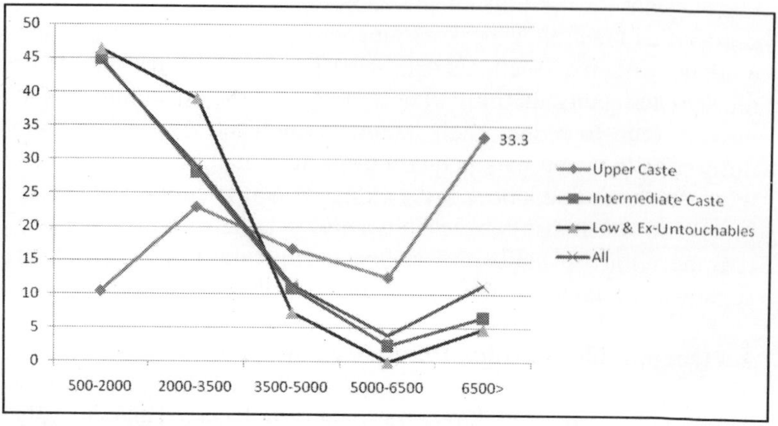

Fig. 3.4: Monthly Earning of Respondents in Ghaziabad

3.6.1 Upper Castes

Table 3.11 on earning and occupation of the upper caste workers shows two things particularly that the highest earning occupational group quite reverses in Ghaziabad, which was not only found in skilled works but some of them were engaged in menial activity as well, secondly, most of the respondents (33.3%) from upper caste are in the earning group of Rs. 6000 and above employed in skilled activities (interestingly under the skilled work respondents mainly belonged to the business activities such as petty grocery shop owner, construction material dealer, readymade garments seller etc.).

Table 3.11: Distribution of the Upper Caste Respondents by Earning (Monthly) and Occupation (in %)

Earning in Rs. / *Occupation*	*Menial*	*Semi-skilled*	*Skilled*	*All*
		Kanpur City		
Below 3000	100	42.9	23.7	30.0
3000-6000	—	57.1	34.2	36.7
Above 6000	—	0	42.1	33.3
All	100.0	100.0	100.0	100.0
		Ghaziabad		
Below 3000	—	75	8.3	18.8
3000-6000	—	25	52.8	47.2
Above 6000	—	0	38.9	34.0
All	—	100.0	100.0	100.0

In Ghaziabad the upper caste workers earned highest in the skilled activities (38.9%), skilled workers also occupy in highest percentage in the Rs. 3000-6000 group (in Kanpur City also the activities mainly concentrated in trade and construction group) and the percentage of workers earning in this earning slab is higher than Kanpur City; 47.2 per cent in Ghaziabad and 36.70 per cent in Kanpur City). Below Rs. 3000 was earned by manufacturing workers while in Kanpur it is found in Menial activities. Workers of upper caste had highest percentage in the earning group Rs. 3000-6000 in both the cities (Table 3.11).

3.6.2 Intermediate Castes

To the total percentage of intermediate caste workers 75.5 per cent were found below Rs. 3000 of earning limits in Kanpur (Table 3.12) and within this limit also 51.9 per cent were from the skilled category. The respondents who earned between Rs. 3000 and 6000 were solely skilled workers from the intermediate caste in Kanpur City.

The table indicates that almost the same percentage of (90%) the respondents were found to be working below Rs. 3000 group and 20% per cent were earning between Rs. 3000 and 6000 who worked in the menial and skilled jobs both in Ghaziabad. Though the variation in the occupation is quite obvious in Ghaziabad yet there is certain polarity in work and earning structure of Intermediate caste respondents (Table 3.12) in Kanpur.

Table 3.12: Distribution of the Intermediate Caste Respondents by Earning and Occupation *(In percentage)*

Earning Rs. / Occupation	Menial	Semi-skilled	Skilled	All
	Ghaziabad			
Below 3000	97	90.6	61.8	70*
3000-6000	3	9.4	25.8	20
>6000	0	0	12.4	10
All	100.0	100.0	100.0	100.0
	Kanpur City			
Below 3000	100	100	51.9	75.5
3000-6000	0	0	46.3	23.6
>6000	0	0	1.9	0.9
All	100.0	100.0	100.0	100.0

* Column per cent, numbers in parentheses.

3.6.3 Lower and Ex-Untouchable Castes

Description of the ex-untouchables earning is almost same as the intermediate caste respondents except the concentration of the ex-untouchable workers is even more than the intermediate caste workers.

Table 3.13: Distribution of the Lower and Ex-untouchable Caste Respondents by Monthly Earning and Occupation *(In percentage)*

Earning (In Rs.)	*Ghaziabad*				*Kanpur city*			
	Menial	Semi-skilled	Skilled	All	Menial	Semi-skilled	Skilled	All
Below 3000	92.3	70	82.4	82.5	93.1	92.3	52.2	75.3
3000-6000	7.7	30	5.9	12.2	6.9	7.7	34.8	19.3
>6000	0	0	11.8	5.3	0	0	13	5.4
All	100.0	100.0	100.0	100.0	100.0	100.0	100.0	100.0

In trade and self-employment activity, as this study has already stated that most of the workers were vendors or petty traders; these workers earn below Rs. 3000 in a month.

Table 3.13 on Ghaziabad also indicated same results as Kanpur City in the ex-untouchables earning section. Kanpur and Ghaziabad reflect almost mirror image of earning differences of caste groups. Still respondents earned better in Kanpur City than Ghaziabad because generally they worked in formal occupational setup (Municipal corporation, railways, public works department etc.)

eventhrough their status being only contractual. Other difference in the share of earning amongst occupations could be because of scale of economic activities only. This study here would like to conclude that wage differences might exist in the same kind of occupations in labour market on the basis of caste categories though occupational segmentation is a more attractive explanation behind earning difference yet there are examples of earning difference in the caste groups even within same type of occupation group.

3.7 Earning, Age Differences and Caste Groups

In this section the effort has been made to throw some light on the highest earning age level by each caste group which is an indirect method to decipher discrimination. According to the theory on earning it is assumed that earning reaches to the peak[29] at the middle age (35-50) level and may remain stagnant or decrease in old age (50 onwards).[30] Here this study proposes that earning by age groups may reflect one level of discrimination if earning of middle age differs amongst caste groups.

3.7.1 Upper Castes

Break up by age of upper caste (Table 3.14) workers shows that the highest percentage lies in the 'below 30' age group in Kanpur City by earning (54.3%) in Rs. 3000-6000 and after proceeding age group (30-45) by almost 14 per cent it stagnates in the the age group of above 45– futher in the Ghaziabad two groups vie with each other and maintain roughly similar earning those are Below 30 and 30-45 in the upper caste workers. In Ghaziabad 30-45 age group is an important age group by percentage distribution where distribution spreads almost equally in all income groups Yet below 30 age group workers earned better than this age group in Kanpur City. Earning is higher in the younger age groups than the older age groups in Kanpur City. Though, there are some higher earning cases found in older age groups too.

3.7.2 Intermediate Castes

The next table on intermediate castes (Table 3.15) for both the study areas shows first that in Kanpur there was no representation of workers in after Rs. 6000 except in the age group of >45. Secondly,

Table 3.14: Distribution of the Upper Caste Respondents by Earning and Age *(In percentage)*

Earning in Rs / Age group	<30	30-45	Above 45	All
		Ghaziabad		
<3000	29.4	34.5	0	29.4
3000-6000	35.3	31	75	35.3
>6000	35.3	34.5	25	33.3
All	100.0	100.0	100.0	100.0
		Kanpur City		
<3000	30.6	13.3	9.4	19.4
3000-6000	54.3	40	45.3	48.3
>6000	15.1	46.7	45.3	32.3
All	100.0	100.0	100.0	100.0

though earning reaches to the highest level in 30-34 age group yet the percentage (23.5%) found in this age group is not very significant and the study finds that highest earning was in the age group of 30-45 in Kanpur. Looking at the Ghaziabad side of distribution the study finds that more than half of the earning is concentrated in the lowest earning group (<3000) and also the highest percentage is found in the age group of 30-45. The distribution of earning though is not very murky, nevertheless as this study has assumed in the beginning that the highest earning might reach to the peak in the age group of (Above 45), in case of the intermediate caste group situation is different; most of the respondents from both the cities have reported to be earning less than Rs. 3000 in a month.

3.7.3 Lower and Ex-untouchables

Table on the ex-untouchable workers (Table 3.16) is not different from the intermediate caste too. Earning is distributed almost equally in all the age groups with very slight differences, though the highest earning is found in the age group of 30-45 at least in the higher earning groups too in both the cities (if the study recalls some workers were working in government offices. Possibly these workers influence the highest

Table 3.15: Distribution of the Intermediate Caste Respondents by Monthly Earning and Age *(In percentage)*

Earning in Rs. / Age group	14-30	30-45	Above 45	Total
		Ghaziabad		
<3000	74.2	69.3	63.3	72.2
3000-6000	18.2	21.2	30.7	21.2
>6000	7.6	9.5	6	6.6
All	100.0	100.0	100.0	100.0
		Kanpur City		
<3000	71.6	89.5	60.0	75.2
3000-6000	28.4	10.5	30.0	23.5
>6000	—	—	10.0	1.3
All	100.0	100.0	100.0	100.0

earner) Middle age groups in both the cities show higher earning trends in this caste group.

Table 3.16: Distribution of the Lower and Ex-untouchables Caste Respondents by Earning and Age

Earning (in Rs.)	14-30	30-45	Above 45	All
		Ghaziabad		
<3000	88	63.6	100	82.5
3000-6000	8	27.3	—	12.2
>6000	4	9.1	—	5.3
All	100.0	100.0	100.0	100.0
		Kanpur City		
<3000	83.4	74.1	75.6	75.1
3000-6000	10.6	22.2	24.4	16.1
>6000	6	3.7	—	8.8
All	100.0	100.0	100.0	100.0

This exercise of comparing earning with the age is very important since it not only gives idea about the age combination of three major caste groups of the study but also surmises earning by age group. The study concludes that workers over all earn less, as they get older yet the picture is not a happy one in the lower caste groups. Another observation worth noticing is that ex-untouchables are better placed comparing the intermediate caste groups. Since they are placed high risk but high earning jobs in the protected occupational sectors.

Summing up

The present study has done three pronged analysis of occupation with education nature of job and earning differential; deliberated one point repetitively that surely underprivileged section is still groping in dark of illiteracy, occupational stagnation and carrying on somehow with just survival instinct. Change, however, is occurring in society but with extremely tardy realization. Between the two cities Kanpur City has distinctly traditional occupational structure which is progressing towards the modernization though slowly yet definitely, and also because migrants too come from nearby areas also reinforces same stereotype behaviour towards the other social groups. There are ample evidences in the study that flow of communication is restricted in the market not only along class lines but also along caste lines. It is not mere rhetoric if this study also finds the need of universal education at a war footing scale. What Morris[31] wrote long back in 1960, still holds a clue for equitable distribution "While industrialism generally increases mobility and engenders consciousness of opportunity, in the absence of universal compulsory education in Indian industrialism has tended to perpetuate traditional social inequalities." Education itself will not be useful until due cognition is awarded to education through validating it in all spheres of activities, or occupations. Apathy of underprivileged mass towards education not only foretells their destiny but also overall reverses the growth of society. Khan[32] proves and stresses in his study that education is imminent to infuse the self-dignity, and not just ordain one with human capital to sell one's labour in market. In this case study of identity formation of Harijan, he declares that majority of the educated and uneducated feel that there is discrimination but more educated than uneducated feel that discrimination is to marginalize them. In another experiment on the belief prevailed in the opinion of innate intelligence of these people of educated Scheduled Caste respondents felt that their caste is no less than that of the caste Hindu. But a sizeable portion of them do not base on low wages rather than innovations and quality improvements."[33]

The present study also shows that there is segregation in the occupations also. Though it cannot be judged if it is because of discrimination yet one such empirical study on Kanpur City has evaluated segregation in the labour market yet this study also could not conclude if it was due to discrimination. Anand Nath Banerjee quotes Fremantle who gave statement 25 years ago (the study quoted here is of 1931):

> "There is no prejudice against mill labour among high castes. Further, caste has no influence whatever on wages or on the class of work in the mill performed by each man. Brahmins and Chhatriya work with Chamars and do not find their touch polluting as they would in their village."

He further adds:

> "Though there is no caste prejudice against mill workers, there are some castes which are especially suited for certain types of work. Thus Koris are usually found I the weaving departments.... Brahmins and Thakurs can adapt themselves very well and they are serving in almost every department."

The sentiments, which are intertwined here in the quotation given by Fremantle is of escapism and in Anandnath Banerjees' statement, reality.[34]

Bardhan[35] connects low wage, education and paternal intervention in injecting children in labour force at tender age, says:

> "Wages very much less by level of education in casual jobs than they do in regular jobs. Perhaps the most important way in which education interacts with poverty is at the inter-generational level: poverty and low levels of education of parents are associated with early drop out from school and labour market entry of children, limiting the possibilities for acquiring educational credentials or training and perpetuating the existence of an unskilled lower stratums of the labour force."

Sharma[36] who refers to the continuous change in the caste and where several changes are occurring which earlier thought were fixed in nature and unalterable social system. Traditionally considered rules of caste orders are taking place in the direction politico-economic formations.

Sociological readings generated many interesting readings and conclusion in caste and egalitarianism focusing on change and mobility and caste as changing phenomena have made more exciting in roads than immobility and stagnation within the caste structure. He sites Swedish Anthropologist who worked on stagnant and poor neighbourhood in Kanpur expressed that everywhere he encountered mobility of entrepreneurial success of caste organisation bargaining effectively with political parties and so forth what he points out that a lot of sociologist while capturing mobility, mobilization, achievements, egalitarianism and kept neglecting growing inequality as well as the process which made this permanently so.

Beteille[37] takes another step in interpretation of the process or mechanism in ranking and grading of service class in Indian Society where from generation to generation keep working in the same grade. Something is working where from reproduction of inequality in which family and caste plays an important role. He argues that caste remains the root proof of the social morphology and it is still manifestly correlated with every occupation, wealth, income, education or some other criterion. In all public institutions, those in inferior positions are likely to be higher and those in inferior position of lower caste. Some of this kind of manifested correlation is a proof that caste is at the bottom the cause of the ranks that we observe in the public life.

The study also proves that wages are low overall for all caste people but ex-untouchables are further very lowly paid people. Wage is very much linked with education in high jobs but for casual jobs like rickshaw pulling, construction work etc. education does not make any difference. Respondents felt that education enhances wage, attitude and nature of jobs. Discrimination has given vent to the segmentation of caste groups in certain occupations[38], featuring inferior setting of job descriptions, with same level of education. Lower caste groups are found in generally unprotected irregular jobs. The methodology which study has adopted to squeeze out discrimination and equity proves that there exists traces of occupational discrimination, wage discrimination in urban labour market also which are shadows looming large in urban scenario too.

NOTES

1. K.P. Kannan "Labour Institutions and the Development Process in Kerala"

studied the labour market in Kerala and institutions like trade unions which is internal factor and external factors like social background of workers, the nature of product market and the attitude of the state control, the forces of recruitment in industries are indeed correlates. In Papola and Rodgers (ed.) (1992). *Labour Institutions and Economic Development in India,* ILO Research Series 97, p. 66.

2. World Labour Report 1988, pp. 113-114.
3. Chitra Joshi, "Hope and Despair: Textile Workers in Kanpur in 1937-38 and the 1990s" in Parry, Bremann, Kapadia (ed.) (1999). *The Worlds of Indian Industrial Labour*, Sage Publications, New Delhi.
4. Backer (1970). *op. cit.*
5. http://www.arthapedia.in/index.php?title=Worker_(Census_Definition)
6. World Labour Report No. 3, 1988 p. 133.
7. Harriss, Kannan and Rodgers (1990). *Urban Labour Market Structure and Job Access in India*, ILO Research Series, 92, p. 12.
8. *Ibid.*
9. *Ibid.,* pp.16-18.
10. Many respondents told that this status as seasonal when other regular jobs are not available in abundance such as in rainy season, summer season when they can sell anything at a very low cost.
11. Intermediate caste respondents included number of artisan caste respondents in this study. These workers were found to be comfortably placed in the unprotected regular short term wage work, shows the demand for the artisan caste respondents is high for regular short term wage works though unprotected. This may lead to conclude that though artisan caste workers are in demand for work yet due to lack of capital they cannot afford to start their own enterprise. (Most of the respondents in this category were carpenters, earthen pot makers, and blacksmith).
12. This study has tried to classify occupation while keeping in mind the overall comparability of the occupations across caste groups on the basis of associated prestige, income potential, growth potential, educational and skill requirements and functional importance given to the occupations. Also referred Albert J. Reiss (1961). *Occupational and Social Status*, The Free Press, New York. p. 86. Occupational differences are explained on the basis of developed classification; however, the study also gives references of minor details of the occupations as an explanation and field experience within the classified occupation. *National Classification of Occupation-2004* though analyse the Indian classification of the Occupation and International Standard Classification of Occupation where the report devise to use standard way of using job (as task and duties), occupation as a set of jobs where bunch of duties of similar nature clubbed together to match with skill level required to carry out the tasks and duties further explained 'skill level' under which complexity and range of tasks involved whereas skill specialization shoes the field of knowledge required, the tools and machinery worked on and the kind of goods and services produced. This study hence tries to adopt the

most acceptable occupational classification to study discrimination though nature of job has been separately discussed in anecdotal method. *The same classification has been followed in the following chapters as well except in the section on fathers occupation cultivator category is separated from the semi-skilled category.*

13. T.B. Bottomore (1971). *Sociology: A Guide to Problems and Literature*, S. Chand Publications, New Delhi. The author refers Hutton and says that there is a particular growing interest among sociologists to find out the widening labour structure and caste system. p. 136.
14. The distinct feature in Kanpur City first there were large number of respondents reported to be shop assistant, rickshaw pullers, vendors and helper in the workshops. In Ghaziabad though in the unskilled category *baildaar* (Loader), cleaner, scavengers were dominating.
15. Lambert (1963). *Workers, Factories and Social Change in India*, Princeton University Press, Bombay, his study finds that Brahmins are in numerical strength in all factories in clerical, supervisor posts. pp. 153-154.
16. Deepak Lal (1988). *Cultural Stability and Economic Stagnation*, Clarendon Press, Oxford, p. 23.
17. Andre Beteille (1969). *Caste, Class and Power: Changing Patterns of Stratification in a Tanjor Village,* Oxford University Press, Bombay.
18. Holmstrom (1985). *op. cit.,* p. 5.
19. Arrow (1985, p. 918) says in his utility analysis of discrimination says that wage and job discrimination have different implications in different condition of jobs.
20. A.U.P. Ranga Rao (1989). *Urbanization, Occupational Mobility and Social Integration: A Study of Scheduled Castes,* Deep and Deep Publication, p. 344.
21. Daily notes during field survey were referred.
22. Rodgers (ed.) (1985). *op. cit.* p. 346.
23. http://www.livemint.com/2010/06/14212328/The-business-of-caste-in-India.html accessed on 22nd June, 2012. In the article Narain and Singh "Business of Caste in India" writes how the plumbing occupations are monopolized (almost 90%) by the Oriya people belonging to low caste in the National capital region of Delhi.
24. Peter Knorringa (1998). "Barriers to flexible specialization in Agra's foot wear industry." p. 298 in Cadene and Holmotrom (1998). (ed.) Incidence of Agra footwear industry where polluted caste background people were 'almost' banned from jobs in hotel and catering industry. John Marris (1989). "Vulnerable Workers in the Indian Urban Labour Market." in Gerry Rodgers (1989). Urban Poverty and the Urban Market also cite an example of Naidus Industrialist in Coimbatore City. These industrialists give preference to the Naidus while not discriminating with other Scheduled Caste but they may not get into permanent salary job.
25. Harbhajan Singh (1990). *Sources of Income Inequality: A Case Study of Delhi*, Patriot Publishers, New Delhi, p. 13. He says that personal income may differ

on the basis of intellectual capacity, dexterity, strength, stamina etc. He also finds application of theories on income on six models: (a) ability model, (b) the scholastic model, (c) the Human capital model, (d) the screening model, (e) the job competition model, and (f) the segmented market. p. 15.

26. Shitla Prasad Saxena (1937). *Wages and Labour Conditions in Cawnpore,* Superintendent, Printing and Stationary, United Province, Allahabad.
27. Williams, Blackstone and Metcalf (1974). *The Academic Labour Market: Economics and Social Aspects of a Profession*, Elsevier Scientific Publishing Company, Netherlands. pp. 10-11 and 12.
28. N.R. Sheth (1968). *The Social Framework of an Indian Factory*. Oxford, Bombay, p. 79.
29. A study in British labour market where authors say that the most manual workers who constitute the bulk of the subject-matter of traditional labour economics reach their peak earning capacity early in life and on the evidences of cross-sectional data at least their relative earnings remain more or less constant until after middle age when declining physical powers tend to reduce their income somewhat. In Williams, Blackstone and Metcalf (1974). *The Academic Labour Market: Economics and Social Aspects of a Profession*, Elsevier Scientific Publishing Company, Netherlands. pp. 10-11.
30. Haworth, Gwartney and Haworth (1975). "Earning, Productivity and Changes in Employment Discrimination During the 1960s", *The American Economic Review*, March, Vol. 65, No. 1, p. 159.
31. M.D. Morris (1960). in Holmstrom (1984). p. 38.
32. Mumtaz Ali Khan (1994). *op. cit.* p. 168, pp. 191-192.
33. Schmitz (1989). in Cadene and Holmstron (1983). *op. cit.*
34. Appendix on Labour Supply by Mr. A. Banerjee in S.P. Saxena (1937). *op. cit.* pp. 108-109.
35. Bardhan (1981). in Gerry Rodgers (ed.) (1989). *op. cit.*, p. 14.
36. K.L. Sharma (1995). *Social Inequity in India*, Rawat Publication, Jaipur. pp. 2-3 and 108-109.
37. Andre Beteille, *The Reproduction of Inequality*, p. 118 in K.L. Sharma *op. cit.*
38. M.N. Panini in his article *Networks and Styles Industrial Entrepreneurs in Faridabad,* gave evidences where upper caste have occupied mostly coveted jobs in the town. In Satish Sabarwal (1978)., *op. cit.* p. 97.

4
Education, Migration and Occupational Mobility

This chapter lays down necessary foundation to capture the pre-market discrimination by identifying the education level exclusively and by cross-analysing the occupation status also. Other major point of enquiry of the pre-market discrimination is by analysing the employment status of the respondents at the time of migration *vis-à-vis* current employment status. In the previous chapter it is found that the caste configuration differed on the basis of occupation and earning both. In this chapter research questions which aimed to find the impact of education, education and occupation, parental status, migration and recruitment aspects in the labour market have been intensely investigated.

The question is if parental standing of the respondents and other inputs in the human capital lead to differences in getting the job and chasing other opportunities then how much does it vary on caste lines? It is often found[1] that parental influence on child's future is a benchmark from where a child steps into a new horizon, this phase is often pre-destined by the status of parents and affects the prospects of their social standing in the society.

Next step of migrated labour in the city has been explored by finding about his journey to the current stage. Questions focusing on "What is the status of employment of the people who migrated at the arrival in the city and after certain duration of stay in the city? Are they still earning their livelihood from traditional occupation? What has been the shift in occupation?" The chapter next explores the questions of recruitment processes like information network, obtainment of work type of contact, skill requirement for jobs, and finally involving regularity, legal protection cutting across the caste lines. Processes are cardinal to understand the magnitude and the levels in all sorts of end product; consumable or non-consumables. One of the important tasks of human geography according to David[2] is to build up more sophisticated knowledge of the process of development and underdevelopment. This involves disentangling complex networks of economic social and cultural relationships. This study though aimed to explore processes in great detail yet with several constraints led to standardize the levels where we can capture the processes of job market such as information of the job, acquiring the job, leaving the job etc.

Answers pulled by all this analysis are thus categorized as pre-market discrimination which largely determines the fate of the people marching in the labour market as a job seeker or trainee in the job.

4.1. Education Profile

This research study believes that there exists inequality in the investment of human capital, which originates at the time of upbringing of a child. This is the discrimination at the pre-market level and at this stage of pre-market discrimination there is not only variation in the investment but also in rate of return due to the social status of the worker. The study attempts to explain this kind of human capital variation (investment in education and return as occupation and earning of the workers).

Earlier analysis in chapter three on age structure has given fair view that the respondents in Kanpur are long settled and mature while Ghaziabad has experienced more mobile transition of workers. This leads to conclude that Ghaziabad has young migrant population. Though Kanpur is now in a mode to revive economic pace yet the city is no more attractive enough to remain a destination of employment whereas Ghaziabad offers many opportunities to the people migrated from other parts of the country. According to this study educational level in Kanpur City is far better than Ghaziabad. People are at the least literate or educated till the primary level if not highly educated. Equal percentage of the respondents reported to have achieved middle and secondary level of education (19.5% in each group) (Table 4.1).

The upper caste respondents were educated till the professional and graduate degree. However, the upper caste respondents (6.2%) also have reported to be illiterate. It is noticeable that in Kanpur the study could find respondents above graduate also who were from upper caste, and intermediate caste both (Table 4.1).

Table 4.2 on educational attainment in Ghaziabad indicates

Table 4.1: Education level amongst Caste groups in Kanpur City

(In per cent)

Education Level	*Upper Castes*	*Intermediate Castes*	*Lower and Ex-Untouch-ables*	*All*
Illiterate	6.2	30.6	24.3	23.70* (63)
Literate	4.2	5.4	3.7	4.5(12)
Primary	18.8	15.3	24.3	19.5(52)
Middle	16.7	19.8	20.6	19.5(52)
Secondary	18.8	18	20.6	19.2(51)
Higher Secondary	14.6	6.3	3.7	6.8(18)
Diptoma/professional	12.5	3.6	1.9	4.5(12)
Graduate and above	8.3	0.9	0.9	2.3(6)
All	100(48)	100(111)	100(107)	100(266)

*Column per cent, numbers in parentheses.

that 33.6 per cent of the sample respondents were illiterate, which is significantly high. Even though the respondents were educated but they were only to the level of primary (35.5%). Secondary, higher secondary and middle level was evenly shared among educational attainment. The upper caste respondents in Ghaziabad also had highest percentage (27.1%) share at the level of primary yet they occupy other education levels also comparing to other caste groups. The intermediate caste respondents have highest percentage share as illiterates followed by primary level educated respondents on the same time they have achieved senior secondary level and professional degree[3] were as well. In the intermediate caste groups 37.1 per cent of the respondents were educated up to primary level and a significant percentage (36.5%) of the respondents were illiterate. Scenario of the lower caste and ex-untouchables group appears to be bleak as a very high percentage (46.3%) of the respondents were illiterate and the rest if they were educated they cleared only primary level (39%) of education. In other education categories a mere 4.9 per cent of the respondents claimed to be literate and 2.4 per cent of the respondents said that they have passed secondary level (Table 4.2).

Overall this study suggests a few important difference between these two cities first can be that Kanpur City has higher percentage of respondents educated in both quantity and quality aspects. Secondly, Kanpur also shows marked difference in terms of awareness for education though sizeable respondents were illiterate.

The difference in the level of education can be contributed to the efforts done by the Municipal Corporation of Kanpur and

Table 4.2: Education level and Caste Groups in Ghaziabad

Education Level	*Upper Castes*	*Intermediate Castes*	*Low and Ex-Untouchables*	*All*
Illiterate	12.5	36.5	46.3	33.60*(86)
Literate	2.1	5.4	4.9	4.70(12)
Primary	27.1	37.1	39	35.5(91)
Middle	12.5	6	2.4	6.6(17)
Secondary	12.5	6.6	2.4	.7(18)
Higher secondary	18.8	7.2	4.9	.9(23)
Diploma/professional	10.4	1.2	0	2.7(7)
Graduate and above	4.2	0	0	0.8(2)
All	100(48)	100(167)	100(41)	100(256)

*Column per cent, numbers in parentheses.

implementation of Government schemes, opening of Anganwadi, while not forgetting that Ghaziabad does not have very old slums where such activities can be organized in a much intensive way. Moreover the sense of belongingness[4] does not prevail in the respondents of Ghaziabad and hence participation and motivation factors were hardly visible even if government schemes exist to support them.

4.2 Education and Occupation

Occupation will not give the qualitative details of occupation until occupation is seen in the background of formal educational attainment. How these respondents are placed in the jobs after having same educational qualifications; it may illustrate lack of opportunity if not totally the magnitude of discrimination. Indeed there is high percentage of respondents belonging to illiterate category, yet it is thought stirring to find the occupational distribution in each education group. Primary level education does not revolutionize occupation pattern. This is only higher secondary level education qualification, which may bring difference in occupation. Rodgers[5] discusses demand side of human capital model and relates the education with urban poverty.

He writes:

> "Human capital models would explain differentiation in terms of relative productivities and such explanations obviously have some validity. But the educational qualifications required for access to any particular job usually rise with the average education level of the population. Evidently education plays a

> rationing, rather than a purely productivity measuring role... urban poverty appears to be particularly closely associated with lack of schooling above the primary level and it is mainly secondary level qualifications which provide desirable labour market entry points."

The study has done cross-section analysis of education, occupation and caste categories.

4.2.1 Upper Castes

It can be interpreted from Table 4.3 that of the total per cent of the upper caste workers 7.9 per cent respondents were in illiterate category working in various skilled occupations like construction, transport, and 28.6 per cent in semi-skilled occupations in Ghaziabad. The middle level educated group of the upper caste respondents is mainly engaged in business activities (39.3% to the total educated respondents). The study finds middle and secondary level of respondents along with graduate and professional in skilled group of activities also.

Table 4.3: Upper Caste Respondents by Education and Occupation

(In per cent)

Education/ Occupation	*Unemplo-yed*	*Menial Activity*	*Semi-Skilled*	*Skilled*	*All*
		Kanpur City			
Illiterate	0.0	0.0	12.5	5.6	6.2
Up to Primary	0.0	0.0	75	13.9	22.99
Up to Secondary	75.0	0.0	12.5	55.6	50.0
Up to Graduation	25.0	0.0	0	25	20.8
All	100.0	0.0	100.0	100.0	100.0
		Ghaziabad			
Illiterate	0.0	50.0	28.6	7.9	12.5
Up to Primary	0.0	0.0	0.0	2.6	2.1
Up to Secondary	100.0	50.0	57.1	50.0	52.1
Up to Graduation	0.0	0.0	14.3	39.5	33.3
All	100.0	100.0	100.0	100.0	100.0

It should be made clear that these workers were either clerk in small establishment, supervising a small group or primary level (*Anganwadi*) teachers. The portion on Kanpur City in the table shows that the majority of illiterate and up to primary level educated upper caste respondents were able to manage their setup in business activities, skilled occupations are occupied (expectedly) by higher educated respondents specifically yet some discreet respondent reported to have managed to be in skilled occupation despite of being illiterate. On the other hand there are some respondents with secondary education level working in semi-skilled jobs both in Kanpur and Ghaziabad. Most important of all the upper caste respondents of any educational level is not visible in unskilled activity (Table 4.3).

4.2.2 Intermediate Castes

In Kanpur, respondents who are secondary level passed found to be unemployed and even menially employed. In Ghaziabad the intermediate caste group (Table 4.4) shows that in this caste group illiterate respondents have high share (36.5%), 49.70 per cent have got education up to secondary level and mere 8.0 per cent are educated till graduation level. Looking at this indirectly the study can say that majority of the respondents could barely read and write found in skilled construction, carpenter, and painter activities. The next important occupation group

Table 4.4: Intermediate Caste Respondents by Education and Occupation

(In per cent)

Education/ Occupation	*Unemployed*	*Menial Activity*	*Semi Skilled*	*Skilled*	*All*
		Kanpur City			
Illiterate	14.3	45	33.3	25.9	30.60
Up to Primary	14.3	25	40	9.3	20.7
Up to Secondary	71.4	30	26.7	55.6	44.1
Up to Graduation	0.0	0.0	0.0	9.3	4.5
All	100.0	100.0	100.0	100.0	100.0
		Ghaziabad			
Illiterate	30.8	63.6	37.5	27	36.5
Up to Primary	23.1	3	6.2	3.4	5.4
Up to Secondary	38.5	33.3	53.1	56.2	49.7
Up to Graduation	7.7	0	3.1	13.5	8.4
All	100.0	100.0	100.0	100.0	100

for this caste group is unskilled menial activities (30.6%), where more than half the respondents were illiterate (45%) and along with is also glaring the presence of (30%) secondary level educated respondents. In the skilled group the respondents are mainly up to secondary educated (55.20%) and only 9.3 per cent are educated till graduation level.

The study do not see anyone particular group of activity which is predominantly have concentration of educated group, rather in the intermediate caste groups educated group is confined till diploma/ professional degree endowed respondents in skilled workers (transport, construction and other skilled work) categories. Nevertheless, illiterate respondents were present in almost all occupations though not in the same percentage as in Ghaziabad.

4.2.3 Lower and Ex-untouchables

It was mentioned in this chapter that a large portion of workers in Kanpur were vendors[6]. While cross-checking the table, the study finds that 36.4 per cent of workers in the ex-untouchables community were in semi-skilled category, of which 25.6 per cent had attained education level up primary level and 30 per cent were illiterate. Of all the respondents in the ex-untouchables category 27.0 per cent were in the unskilled menial jobs of which 35.0 per cent were illiterate but even in high level of education level (20% and 25% in middle and secondary level) also the study finds presence of ex-untouchables in unskilled activity section (Table 4.4).

To the total percentage of workers in the ex-untouchable workers in Ghaziabad, 31.7 per cent were in unskilled menial activity segment, 38.5 per cent were illiterate, and 61.5 per cent were up to secondary level educated. This study does not find the ex-untouchable workers in higher education group. The Table indicates that the ex-untouchables have not reached to the level even where they can be compared especially in Ghaziabad (Table 4.5).

Ghaziabad also shows more or less same pattern of occupation distribution like Kanpur but the study witnessed greater segmentation of occupations in Ghaziabad than Kanpur City. Two things emerged from Table 4.3 on Ghaziabad, first upper caste respondents worked in protective services and other respectable jobs, second intermediate caste respondents found accomplishing task of supervisor and business within illiterate category experience and loyalty may be the decisive factors. Ex-untouchables have highest share in services like transport

Table 4.5: Low and Ex-untouchables castes Respondents by Education and Occupation

(In per cent)

Education/ Occupation	*Unem-ployed*	*Menial Activ-ity*	*Semi Skilled*	*Skilled*	*All*
		Kanpur City			
Illiterate	12.5	27.6	30.8	17.4	24.3
Up to Primary	31.2	34.5	25.6	21.7	28
Up to Secondary	43.8	37.9	43.6	56.5	44.9
Up to Graduation	12.5	0.0	0.0	4.3	2.8
All	100.0	100.0	100.0	100.0	100.0
		Ghaziabad			
Illiterate	100	38.5	80	29.4	46.3
Up to Primary	0.0	0.0	20	0.0	4.9
Up to Secondary	0.0	61.5	0.0	58.8	43.9
Up to Graduation	0.0	0.0	0.0	11.8	4.9
All	100.0	100.0	100.0	100.0	100.0

equipment operator, machinery fitters, shoemaker, and construction work. Seeing the distribution of all four major caste groups in Kanpur City this study would like to assume that upper caste workers are privileged in terms of education and occupation both, however, they were present in the menial activities too. Intermediate caste group is not only found in the dignified occupations but are also in other occupations groups which are understandably of low importance though this group of caste shows better placement than the lower and ex-untouchables in Kanpur City.

The analysis on education, occupation and caste groups justify earlier statement of Rodgers[7]. Distribution of caste in even the lowest rungs of occupations and education combination evinced substantial difference by all caste groups. The occupations like construction workers (there are many who graduated to *Rajmistry* level in construction workers category) other low skilled occupations do not essentially require educated workers, are virtually inherited by ex-untouchables not only on the grounds of education but also employers do not mind employing them as far as they remain less in physical contact and can be easily manipulated for lower wages. The other thing, which may bring difference in earning, is age factor. One such study in Andhra Pradesh finds that the discrimination coefficient raises as age increases thus indicating higher discrimination at later ages[8].

One more thing, which needs to be mentioned, is that the contractors in the building industry were mistry contractors, working along with labourers and also supervising workers alongside. One such study on urban informal section in Kanpur comments on the caste and occupation relations; this study infers[9]:

> "informal sector, most of the entrepreneurs (30.04%) originated from Baniya Caste, the well known traditional business community of the State, 18 per cent come from Muslims, 17.19 per cent from Brahmins, 11.74 per cent from Chhatriya, 10.41 per cent from SC and ST, 8.47 per cent from other castes, 3.87 per cent from Kayastha. In the independent establishment sectors, a majority of entrepreneurship comes from S.C. and S.T. (31.84%)."

The present study also closely agree with the statement since the study had also encountered situations where shop owners were mainly from Baniya Caste (upper caste) and Carpenters were from Badhai Caste, pot makers were Kumhars (or Prajapati). Education has assisted in the perpetration of segmentation and checked the equitable distribution of occupation. Commenting on education and Caste, Quigley[10] felt:

> "Literacy makes possible cultural and cognitive centralization and dramatically alters the potential for social organization. The formalization of the written word also introduces a huge gulf between the great tradition of the elites and the cults of the majority who remain illiterate."

Rodgers[11] gives different opinion on the segmentation in market and feels that education is not the only variable which controls occupation assigning[12] function but caste identity affects the entry to particular segment in labour market, generally controlled by one particular caste or community. Education is considered to be of prime importance for quality of livelihood. Literature dealing with the human capital approach has given a consequential status to education. In a study[13] done on the educational stagnation and opportunity grabbed by one segment of the society the author says that equality of opportunity in a society depended on the ability of its members to notice and support merit whenever it is found irrespective of caste, class, race, religion or language difference. Education can do a great deal to promote this attitude of mind. It is not just assumed or necessary that only educated persons are more likely to fetch right job opportunity but education helps and becomes an instrument in fostering right attitude to open up for other available opportunity. The human capital approach includes within its purview on the job training, apprentice etc. Becker and Cheswick[14] explained existing inequality in the society due to the difference in the human capital investment by pointing out (1) the inequality in investment in the human capital, (2) the average level of investment in the human capital, (3) the average level of the return of human capital, and (4) the inequality in the rate of return to human capital. The extension for human capital is also 'imperfect' since parents make decisions on behalf of their children. In the World Development Report, it has been assessed that expected rate of returns are influenced by location, contacts and discrimination on ground of gender, caste, religion or race. "Discrimination and stereotyping mechanism for the reproduction of inequality between groups have been found to lower self-esteem, effort, and performance of individuals in the groups discriminated against."[15]

Another significant difference in the occupation structure, which emerges from the occupation and education analysis is that the people pick up jobs like (kept in menial activities) rickshaw puller because opportunities around in other menial or lowly skilled jobs are less. Lack of city auto transportation leaves space for them an easy option of living. Next available earning option is by becoming Vendor (mostly vegetable, scrap metal and textile Vendors) because investment in such alternate occupations is the lowest and leaves them with ample time to go for any other random job too whenever time allows and also because industries consuming and needing such products and services in local market. Does it mean that there is no discrimination? Perhaps this study at this juncture pre-proposes that these workers may not be a case of discrimination but overall lack of opportunities. The figment of discrimination is still unclear. Now the study looks into the nature of job aspect within occupations.

4.3 Background Information of the Respondents

4.3.1 Education of Respondents Father

There is absolutely no distinction among all caste respondents when it comes to the level of illiteracy in respondents' father in Ghaziabad. There is marginal difference in the level of education where the upper caste respondents and to some extent intermediate caste respondents show literacy trend and the study also found that the level of education sometimes go up to the higher secondary level but insignificant (.9%).

Table 4.6: Education Level amongst Father of the Respondents[16]

(In per cent)

Education Level	*Upper Castes*	*Intermediate Castes*	*Low and Ex-Untouchables*	*All*
		Kanpur City		
Illiterate	20.8	61.3	66.4	56.0*(149)
Literate	8.3	6.3	5.6	6.4(17)
Primary	33.3	17.1	12.1	18(48)
Middle	18.8	10.8	10.3	12(32)
Secondary and above	18.8	4.5	5.6	7.5(20)
All	100.0(48)	100.0(111)	100.0(107)	100(266)
		Ghaziabad		
Illiterate	29.2	65.3	80.5	60.9*(156)
Literate	22.9	9	7.3	11.3(29)
Primary	20.8	13.2	4.9	13.3(34)
Middle	18.8	9.6	2.4	10.2(26)
Secondary and above	8.3	3	4.9	4.3(10)
All	100(48)	100(167)	100(36)	100(256)

*Column percent, numbers in parentheses.

Educational attainment has slightly improved when this study compares son (Table 4.6) and father still there is much to be done in the field of education.

In Kanpur City also the study does not see variability in educational achievement in respondents' father. Except the upper caste, respondents all other caste groups show a very higher percentage of illiterate fathers. Education standard of father of the upper caste workers is noticeably higher than the fathers of the other low caste workers' (Table 4.6).

Comparison between Kanpur and Ghaziabad shows that the fathers of the lower caste groups are better off in Kanpur than Ghaziabad. Again the fathers of the upper caste workers have overall dominance in all education categories. Comparing the education level of workers and their fathers' education, this study finds that there is no drastic drift in the education profile of the respondents and their fathers. The study assumes that there is a close relationship between father's education and the education of the offspring. In the light of this summation it can be hypothesized that the government departments in the urban areas should concentrate in the mobilization of the masses and rationalization[17] of education.

4.3.2 Education of the Respondents' Mother

Education analysis of mother's education of the respondents generalize the fact that the female education was never a priority in the Indian society be it the upper caste or the lower caste. Here the study has first brought into the focus of mother's education as an educated mother teaches the generations[18].

What has been the point of interest in the respondents' mother education finding is that Ghaziabad is better presented than Kanpur City. Illiteracy level though is high yet less than Kanpur City (89.3%) have shown uptrend in the upper caste and intermediate caste respondents' mother (20.8% and 8.4% clubbing literate and primary educated mother in respective caste categories). This diversion could be appropriated to the educated upper caste in Ghaziabad who is positively affected with the process of modern environment of the Delhi and surrounding while Kanpur City is yet to show this effect of modernization especially to the female education is concerning.

What this study has gathered from other tables on the level of education of fathers highlights the same points as far as the mother's education is concerned. Evidently respondents' fathers in Kanpur city have shown a trend towards literacy but so far the mother's education does not emerge to be an important factor in Kanpur City. According to Table 4.7 the lower and ex-untouchable caste group, and intermediate caste respondents' mother are illiterate (97.3% and 93.5% respectively) only the upper caste respondents show lower percentage (77.1%,) share in illiterate group in Kanpur City.

This study can conclude after analysis of tables on the level of education of parents and the respondents that concerted efforts are required to make education a meaningful tool towards gainful employment. Using NSSO 61st round data paper[19] on skill mapping of labour market confirms a low skill base of Indian labour force while higher skill labour force remain outside of the labour force for various reasons.

Table 4.7: Education Level in Respondents' Mother

(In per cent)

	Upper Castes	*Intermediate Castes*	*Low and Ex-Untouchables*	*All*
		Kanpur City		
Illiterate	77.1	97.3	93.5	92.1*(245)
Literate	10.4	2.7	3.7	4.5(12)
Primary	10.4	0.0	0.0	3.0(8)
Middle	2.1	0.0	0.0	0.4(1)
All	100**(48)	100(111)	100(107)	100(266)
		Ghaziabad		
Illiterate	79.2	91.6	95.1	89.5(230)
Literate	14.6	4.2	0.0	5.5(14)
Primary	6.2	3	0.0	3.1(8)
Middle	0.0	1.2	2.6	2.9(4)
All	100**(48)	100(167)	100(41)	100(256)

*Column per cent, numbers in parentheses.

4.3.3 Occupation of Father

The occupation of father presumably brings stability and security not only for the entire family but also to a child also. Father's livelihood becomes important for his self-esteem, educational and other requirements. The aspect became vital from the point of view to know the current occupation of the father, if they were following caste occupations or do they have opted for modern methods of livelihood or if they were able to bring a balance between their caste occupations with other modern available occupations (Table 4.8).

Occupation of the respondents' father in Kanpur does not have much similarity with Ghaziabad. The percentage share of cultivators is lower in Kanpur than Ghaziabad. The fathers of the lower and ex-untouchables found place in the cultivators category yet the size of the land holding is miserably low which is deficient to support the large family and hence these respondents though reported to be cultivators but simultaneously worked as agricultural labour as well. The study found that 14.6 per cent of the upper caste respondents' fathers were engaged in professional occupation such as teaching, clerk etc. though only 3.0 per cent intermediate caste respondents also said to be working

Table 4.8: Occupational Status of the Respondents' Father

(In per cent)

Occupation Category	*Upper Castes*	*Intermediate Castes*	*Low and Ex-Untouchables*	*All*
		Kanpur City		
Professional	14.6	2.7	—	3.8(10)
Skilled Workers	47.9	49.1	30.2	41.3(109)
Cultivators	37.5	18.5	10.4	18.1(49)
Semi-Skilled	0.0	16.4	27.4	17.8(47)
Menial Activities/ Unskilled	0.0	15.5	32.1	19.3(51)
All	100**(48)	100(111)	100(107)	100 (266)
		Ghaziabad		
Professional	10.4	3.0	—	3.9*(10)
Skilled Workers	41.7	28.7	22	30.1(77)
Cultivators	41.7	45.5	31.7	42.6(109)
Semi-Skilled	6.2	16.2	34.1	17.2(44)
Menial Activities/ Unskilled	0.0	6.6	12.2	6.2(16)
All	100*(48)	100(167)	100(41)	100(256)

*Column per cent, numbers in parentheses.

in the professional jobs in Kanpur City[20]. Unskilled menial activities are dominated by the lower and ex-untouchable caste respondents 66.7 per cent in Kanpur City and 31.2 per cent in Ghaziabad. Semi-skilled occupations with marginal difference are shared highly by the Low and ex-untouchables in both the cities (27.4% and 34.1% in Kanpur city and Ghaziabad respectively).

It is interesting to know that in Ghaziabad 42.6 per cent of the total respondents' father said to be engaged in cultivation of which intermediate caste have the highest (69.7%) share among all caste categories and also within the intermediate caste category. The reason behind this is that in Ghaziabad percentage of migrants is high and therefore, the majority of the respondents have told their father either cultivators or agricultural labourer. The upper caste respondents' father were mainly engaged in skilled occupation or as cultivators (for both 41.7%) while 10.4 per cent of the fathers also enjoyed being in the professional occupation category. There are other occupational categories which were important such as skilled workers in construction, transport and other skilled jobs (Table 4.8).

The hypothesis that parents influences the future path of their children is proved here since occupational structure of sons rarely deflects from their fathers or *vice versa*. Children in Kanpur were slightly fortunate because their father at least could provide (pensions given by the closed mills) them some resources to have their own establishment or constant source of income.

4.3.4 Occupation of Mother

The occupation of mother has essentially never been an important source of sustenance and generally considered a secondary source of income[21]. Table 4.9 on the employment status of mothers shows that only 28 mothers in Ghaziabad and 59 mothers in Kanpur found to be working and rest of the mothers were in the status of house wife.

Table 4.9: Status of Employment of the Respondents' Mother

(In per cent)

Status of Employment	*Upper Castes*	*Intermediate Castes*	Low and Ex-Untouchables	All
		Kanpur City		
Non-Working/House wife	92.5	83.8	66.2	79.1*(207)
Working	7.5	16.2	33.8	20.9(59)
All	100**(48)	100(111)	100(107)	100 (266)
		Ghaziabad		
Non-Working/House wife	97.6	89.1	80.6	89.3(228)
Working	2.4	10.9	19.4	10.7(28)
All	100**(48)	100(167)	100(41)	100(256)

*Column per cent, numbers in parentheses.

In Ghaziabad most of the mothers said to be working as agricultural labour. This study though did not insist to probe further yet it can be assumed that they were helping during the preparation of the field and harvesting time. There is no other observation except the mothers found to be helping in financial support of the family by working as domestic helper.

There is no drastically difference in these two cities seeing the mothers' occupational structure; even in Kanpur respondents' mothers found to be working as domestic helper, vegetable vendors, tailor and agricultural labourer.

4.3.5 Size of the Household

This sub-section desires to deduce the impact of the size of the household of the workers when they were living with their fathers. The purpose is to roughly ascertain the size of the household during the father's time and attempt at a possible comparison with the size of household of the workers at present.

Table 4.10: Average Size of the Household

(In per cent)

Caste Groups	HH Size	
	Ghaziabad	Kanpur City
Upper Caste	5.4	5.0
Intermediate Caste	5.2	5.2
Lower Caste and Ex-Untouchables	5.5	5.9

The highest percentage of the respondents belongs to the household size of 7-9 in both the cities. In the group of 7-9 the lower and ex-untouchables and upper caste respondents told to have high percentage (47.66% and 47.92%) share while intermediate castes have 49.55 per cent of the households in the category of less than six per household in Kanpur City (Table 4.11). Apparently the upper caste has large size of the households, i.e., 10-12 and and above 12 members per household having the percentage figure of 16.67 per cent in each category. This perhaps indicates the upper caste respondents were living together for the reason that the families are settled long time back and lived with the extended family. Even in Ghaziabad 7-9 size of family has reported mainly (41.0%) of which 52.08 per cent upper caste respondents, 40.12 per cent of intermediate caste and 31.71 per cent of ex-untouchables stated to have family size of between 7-9 though bigger family (10-12) size also reported by significant per cent of the respondents[22].

In comparison to Kanpur City, Ghaziabad has large number of families in above 12 groups. Thus there is a dominance of large families in Ghaziabad during the life spent at the father's place.

Comparing the household size of the fathers with the household size of the workers at present, the study finds that the workers of Kanpur City has larger size of the households at present and Ghaziabad workers

Table 4.11: Size of the Household during the stay with father

(In per cent)

Size of the HH	*upper castes*	*intermediate castes*	*Low and Ex-untouchables*	*All*
		Kanpur City		
< 6	18.75	49.55	21.5	32.71*(87)
7-9	47.92	33.33	47.66	41.73(111)
10-12	16.67	17.12	21.5	18.8(50)
12 <	16.67	0	9.35	6.77(18)
All	100(48)	100(111)	100(107)	100(266)
		Ghaziabad		
< 6	16.67	16.77	29.27	18.8(48)
7-9	52.08	40.12	31.7	41(105)
10-12	18.75	31.14	24.39	27.7(71)
12 <	12.5	11.98	14.63	12.05(32)
All	100(48)	100(167)	100(41)	100(256)

*Column per cent, numbers in parentheses.

have smaller size. The phenomenon reverses when the study looks at the distribution of size of household during stay of the respondents. The present study thus may conclude that Kanpur City has witnessed a stable household size for a long time. But in the case of Ghaziabad, the study finds that there is a tremendous pressure for the job-hunting, which has led to the migration of the people from their native places. Perhaps, Delhi has served as a great attraction point for jobs getting migrants from distant places.

4.3.6 Land Holding Size

Not a significant per cent of the respondents who said that their father owned land. Kanpur City thus portrays different picture when this study finds the landholding size in Kanpur City either for the reason that agricultural land has been taken over by the industries historically or for housing purpose in other words the mainstay of their life was either industries in Kanpur City or some other urban occupations.

Of the total 51.13 per cent respondents' fathers are landless. Along caste group distribution, 58.8 per cent of the ex-untouchables, 46.85 per cent of the other intermediate castes, 43.75 per cent of the upper caste respondents' father were landless (Vaishya caste reported of having no agricultural land). The second highest group is 1-5 size category

Table 4.12: Land holding size by caste groups

(In per cent)

	Upper caste	*Intermediate caste*	*Low and Ex-untouchables*	*All*
		Kanpur City		
Landless	43.75	46.85	58.88	51.13*(136)
1-5	25	39.64	34.58	34.96(193)
5 <	31.25	13.51	6.54	13.91(37)
All	100(48)	100(111)	100(107)	100(266)
		Ghaziabad		
Landless	18.75	29.34	73.17	34.08(86)
1-5	37.5	42.51	19.51	38.4(99)
5 <	43.75	28.14	7.32	27.52(71)
All	100(48)	100(167)	100(41)	100(256)

*Column per cent, numbers in parentheses.

which has the percentage share 34.9. In this group the Intermediate caste has the highest percentage (39.6%) followed by the lower caste persons. In the bigger land ownership 31.2 per cent respondents from upper caste said to have above five acre land holding. In Ghaziabad the study concludes that workers are better off in terms of land possession, however, lower and ex-untouchables are still at the bottom so far as bigger land holding size is to be considered. Only 33.08 per cent of the workers reported to be landless and is less than Kanpur City fathers. Major chunk of the respondents are in the '1-5' category (36.4%) and the rest of the land holding size groups hover around 30 per cent (Table 4.12).

Comparing these two cities this study infers that Kanpur City is predominantly inhabited by the industrial workers who either had migrated to Kanpur in the wake of opening of the industries in the historical past or industries encroached into their cultivable land. Ghaziabad has attracted agricultural workers possessing very small piece of land, which may not have been sustainable for a large family. In human capital approach of discrimination, parental education has found a place of crucial investigation. A study done by Dhesi and Gumber[23] on earning difference of migrant workers found that parent's education and number of siblings determined years of schooling of workers (in other words level of education also). The study may conclude that upper caste respondents had slightly better human capital investment and richer source of physical capital as well.

4.4. Migration

Once again recalling the objective of the study, migration is seen here as a transition stage in the respondents life. The analysis on the migration necessarily[24] need to be seen in detail by breaking up further the migration pattern or the history but here the objective behind migration analysis is limited to know first if the respondent was migrated second if migrated what was the reason and if finding occupation was the main reason then what was the waiting period and how did he approached the job market?

Migration can prove to be an effective indicator of well being of a society. Especially, in the case of discrimination and poverty which forces people to migrate from rural area to urban centres not just in search of a job but also as a haven to hide one's identity. Literature on migration studies suggests the root cause for migration for such poor people are moribund and stagnant status of agriculture, multiplying population, lack of resources and attraction of job opportunities.

Table 4.13: Respondents by the Migration Status

	Frequency	*Per cent*
	Ghaziabad	
Non-migrants	36	14.0
Migrants	220	86.0
All	256	100.0
	Kanpur City	
Non-Migrants	106	40.0
Migrants	160	60.0
All	266	100.0

Table 4.13 on migration indicates that Ghaziabad had higher percentage of migrants in comparison to Kanpur City. The study has though already stated on the industrial status in both the study areas yet, the Table again confirms that new and growing industrial demands have attracted many people from distant areas of Ghaziabad. In early 1930s Royal Commission on Labour very well commented on the pull factor for the people who throng to the industrial areas, it says:

> "The driving force in migration comes almost entirely from the one end of the channel, i.e., the village end. The industrial worker is not prompted by the lure of city life or any great

> ambition. The city, as such, has no attraction for him and when he leaves the village he has seldom an ambition beyond that of security in the necessities of life. Few industrial workers would remain in the industry if they could secure sufficient food clothing in the village; they are pushed and pulled to the city."

The study adds that circumstances and easy forward link (mostly natives, relatives) also brace them to migrate while both the factors of pull and push intensify the judgement of the person to migrate.

Table 4.14 on migration status by caste groups amplifies that the employment opportunities are scarce so far as the lower caste people are concerned. The study surmises that the migration is higher amongst lower caste people irrespective of the city yet percentage is higher in Ghaziabad City.

Table 4.14: Migration status by Caste Groups

	Frequency	*Per cent*
	Kanpur City	
Upper castes	35	21.9
Intermediate castes	65	40.6
Low and ex-untouchables	60	37.5
All	160	100
	Ghaziabad	
Upper castes	39	17.7
Intermediate castes	68	30.8
Low and ex-untouchables	113	51.5
All	220	100

4.4.2 Age at Migration

Respondents from lower and ex-untouchable castes migrated to Kanpur City at a very tender age (likely to be below 15 years) though by approximately 30 per cent less in Ghaziabad. Upper caste and intermediate caste respondents were found to have migrated in the age group of 15-19 years which is no less a vulnerable age group than below fifteen years old age group. Both the cities generally have same trend in migration age group (Table 4.15).

4.4.3 Purpose of Migration

Nearly 81.3 per cent migrated in Ghaziabad and 66.2 per cent in Kanpur City reported to have migrated in search of jobs. Amongst the caste

Table 4.15: Age at Migration by Caste Groups

(In per cent)

	Upper castes	*Intermediate Castes*	*Low and Ex-Untouchables*	*All*
		Kanpur city		
Below 15	22.86	30.77	66.67	42.5*(68)
15-19	77.14	56.92	21.67	48.13(77)
30-49	0.0	12.31	11.67	9.38(15)
All	100(35)	100(65)	100(60)	100(160)
		Ghaziabad		
Below 15	20.51	38.24	28.32	30(66)
15-19	69.23	51.47	61.95	60(132)
30-49	10.26	10.29	9.73	10(22)
All	100(39)	100(68)	100(113)	100(220)

*Column per cent, numbers in parentheses.

categories 76.6 per cent of the lower and ex-untouchables and 69.2 per cent of Intermediate caste in Kanpur City have given reason to find a job and in Ghaziabad the per cent goes very high for all caste groups. It is noticeable to find that 20 per cent of the upper caste respondents in Kanpur migrated due to family problems. While respondents from intermediate caste (15.38%) and lower caste (15.0%) also gave reason that they came along with family. Percentage due to this reason is low amongst all caste groups in Ghaziabad may be because the age group which has migrated is younger and arrived in the recent past. This study hence find that people migrate to the cities for various reasons yet majority of the populace move in search of occupational opportunity (Table 4.16).

4.4.4 Occupation at Migration

Analysis of the previous tables indicates that this study can assume at this juncture that most of the respondents were either unemployed or lowly employed at the time of arrival in the city. Table (4.17) shows that the respondents were overwhelmingly unemployed in Kanpur City and Ghaziabad. Migrants who were engaged in agriculture activities are though present in high per cent in both the cities yet less by almost 10 per cent in Kanpur City. Second important observation is that the respondents reported to be engaged in menial activities at a high percentage (23.13% and 25.45%) at the time of migration in Kanpur and Ghaziabad respectively. However, these menial activities are reported by only intermediate caste and lower caste respondents. It is important to report here that it could

Table 4.16: Respondents by the Purpose of Migration

(In per cent)

	Upper Castes	*Intermediate Castes*	*Low and Ex-untouchables*	*All*
		Kanpur city		
In search of Job	42.86	69.23	76.67	66.25*(106)
Due to Family Problems	20	4.62	3.33	7.5(12)
Came along with family	5.71	15.38	15.0	13.13(21)
All	100.0 (35)	100.0(65)	100.0(60)	100 (160)
		Ghaziabad		
In search of Job	61.54	79.41	89.38	81.36(179)
Due to Family Problems	10.26	5.88	7.08	7.27(16)
Came along with family	0	7.35	3.54	4.09(9)
Any Other	28.21	7.35	0	7.27(16)
All	100.0(39)	100.0(68)	100.0(113)	100 (220)

*Column per cent, numbers in parentheses.

be undermining if the study simply considers unemployed status of the respondents because there were several incidences where respondents said that they could go back and start working in the fields as and when they wish to especially in Ghaziabad[25]. Temporary wage workers from upper caste were high (28.5%) in Ghaziabad whereas the upper caste respondents found to be working on the permanent positions in Kanpur.

The picture which has emerged after the analysis on pre-market discrimination indicators is somber because this study witnessed a picture where two poles (upper and lower ex-untouchables) exist in the Indian society and also exists the middle world (intermediate caste). In the beginning the study had assumed that the education is one decisive factor in the labour market, emerges as an established fact and reinforces many other studies on the achievement in urban labour market. Education has become a necessary qualifier to get a job in the labour market yet the older people are still not convinced with the importance of education to broaden the prospects of education. With marginal variability all respondents showed that education is important to get good job still for various reasons they could not achieve satisfactory level of education and got sucked in the job market in the early years of their teens.

The parental background seems to have profound impact on the future of the offsprings. Though hiatus has emerged in the age old caste hierarchy yet, this enjoyed the fruits of development by passing on

Table 4.17: Respondents by Status of Employment at Migration

(In per cent)

Employment Status	*Upper Castes*	*Inter-mediate Castes*	*Lower and Ex-untoucha-bles*	*All*
		Kanpur City		
Unemployed/Seeking Job	42.86	44.62	23.33	36.25*(58)
Menial activity	0	15.38	45	23.13(37)
Wage Worker (temp)	28.57	3.08	5	9.38(15)
Wage Worker (permanent)	2.86	1.54	0.0	1.25(2)
Self employed	8.57	7.69	3.33	6.25(10)
Agriculture Activities	17.14	27.69	23.33	23.75(38)
All	100.0(35)	100.0(65)	100.0(60)	100.0(160)
		Ghaziabad		
Unemployed/Seeking Job	58.97	39.71	30.97	38.64(83)
Menial activity	0	17.65	38.94	25.45(58)
Wage Worker (permanent)	7.69	0.0	0.0	1.36(3)
Self-employed	5.13	4.41	0.0	2.27(5)
Agriculture Activities	28.21	38.24	30.09	32.27(71)
All	100.0(39)	100.0(68)	100.0(113)	100.0(220)

*Column per cent, numbers in parentheses.

the inherited blessing of forefathers to the next generation. D'souza[26] in his case study of three villages in Punjab and Haryana border found that,

> "By and large the fruits of development have gone to the members of different castes according to the positions of their caste hierarchy..., there is high degree of correlation between the occupational prestige of father and sons. This has resulted in the population of the inequalities existing in the caste system."

Borjas[27] points out that primarily the link between the skills of the parents and children needs to be understood because parents invest in the human capital of their children. Secondly, child's quality not only depends on the parental inputs but also on the average quality of the ethnic environment where the child has been raised. He also refers to the Coleman's concept of social capital common to all members of that group, alters his opportunity set which has significant effect on behaviour, human capital formation and labour market outcome. He puts ethnic capital equal to social capital in this article.

Though not done an in-depth analysis, migration has brought some very interesting findings that unemployed respondents were higher in Kanpur than Ghaziabad. In the introductory chapter on urban poverty and labour market Rodgers[28] writes "recent migrants often suffer distinctly less unemployment than longer term residents and their occupational and work status structure is not significantly worse." The present study also proves that since Kanpur City has higher percentage of natives facing unemployment than Ghaziabad which receives good flow of migrants entering fresh in the labour structures. Gleaning over the purpose of migration and migration decisions are very much related to the availability of employment at the target area especially to the lower caste (lower stratum) people. Behavioural models on migration paid attention to the decision making process of individuals.

> "Migration pattern is a composite aspirations, needs and perceptions of real persons and mobility behaviour is one of several means by which individuals can seek well being or utility maximization"[29]

People from distant parts come loaded with many expectations and one of them is to earn more without breaking ties back at the place of origin especially in informal sector where insecurity is more.

4.5 Occupational mobility

In this section of the present chapter, there are three levels of enquiry. First is the comparison of age at which workers join the work force, It is assumed in this method that people from lower caste join labour force at early age while upper caste devotes early years of life as opportunity cost investing in education. Second is the duration of work and change in the status of first and current occupation. Third is to evaluate the occupational mobility between present generation (respondents) and past generation (fathers).

4.5.1 Age at First Occupation

The highest percentage of the upper caste respondents joined their first job between 15 and 20 age (Table 4.18). The average of the intermediate caste at first joining is same but there is also very late entry in the job market. It could be because they did not handle financial matter independently being in a joint family or may be for some other unidentifiable reason. The other Intermediate caste joins at previous age group 15-19 and group 25-29 (28.6%). The lower and ex-untouchables also show the highest percentage (68.2%) in the below 15 age group. Distinguishable point in this Table is that the late entry of all caste group respondents as late as 40 and constant entry of people in the later stage of life. It is visible from the Table that even (4.2%) respondents in ex-untouchables category also entered in the labour force >45. The study perceives from this observation could be the economic fluidity and crisis at family level or wrong perception of the respondents of age at the first job.

Table 4.18: Respondents by Age at First Occupation

(In per cent)

Age Group	*Upper Castes*	*Intermediate Castes*	*Ex-Untouchables*	*All*
		Kanpur City		
<15	26.53	70.8	68.27	62.03*(165)
15-29	67.35	20.35	26.92	31.2(83)
30-49	6.12	8.85	4.81	6.77(18)
All	100.0 (48)	100.0 (111)	100.0 (107)	100.0(266)
		Ghaziabad		
<15	22.92	59.28	68.29	55.86(143)
15-29	77.08	37.72	19.51	40.23(103)
30-49	0.0	2.99	12.2	3.91(10)
All	100.0 (48)	100.0 (167)	100.0 (41)	100.0(256)

*Column per cent, numbers in parentheses.

Ghaziabad (Table 4.18) also follows more or less same pattern like Kanpur. The upper caste respondents have the highest percentage in 15-29 age group. The other Intermediate caste, lower and ex-untouchables also have the highest percentage in younger age group

(<15). The lower and ex-untouchables have the largest percentage (68.3%) share in 'below 15' age group. Second observation in the lower and ex-untouchables' category is that there are respondents in the late age groups as well. The group of 15-29 age has the second highest percentage to the total percentage of the respondents. The artisan caste (clubbed in the intermediate caste) respondents have an early joining in the labour force.[30] Inter-city comparison leads to conclude that respondents entered at a very early age in Kanpur City while in Ghaziabad respondents have entered at mature age, still 40.23 per cent of the respondents started working between the age of 15 and 29.

4.5.2 First Occupation and Current Occupation

By the method of matching the 'joining age of labour force' with the first occupation will give a more comprehensive picture to visualize the entry age, and the kind of occupation they worked in and are working at present. In this section the occupational categories has changed and clubbed together so that the number of observation in each classification increases. Table 4.19 divulges a very interesting phenomenon as this study compares first occupation with the current occupation. In this section unskilled and unemployed are clubbed together since the attainment in learning and earning was lowest as told by the respondents.

The Upper caste respondents were the sole occupants of the professional jobs in the first job, later intermediate caste and ex-untouchables were also found in the professional category. Skilled group of jobs has significant percentage (27.3%) in the first occupation in Kanpur. In these occupations the upper caste workers share the second highest percentage (31.2%). The configuration changed in the current occupations and the ex-untouchables, intermediate caste workers gain. Besides analysing the occupational shift here the study would like to state that the reduced percentage in the manufacturing group of respondents also indicates the change in the economic variables in Kanpur where industrial shift rapidly changing in favour of other types of industries. Looking at other occupational change the study would like to say that there is a great shift towards the self-employment in Kanpur. The share of the low and ex-untouchables increases in the self-employment. The study also found the decrease in the percentage of menial activities. In the unskilled menial activities the share of the ex-untouchables has reduced. The workers in Kanpur

City have shifted in significant number from occupations like assistant, salesman, agriculture labour, and cultivators to the other kind of jobs, which have emerged as more lucrative job. Even within one type of job for instance vendors can be put into different categories as non-perishable items and perishable items (*Katchcha Sauda,* and *Pakka Sauda*) since former fetches more money though risk factor is higher (Table 4.19).

The respondents from low and ex-untouchable castes found to be working as sweeper, and other Intermediate caste respondents as

Table 4.19: Respondents by their first and current occupation in Kanpur City

(In per cent)

Occupation Groups	*Upper Caste*	*Intermediate Caste*	*Low and ex-untouchables*	*All*
		First Job		
Professional	12.5	0.0	0.0	2.34*(6)
Skilled	31.25	27.03	32.71	27.34(70)
Semi-skilled	35.42	36.94	29.91	35.16(62)
Unskilled/unemployed	20.83	36.04	37.38	35.16(128)
All	100.0(48)	100.0(111)	100.0(107)	100.0(266)
		Current Job		
Professional	20.8	8.1	2.8	8.3(22)
Skilled	54.2	39.6	18.7	33.8(90)
Semi-skilled	16.7	27.9	36.4	29.3(78)
Unskilled	0	18.0	27.1	18.4(49)
Unemployed	8.3	6.3	15.0	10.2(27)
All	100.0(48)	100.0(111)	100.0(107)	100(266)

*Column per cent, numbers in parentheses.

washerman. The study on this observation feels that the low caste people may indulge in the economic activities, which are basically designated untouchable activities and also in circumstances when there are not many economic opportunities available. Workers may start doing anything which requires the lowest capital and also jobs which are not very popular and considered unclean.

As this study had found that there is a shift from the manufacturing to the other types of occupation in Kanpur, but in Ghaziabad the manufacturing occupations gain (Tables 4.19 and 4.20). The shift is pronounced, but the intermediate caste group increases the share considerably in construction group of jobs in Ghaziabad. In trade and self-employment occupations the upper caste workers had monopoly in first occupations table. Later other caste groups also indulged in this activity. There is no visible change in the menial activities and the share of all caste categories remains more or less same.

The essence, which emerges after this whole investigation that there is no remarkable change or shift in the first and current job but the percentage share by caste categories changes. This study concludes that primarily there is no choice for workers and the change in the occupations is according to the demand in particular industry, secondly, skill enrichment opportunities are but few in such moribund jobs even after working for several years[31]. The nature of activity hardly

Table 4.20: Workers by their First Job and Current Job in Ghaziabad

Occupation Group	*Upper Castes*	*Intermediate Castes*	*Low and ex- un-touchables*	*All*
		First Job		
Professional	14.58	0.0	0.0	2.73*(7)
Skilled	54.17	23.35	9.76	26.95(69)
Semi-Skilled	22.92	29.94	19.51	26.95(69)
Unskilled/unem-ployed	8.33	46.71	70.73	43.36(111)
All	100.0 (48)	100.0 (167)	100.0 (41)	100(256)
		Current Job		
Professional	14.6	1.2	0.0	3.5(9)
Skilled	64.6	51.5	43.9	52.7(135)
Semi-Skilled	14.6	19.8	22	19.1(49)
Unskilled	4.2	19.8	31.7	18.8(48)
Unemployed	2.1	7.8	20.4	5.9(15)
All	100.0 (48)	100.0 (167)	100.0 (41)	100.00 (256)

*Column per cent, numbers in parentheses.

changed and conditions of workers belonging to different caste groups in such industries remain almost same.

4.5.4 Occupation Mobility in the Occupation of Father and Worker

Modern industrial occupation structure has not only provided liberty to select jobs but has also democratized the occupational structure in 'growing cities' and so far none is left unruffled from the effect of globalization and intercity exchange of manpower which means to say that distances between places have further reduced to attract people from far-flung areas. Permissibility of occupations have gone very high and in recent past due to several state policies and therefore, the airtight compartmentalization of jobs have become loose to accommodate people from any social strata.

This section would like to explore the occupational mobility of the respondents in the current job and also in the context of fathers' occupation across the caste groups. Occupational classification as adopted in this study has been the basis of analysis. Education level is cross tabulated with the occupational placement of both generations and looked into the difference in the mobility or *vice versa* in the labour market. Only one change from the previous chapters can be noticed in this analysis where cultivators get exclusive space; most of the respondents reported their father as a cultivator and agriculture labour, are included in semi-skilled occupations in the present analysis.

The foremost and obvious aspect is that the unemployed people are present only in the son's category and cultivators are present only in fathers' category which is expected in both the cities. Till now the study has maintained that Kanpur City has literate and aware respondents about the economy and politics both which is reflected in the generation shift in the occupation too. From Table 4.21 one can understand that even in illiterate category people from all castes has gained in skill from one generation to other especially ex-untouchables (from 12.8% in fathers section to 46.15% in sons' section). However, there is increase in the Intermediate caste sons sections to the total per cent of Intermediate caste. In higher educated group the low and intermediate caste sons have achieved better than their upper caste counterparts in the professional group of occupations yet failed miserably in unskilled category where they have higher percentage than their father.

Illiterate and higher educated group emerge to be the most important sections to see the mobility in Ghaziabad (Table 4.22). Fathers of the upper caste respondents in the illiterate education level worked in higher per cent (28.5%) as business or in trade occupation group. The precariousness of occupation has equally increased in the sons' time for all caste categories but at higher magnitude in intermediate caste category while looking at the menial activities. Searching the difference in the higher educated group it can be surmised that low and ex-untouchables (15%) though have gained in the professional occupation but upper and intermediate caste sons have decreased, especially intermediate caste sons (from 20% in fathers section to 7% in sons section). There is positive and effective increase in the skilled work

Table 4.21: Occupation Mobility in Kanpur City

	Father						*Son*				
	Occupation group	*Upper Caste*	*Intermediate Caste*	*Low and Ex-untouch-ables*	*All*		*Occupation Group*	*Upper Caste*	*Intermedi-ate Caste*	*Low and Ex-un-touchables*	*All*
Illiterate	Business/Trade	10.00	2.98	0.00	2.0(3)	Illiterate	Business/Trade	66.67	8.82	3.85	9.52(6)
	Skilled Workers	10.00	43.28	12.85	26.5(39)		Skilled Worker	33.33	50.00	46.15	47.62(30)
	Cultivators	80.00	14.92	8.57	16.3(24)		Cultivator	0.00	0.00	3.85	1.59(1)
	Semi Skilled	0.00	19.40	41.42	28.5(42)		Semi-Skilled	0.00	11.76	7.69	9.52(6)
	Menial /Un-skilled	0.00	19.40	37.14	26.5(39)		Menial /Un-skilled	0.00	26.47	30.77	26.98(17)
							Unemployed	0.00	2.94	7.69	4.76(3)
	All	100(10)	100(67)	100(70)	100(147)		All	100.0(3)	100.0(34)	100.0(26)	100.0(63)
Literate and Primary level	Professional	5.00	7.69	0.00	4.62(3)	Literate and Primary level	Professional	9.09	0.00	0.00	1.56(1)
	Business/Trade	20.00	0.00	5.26	7.69(5)		Business/Trade	27.27	8.70	3.33	9.38(6)
	Skilled Workers	35.00	46.15	63.16	47.69(31)		Skilled Worker	54.55	65.22	43.33	53.13(34)
	Cultivators	40.00	15.38	0.00	18.46						
	Semi-Skilled	0.00	15.38	0.00	6.15		Semi-Skilled	9.09	0.00	0.00	1.56(1)
	Menial /Un-skilled	0.00	15.38	31.58	15.38		Menial /Un-skilled	0.00	21.74	36.67	25.00(16)
							Unemployed	0.00	4.35	16.67	9.38(6)
	All	100(20)	100.0(26)	100.0(19)	100.0(65)		All	100.0(11)	100.0(23)	100.0(30)	100.0(64)

(Contd.)

	Father						Son				
	Occupation group	*Upper Caste*	*Intermediate Caste*	*Low and Ex-untouchables*	*All*		*Occupation Group*	*Upper Caste*	*Intermediate Caste*	*Low and Ex-untouchables*	*All*
Middle to Graduation	Professional	33.33	5.56	0.00	13.21	Middle to Graduation	Professional	29.41	20.37	7.84	17.9(25)
	Business/Trade	16.67	0.00	5.88	7.55		Business/Trade	29.41	5.56	1.96	10.0(14)
	Skilled Workers	38.89	66.67	52.94	52.83		Skilled Worker	26.47	51.85	43.14	42.4(59)
	Cultivators	11.11	22.22	29.41	20.75						
	Menial Unskilled	0.00	5.56	11.76	5.66		Menial Unskilled	0.00	11.11	23.53	12.9(18)
							Semi-Skilled	2.94	1.85	5.88	3.6(5)
							Unemployed	11.7	9.26	17.65	12.9(18)
	All	100.0(18)	100.0(18)	100.0(17)	100.0(53)		All	100.0(34)	100.0(54)	100.0(51)	100.0(139)

Table 4.22: Occupational Mobility in Ghaziabad

	Father						Son				
	Occupation group	*Upper Caste*	*Intermediate Caste*	*Low and Ex-Untouchables*	*All*		*Occupation group*	*Upper Caste*	*Intermediate Caste*	*Low and Ex-Untouchables*	*All*
Illiterate	Business/Trade	28.57	0.00	0.00	2.56(4)	Illiterate	Business/Trade	0	3.28	0.00	2.3(2)
	Skilled Work	7.14	22.02	15.15	19.23(30)		Skilled Workers	83.33	54.10	57.89	56.9(49)
	Cultivator	42.86	44.95	27.27	41.03(64)						
	Semi-Skilled	21.43	23.85	42.42	27.56(43)		Semi-Skilled	0.00	3.28	15.79	5.8(5)
	Menial/Unskilled	0.00	9.17	15.15	9.62(15)		Menial Activities	16.67	32.79	26.32	30.2(26)
							Unemployed	0.00	6.56	0.00	4.6(4)
	All	**100.0(14)**	**100.0(109)**	**100.0(33)**	**100.00(156)**		**All**	**100.0(6)**	**100.0(61)**	**100.0(19)**	**100.0(86)**

(Contd.)

(Contd.)

	Father						Son				
	Occupation group	*Upper Caste*	*Intermediate Caste*	*Low and Ex-Untouchables*	*All*		*Occupation group*	*Upper Caste*	*Intermediate Caste*	*Low and Ex-Untouchables*	*All*
Liter-ate and Primary	Business/Trade	28.57	13.51	20.00	19.05(12)	Liter-ate and Primary	Business/Trade	100.00	0.00	0.00	8.3(1)
	Skilled Work	14.29	37.84	20.00	28.57(18)		Skilled Workers	0.00	44.44	0.00	33.3(4)
	Cultivator	57.14	45.95	60.00	50.79(32)						
	Semi-Skilled	0.00	2.70	0.00	1.59(1)		Semi-Skilled	0.00	11.11	50.00	16.6(2)
							Menial Activities	0.00	11.11	50.00	16.6(2)
							Unemployed	0.00	33.33	0.00	25.0(3)
	All	**100.0(21)**	**100.0(37)**	**100.0(5)**	**100.0(63)**		**All**	**100.0(1)**	**100.0(9)**	**100.0(2)**	**100.0(12)**
Middle to Gradua-tion	Profess	27.78	20.00	0.00	21.74(10)	Middle to Gradua-tion	professional	26.82	7.21	15.0	13.29(21)
	Business/Trade	16.67	8.00	0.00	10.87(5)		Business/Trade	19.5	4.12	0.0	7.59(12)
	Skilled Work	16.67	12.00	66.67	17.39(8)		Skilled Workers	46.34	69.07	45.0	60.12(95)
	Cultivator	11.11	40.00	33.33	28.26(13)		Cultivators	2.43	0	0.0	0.63(1)
							Semi-Skilled	0	2.06	0.0	1.26(2)
							Menial Activities	2.43	11.3	40.0	12.65(20)
							unemployed	2.43	6.18	0.0	4.43(7)
	All	**100.00**	**100.00**	**100.00**	**100.00(46)**		**All**	**100(41)**	**100(97)**	**100(20)**	**100(158)**

force of the sons' yet sons can be found in unskilled works in higher percentage (12.6%) where low ex-untouchables and intermediate caste sons have high percentage (40%) to the total percentage of the low ex-untouchables and intermediate sons. The picture which emerges is of both satisfaction and dissatisfaction where sons from the Intermediate caste and low ex-untouchables have increased their presence in the professional and skilled category but on the other side high presence in the unskilled category is equally worrisome.

Overall it can be said that local market and economy though have greatly influenced the overall structure of the labour market yet the situation of the low and ex-untouchables from one generation to other has not improved. A study by Motiram and Singh[32] on intergenerational mobility suggests occupational immobility and higher downward mobility among SC/STs. Substantial level of immobility particularly among low skilled and low paying occupations. This study used data from Indian Human Development Survey (IHDS), 2005. Another study by Hnatkovska, Lahiri and Paul[33] found that the intergenerational mobility of the SC/STs have converged to non-SC/ST levels from 1983 to 2005 especially of the middle income households.

After probing the pre-market dissemination and traversing through some of the migration information, the present study steps into a world where worker stand in the market looking for job from entirely new angle, aspirations or for improvement from previous job. This section thus enters into the realm of recruitment of the workers.

4.6 Recruitment and Other Processes in the Market

Studies on discrimination have considered the role of recruitment process, methods of job search, duration in job, promotion and tenure in the job, status and the sector of industry of workers absorption as very significant points of inquiry[34]. Recruitment is a very crucial point of argument in discrimination analysis. It is an entry stage (port of entry) where people may or may not find job according to their qualification, expectations.

After probing the pre-market dissemination and traversing through some of the migration information, the present study steps into a world where worker stand in the market looking for job from entirely new angle, aspirations or for improvement from previous job. This section on job processes thus enters into the realm of recruitment of the workers.

4.6.1 Information Networks

Generally, it is believed that unorganized and organized workforce, at some point of time in their job tenure may have resorted to the information through informal channel and this was the method to obtain a job. There is no dearth of studies showing that the informal mechanism play pivotal role in selecting the employees. One such study done by Rees[35] in Chicago labour market information networks, points out that "out of the four white colour occupations under study, informal sources account for about half of all hires in the eight blue colour occupations, informal sources account for more than four-fifth of all hires." In case of unorganized sector this method is a rule rather than exception. It is the informal method of recruitment, which has given a solid footing to '*Badli* workers' in manufacturing sectors and also since jobbers, or entrepreneurs give contractors a legitimate and valuable role to obtain workers for unskilled and semi-skilled jobs[36].

During the British rule job of collecting workers, was performed ceremoniously by jobbers (known as *mukkadams* or *sirdars*). Holmstrom mentions the constant uselessness of jobbers after 1970s onwards and due to the superfluity of labourers. The jobbers may not be existing any more to recruit or fetch labourers from farfetched villages, yet in highly industrialized cities, the work of getting workers is resumed by contractors. Many entrepreneurs still rely on them for workers, which are inducted on temporary rolls (it is sometimes dubious distinction given by industrialists to evade legal implications).[37] These contractors may be from the same caste of the labourers or from other caste.

Table 4.23 on information network in Ghaziabad and Kanpur City reveals distinctly quite different details on source of information of jobs. For information (Table 4.23) on jobs, the highest percentage is in 'other personal contacts' in Ghaziabad and Kanpur City both (44% in Ghaziabad, 42% in Kanpur City). Upper caste respondents (41.6%) and intermediate caste (51.8%) respondents seems to be depending heavily on the other personal contacts while ex-untouchables (17.6%) show poor information backup on personal contacts. Ex-untouchables have said that there is no particular place for information check on the availability of work but they go to the market every morning for job (most of them are construction workers) in Ghaziabad. Family connections (19%) are found to be performing links to obtain jobs in Ghaziabad for all caste categories though slightly less through caste contacts (7.9%).

Table 4.23 suggests that 42.04 per cent of respondents got information from personal contacts in Kanpur City; the study found that the respondents either collected information from neighbour or

Table 4.23: Respondents by Source of Information of Job and Caste Groups

(In per cent)

Source of Information	*Upper Castes*	*Intermediate Castes*	*Low Caste and Ex-untouchables*	*All*
		Ghaziabad		
Through family connections	23.87	18.8	20.59	19.97*(40)
Through caste contacts	11.51	5.26	14.71	7.93(16)
Through Advertisement	8.63	5.26	2.94	5.45(11)
Other personal contacts	41.61	51.88	17.65	44.34(89)
Any other	14.38	18.8	44.12	22.3(45)
All	100.0 (35)	100.0 (133)	100.0 (34)	100.0 (202)
		Kanpur City		
Through family connections	32.26	30.99	23.13	28.14(45)
Through caste contacts	14.6	10.78	17.54	13.99(23)
Through Advertisement	19.58	1.64	1.94	4.51(8)
Other personal contacts	28.23	45.81	43.04	42.04(68)
Any other	5.34	10.78	14.35	11.33(18)
All	100.0 (25)	100.0 (74)	100.0(63)	100.0(162)

*Column per cent, Numbers in parentheses.

from previous work place. The ex-untouchables are discreet to tell about the information they gathered for current occupation. Some of them show confusion on this question and some replied that the people come searching for small jobs like cleaning and related works in the residential areas of the city. Of all the upper caste respondents 32.2 per cent said to get it due to family connections in Kanpur City, 30.9 per cent and 23.1 per cent of the intermediate caste and lower castes respondents told to have learnt about the current job through family connections respectively.[38] The ex-untouchables (14.7%) and upper caste (11.5%) workers give equal weightage to caste contacts for jobs in Kanpur City.

There is visible difference between Ghaziabad and Kanpur City for information network in a job. If this study assumes family relations equivalent to caste contacts (considering that family relations also revolve around the same kind of people like upper caste people are in close contact with the upper caste and lower caste people get friendly with the same kind of group) thus if adding both these groups of first 'through family connections' and 'caste contacts' then both the cities evinces highest percentage (39% in case of Kanpur City and 17.2% in Ghaziabad) in the caste contact category. This may prove that caste contacts are vital in case of Kanpur City. Again the study would like to clear here that family relations and caste contacts are two distinct variables nevertheless it is just an assumption of the study that family connections are more with either their own caste circle or are some times beyond caste circles. A study on Ahemdabad manufacturing units by Papola and Subrahmaniam[39] dealt this topic in great detail, however, they also do not give further break up by friends, relatives, neighbours and gave total percentage combining neighbours, friends and relatives. They say,

> "The picture is one of a highly informal mechanism in the labour market. There may not be any virtue in the preferring of the use of formalized channels, so long as the informal channel can discriminate information effectively and equitably. They further feel with utter disgust the role-play, which enacted by Employment Exchange and other such agencies in providing information and occupations."

Respondents were asked to put in preference if they know local requirement of the jobs in the area where they work. They ranked first, family, friends, neighbour and natives to recommend for the job.[40]

4.6.2 Contract for Job

The study is not very ambitious on the aspect to find the permanency in jobs since most of the workers worked through informal channel as it has been analysed in the previous table. Still it is but pertinent to see the difference between two cities to judge intra-caste difference in the type of contract (Table 4.24). 41.3 per cent respondents stated to have no contract at all in Kanpur City. The upper caste column though indicates 27.76 per cent respondents in written contract, and 7.94 per cent of ex-untouchables category and also 36.5 per cent respondents show the contract without time period.

The study explains this (written contract without time period) that though employers keep workers on contract yet it was up to the willingness of employer to keep them in job. The intermediate caste group has have the largest share (64.18%) of the respondents in the highest percentage in the 'No Contract' category in Kanpur City though in Ghaziabad it is ex-untouchables (55.3% to total) caste respondents who have no contract.

Table 4.24: Respondents by Type of Contract for Job and Caste Groups

(In per cent)

	Upper Castes	*Intermediate Castes*	*Low Caste and Ex-untouchables*	*All*
	Ghaziabad			
Written Contract	14.19	20.3	14.57	18.32*(37)
Written Contract without time period	19.73	9.02	6.73	10.52(21)
Oral Contract	3.3	9.02	23.32	10.48(21)
No Contract	25.55	32.33	55.38	35.15(71)
Did not tell	37.23	29.32	0	25.8(52)
All	100.00 (35)	100.00 (133)	100.00 (34)	100.00 (202)
	Kanpur city			
Written Contract	27.76	12.16	7.94	12.95(21)
Written Contract Without time period	4.81	9.46	36.51	19.24(31)
Oral Contract	23.8	20.27	42.86	29.59(48)
No Contract	43.63	58.11	20.63	41.3(67)
All	100.00 (25)	100.00 (74)	100.00(63)	100.00(162)

*Column per cent, numbers in parentheses.

Ghaziabad (Table 4.24) have lesser number of respondents replying for no contract (35.1%), 18.3 per cent replying in favour of 'Written Contract' of which Intermediate caste respondents have highest percentage (20.3%), upper caste 14.1 per cent and 14.5 per cent of the ex-untouchables fall in this group category. In the group of 'Contract Without Time' upper caste dominates the group by enjoying highest percentage (19.7%) amongst caste groups and second highest in the upper caste category itself. The revelation on the contract type also tells the marginalized situation of the ex-untouchables while upper caste people are in stronger position.

4.6.3 Skill Requirement

The question of employees looking for skilled job becomes the point of enquiry. In the unorganized sector the quality and requirement in jobs are seldom challenging and often cluster routine unskilled jobs only. This may be chief reason why employer do not like investing money in the advertising the posts and collecting information on potential employees.[41]

There is significant difference in the respondents of the two surveyed cities (Table 4.25). In the 'no skill required' category (Kanpur City 52% and Ghaziabad 33.6%). There is a very minute difference

Table 4.25: Respondents by Skill Requirements for Job and Caste Groups

(In per cent)

	Upper Castes	*Intermediate Castes*	*Low Caste and Ex-untouchables*	*All*
		Ghaziabad		
Family Occupation	14.29	6.02	14.65	8.9* (18)
Apprenticeship	25.71	9.77	12.13	12.93 (26)
Training on the job	17.14	14.29	5.84	13.35 (27)
Learnt job afterwards	28.57	33.83	23.44	31.17(63)
No skill required	14.29	36.09	43.94	33.64(68)
All	100.0(35)	100.0 (133)	100.0 (34)	100.0 (202)
		Kanpur City		
Family Occupation	28.0	7.01	4.76	9.37(15)
Apprenticeship	4.0	7.24	11.11	8.24(13)
Training on the job	12.0	11.65	12.7	12.11(20)
Learnt job afterwards	20.0	17.52	17.46	17.88(29)
No skill required	36.0	56.59	53.97	52.4(85)
All	100.0 (25)	100.0 (74)	100.0(63)	100.0(162)

*Column per cent, numbers in parentheses.

between two cities the distribution of the rest of the classification for skill. A considerable percentage (31.1%) of the respondents in Ghaziabad said to have learnt job after joining while in Kanpur only 17.8 per cent of the respondents said to have learnt job after joining.

Family Occupation is considered the one inherited from father or guardian; it could be traditional caste occupation or any other job followed by the respondents such as business. In most of the cases upper caste respondents took over business of their father and relatives, amongst the intermediate caste respondents chiefly the artisan caste respondents also chose to do traditional caste occupation, yet may have not switched over to father's establishment but have followed only caste occupation. The ex-untouchable workers replying to the question of the family occupation by meaning as the occupation which their forefathers were doing, which means they were following the caste occupation but may not have essentially own the establishment of their own and working in some other enterprise as a labour. To state further ex-untouchables (leather workers) said to have been doing the shoe-making job in private company. This automatically replied by them as their family occupation.

Then comes the final question how they finally obtain the jobs because if skill is not the sole criteria of judging a person what leads an employer or employee to choose a job? Table 4.26 also shows difference from the respondents of Kanpur City, viz. the demand and supply of labour matches in Ghaziabad and Kanpur City (20.8 per cent said that the employer came looking for the workers and 15.3 per cent workers said that they contacted employers directly in Ghaziabad while in Kanpur a large percentage (31.2%) said they were first contacted by the employer but only 9 per cent said they contacted employer directly. This observation may give an elusive view because daily

Table 4.26: Respondents by Obtainment of the Job and Caste Groups

(In per cent)

	Upper Castes	*Intermediate Castes*	*Low Caste and Ex-untouchables*	*All*
		Kanpur City		
Through Family relations	28.45	35.22	17.61	31.19*(63)
Caste contacts	8.53	5.25	17.61	7.92(16)
Desired Qualifications	22.76	14.99	6.74	15(30)
Employer looking for	19.91	20.23	23.49	20.79(42)
Passed selection test	0	0	2.94	0.49(1)
Direct Contact with Employer	17.07	12.74	23.49	15.35(31)
Any Other	3.29	7.49	0	5.52(11)
Did not tell	0	3.75	8.81	3.96(8)
All	100.0 (35)	100.0(133)	100.0 (34)	100.0 (202)
		Ghaziabad		
Through Family relations	4.97	19.01	22.33	18.04(29)
Caste contacts	4.95	9.51	12.76	10.01(16)
Desired Qualifications	40.76	24.45	15.95	23.46(38)
Employer looking for	14.74	35.31	33.5	31.25(51)
Passed selection test	14.2	0	5.56	4.3(7)
Direct Contact with Employer	20.38	6.78	7.96	9.25(15)
Any Other	0.0	4.95	1.94	3(5)
All	100.0 (25)	100.0 (74)	100.0(63)	100.0(162)

*Column per cent, numbers in parentheses.

wage workers also go to the market everyday in search of jobs. At such market joints they meet potential employer. Many potential employers also throng to these market joints, knowing the availability of plenty of workers (especially for construction jobs where ex-untouchables have highest representation in comparison to other caste groups in case of Ghaziabad).

After judging the mechanism of recruitment and job engagement in unorganized market it can be said that it banks on a highly varied type of contacts. Employees also trust in this method of new employee linked with older employee since method "generally reduces the risk of indolence behaviour and protest by new employee."[42] Ultimately this pattern of information network and recruitment leads to perpetuation of already existing inequalities, Papola and Subramaniam[43] who surveyed Ahmedabad industrial setting to see labour mobility, says:

> "The information channels are mainly informal in the Ahmedabad labour market, and even though the majority of workers reveal awareness of the market situation, it is difficult to ensure under such a system that the information is equitably disseminated. The inherent bias of informal system in favour of discriminatory discrimination."

Problem gets multiplied when employer do not get true picture of employee's skills because the worker in question may not be educated, or have learned skill through apprenticeship or by any other source, therefore, the employer rather believe the employee who introduces the potential employee for the skill and behavioural requirement for the job. Piore and Doeringer[44] too assert that the constant contact with some workers result in same community, group crowds in certain jobs. This study envisages here that under such circumstances, workers in Ghaziabad would have found the jobs, since the workers in one particular slum belonged to the same place and worked in the same or neighbour company. Holmstrom[45] also confirms the outcome of the information network based on caste contacts and neighbours.

It can be observed that the ex-untouchables in Kanpur City are more skilled than Ghaziabad. Good percentages of workers in both cities were leather workers. Leather workers in Kanpur City are hired for skilled occupations by in the companies and also managed independent shoe repair and small workshops while in Ghaziabad most of the leather workers respondents were construction labourers[46].

Most of the authors have written at length on the pattern and type of recruitment procedures, which are followed in organized and unorganized sectors. William[47] studied the recruitment phases in academics in British Universities wrote on the essentials of job search in professional labour and manual labour. Authors quoted Becker and his successor who wrote how profession of different amounts and different types of human capital can help to account for differences in earnings that economic theory otherwise finds difficult in accounting for.life time earning profile. He also said that most manual workers who constitute the bulk of the subject matter of traditional labour economics reach their peak earning capacity early in life and on the evidences of cross sectional data at least their relative earnings remain more or less constant until after middle age when declining physical powers tend to reduce their income somewhat.

Holmstrom[48] refers to Deshpande, who is doubtful of 'graduation hypothesis' (casual workers in small establishments promoted to permanent factory workers after a certain span of time) and comments that recruitment through relatives, friends further intensifies stratification and fairness in recruitment get subdivided by the known cycle of contacts. In this section of recruitment first two (information for the job and contract for the job) workers in the private, public and casual work force division were probed while skill requirement includes all the workers even unemployed or available for job.

This study suggests that main fault could be the information channel and recruitment process that does not allow primarily workers to show real skill, secondly this kind of introduction in labour market hinders the improvement in skill up gradation because workers might not get chances to improve his/her skill. This is a serious impediment for workers in unorganized labour market. This fact of technological advancement becomes more important in the backdrop of new arrival of industries in Indian economy.[49] The lack of effective mechanism to match the skills required for currently available jobs is also a perpetrator of segregation in the market.[50] The study would like to quote Holmstrom, which is very relevant here "the use of caste as distinct from particular relatives to get job and favours, is seen as a necessity in a phase of cut-throat competition and unemployment and is not as universal as some people suggest." The gist in this quote is that the caste as a tradition is disappearing gradually yet rephrasing its value in modern and urban job conditions. According to Dual Labour Market theory of discrimination, where internal labour market and external labour market have set pattern of recruitment and other economic variables, but distinguished by certain job classifications and ports of entry (the study presumes the port of entry as mark of recruitment).

Holmstrom[51] commented on the erstwhile jobbers institutionalized by the British administration and present day contractor who have rather endangered the already stacked security of contract labourers. He says,

> "It seems that outside contractors were taking over the jobber's role of recruiting extra labour when it was needed, and that these contract workers had a different statusless secure and worse paid from directly employed workers, when they stood side by side doing the same work: a situation which has recurrent in recent years."

Succinctly stating most of the workers belonged to informal nature of work. There is not a very distinguished trend in recruitment and labour status analysis from the past. This study has observed that the workers still rely mostly on the information provided by relatives, neighbours and natives. The two levels of sector, i.e. internal labour market is crowded with first ex-untouchables in lowest status; intermediate and the artisan caste slightly better in position from the ex-untouchables. Indirectly caste connections, family ties become an important tool to know the availability of jobs and working under the umbrella of the other side of external labour market.[52] Srinivas[53] in the conclusion of study on Okhala, finds that although kinship, caste and religion have no part in the formal procedures of recruitment they nevertheless play an important role in its actual operations. He writes "The adoption of an industrial career does not lead automatically to the collapse of traditional principles of organization among either entrepreneurs or workers, nor such principles continue to operate without some modification. The outcome there is a partial segregation of roles, norms expectations."

This study finds that social background casts its shadow in the urban labour market for not only in the ritual and other social pursuits but also in economic behaviour for favouritism through the recruitment and information process. Derek[54] studied the bargaining power and information network of racially different set of workers. He quotes studies by Mickel 1999 and Caputo where the authors said the meaning of money is partly determined by early childhood experiences and members of certain groups are more likely to grow up poor. He finds logic behind such examples that it is due to poor social network since social networks provide information to applicants about an organization that might prove advantageous during salary negotiations. Thus, it may appear that minorities' relative lack of social networks may result in discrepant perceptions of starting salaries.

This study also indicates from the exercise of recruitment and job attainment that though caste asserts its identity in the labour market yet it is a dubious covert outlook of caste solidarity and not the ugly demonstration of caste oppression. People use caste as an information channel for establishing contacts in the labour market especially in the unorganized market. A study[55] on the labour problems in India states that "the system of recruitment in India has grown up in a haphazard manner and consequently there has been no application of any scientific principles of labour administration and labour management." Andre Beteille takes another step in interpretation of the process or mechanism in ranking and grading of service class in Indian Society where from generation to generation keep working in the same grade. Something is working where from reproduction of inequality in which family and caste plays an important role. He argues that caste remains the root proof that of social morphology and it is still manifestly correlated with every occupation, wealth, income, education or some other criterion. In all public institutions, those in inferior positions are likely to be higher and those in inferior position of lower caste. Some of this kind manifests correlation as proof that caste is at the bottom the cause of the ranks that we observe in the public life[56]. The study thus plainly believes that the recruitment system needs to be systematized especially in unorganised sector where lot of personal links work while employer bank on the references from these old employees.

Summing Up

This chapter on the background characteristics and migration concludes that,

Parents' education and occupational status influences the future prospects of the child. This is not only true in case of the fathers from the well-off section but also proves that fathers who are less educated, working in the lowest dead end jobs, can hardly change the future of their children. People from the upper caste have enjoyed the place of privilege for centuries, which have given them an over other caste groups. The situation of the ex-untouchables has not improved to a satisfactory level. Experience in Kanpur City definitely enforces the ideology that higher the education level, greater is the chance of overall welfare of the society.

Migration status of the workers has revealed that people migrate due to unsatisfactory situation at native place. The caste-wise analysis of migration depicts that lower caste people migrate in large number and their occupational status does not change drastically even after a good span of time spent at one place but certainly provides a sense of stability for a longer period.

In the recruitment processes caste plays as a shield of opportunity initially in the basic absence of good education qualifications and people enter in the informal market through relatives, native residents or friends which ultimately recycles the unskilled people in same type of jobs and those who have some skill to scale up to just another level.

The analysis of journey of the respondents from his native place till the entry point at destination has opened up a new chapter in the life of a worker that is processes involved in search for a job, recruitment, labour market network.

NOTES

1. Several studies have emphasised the role of parents in socio-economic status, educational attainment, determinants of earning of their offspring's. Avtar Singh Dhesi and Harbans Singh (1995) "Education, Labour Market Distortions and Relative Earning of Different Religion, Caste Categories in India: A Case Study of Delhi", *Canadian Journal for Development Studies*, December. p. 79. Beach and Finnie (1988) "Family Background in an Extended Earning-Generation Model: Further Evidence", *Eastern Economic Journal,* Vol. XIV, No. 1, January-March 1988, analysed Canadian micro data that included extensive family background variablcs which were separated as endogenous variables (educational, occupation status and earning in current job, work experience) and background variables. In this study it was found that the education background accounts for 70-80 per cent of the indirect and total effect on the earning of the offspring (pp. 44-47). World Development Report (2006) co-published by the World Bank and Oxford University Press, New York. pp. 3-8.
2. David Smith (1977) *Human Geography,* p. 18.
3. Computer Diploma was the most sought after course in this city.
4. It is field observation that respondents in Ghaziabad are more towards earning enough to either go back their native place or to other place where they get better opportunity.
5. Gerry Rodgers (ed.) (1989) *op. cit.,* p. 13.

6. This study has found the difference that the ex-untouchables if self-employed were mainly vendors while in upper caste workers owned small level establishment.
7. Page 105 of this thesis.
8. J.B.G. Tilak (1980) "Education and Labour Market Discrimination", *Indian Journal of Industrial Relations*, Vol. 16, No. 1, July, p. 108.
9. R.S. Tiwari (1990), *Role of Informal Sector in Urban Communities: A Study of Kanpur*", Giri Institute of Development Studies, Lucknow, p. 136.
10. Declan Quigeley (1993), *The Interpretation of Caste,* Clarendon Press, Oxford, p. 144.
11. Rodgers (1989) (ed.), p. 14.
12. Lambert (1963), *op. cit.* Writes that education and castes are great correlates. p. 216.
13. B.D. Soni (1975) *Educational Problems in U.P. (West*). ICSSR, New Delhi with Agra University. pp. 36-38.
14. Becker and Cheswick (1966) "Education and Distribution of Earning". *American Economic Review*, Vol. VI, p. 366.
15. *Op. cit.* World Development Report, 3, p. 8.
16. In this analysis siblings are not clubbed for two reasons first number of sample would reduce second every individual has different approach to life and efficiency and hence all workers are analysed individually.
17. This study when working in the survey area, found difficult to conduct a survey since all respondents wanted to know the objective of the survey (as always happens) and while telling them the objective which may connect them somewhere with education and their livelihood question at this point generally people interrupted and questioned back that 'education does not guarantee employment in Sarkari department so why to study at all'. It was felt that commoners generally assume that after studying they should get into the Government Department and that should remain the only purpose of getting education. The study, therefore, found that rarely people are told the rationality of education in their own way.
18. It is a famous quote by Jawaharlal Nehru who once said "educate a woman and you educate the whole family".
19. S.K. Sasikumar and Anup K. Karen (2010) "Skill Mapping in Indian Labour market: Supply Side Potential and emerging Demand Scenario", *Labour and Development*, Vol. 16-17, June 2010.
20. M.N. Panini in his study titled *Network and Style Industrial Entrepreneurs in Faridabad*, stated that most of the executive entrepreneurs' fathers were of high urban profession executives of supervisory and craftsman entrepreneurs were from lower social strata and fathers were of lesser urban occupations. In Satish Sabarwal (1978), *Process and Institution in Urban India*, Vikas Publishing House, New Delhi, p. 98.
21. Besides secondary role of women in agricultural economy the labour participation rate for women in rural India has been declining. http://www.scmp.com/comment/insight-opinion/article/1307072/indias-bias-against-

women-workplace-saps-economic-growth.

22. There could be some misreporting also by the respondents since they include all family members who are not sharing or living with them when interviewed.
23. A.S. Dhesi and Gumbar (1983) "Earning Determination, Earning Diffrential and Settlement Behaviour of Migrant Workers: Amritsar City", *Arth Vijnana*, N.1, p. 58.
24. N.R. Seth (1968) *op. cit.*, p. 77, says in his study that migrants absolve in the urban labour force are mainly from low castes and ex-untouchables since they are the worst off. The study has also found that the organized work force mainly constitute migrants from lower caste section of the society. It could be painful to find that the workers of unorganized section are deprived of any decent living standard of human existence.
25. Daily field record suggested that even if people consider themselves unemployed yet village bond never perishes.
26. D'Souza (1985), *Economic and Social Structure and Population Growth*, Sage Publications, New Delhi. p. 129.
27. George Borjas (1992), "Ethnic Capital and Intergenerational Mobility", *Quarterly Journal of Economics,* Vol. 107, No. 1., pp. 124 and 126,
28. Rodgers (ed.) (1989) *op. cit.*
29. Huw Johne's (1990) *Population Geography*, West View; Buolder and London, p. 199.
30. Their real caste identity is hidden at work places to get the job in industry.
31. Report on The Re-sturcturalisation of the Unorganised Sector in India, 2003, by Sheila Bhalla. Where she states that Mechanisation of transport has affected the increased trend of entry in this sector.
32. Sripad Motiram and Ashish Singh (2012), "How Close does the Apple Fall to the Tree? Some Evidence on Intergenerational Occupational Mobility from India", Working Paper-2012-2017. http://www.igidr.ac.in/pdf/publication/WP-20120017.pdf
33. Hnatkovska, Lahiri and Paul (2011), "Breaking the Caste Barrier: Intergenerational Mobility in India", http://faculty.arts.ubc.ca/alahiri/intergenration_4.pdf
34. Michael Fix, George C. Craslster and Struyk in their study on the "Audition Method" in discrimination claims that the selection point is partially due to the residential segregation. Some respondents also gave similar point of view in the present study that they were not able to find jobs because the constraints posed by their residential areas. But a few, in reverse told that people come looking for them in this area. (Mainly for domestic services, cleaning and other petty jobs. In Darity Williams Jr. (ed.) (1995) *Economics and Discrimination*, An Elgar Reference Collection, U.K. pp. 376-386.
35. Rees (1966), "Information Networks in Labour Markets", *American Economic Review*, p. 561.
36. N.R. Sheth (1968), *The Social Framework of Indian Factory*, Oxford, Bombay. p. 76.
37. Mark Holmstrom (1993), "Flexible Specialization in India?" *Economic and*

Political Weekly, August 28th, Vol. XXVIII, No. 35, p. 82.

38. N.R. Sheth (1969), *op. cit.* Also mentioned in his study that the artisan caste have monopolized their traditional occupations, p. 72.
39. Papola and Subrahmaniam (1975), *op. cit.* p. 45.
40. This information was not focused in the interview session yet the study became curious after such monotonous response and hence felt to bring some variability in the study.
41. Rees (1966), "Information Network in Labour Markets," *American Economic Review,* p. 561.
42. Holmstrom (1985), p. 4 a. Rees also confirms this observation in his study of Chicago Labour Market, *op. cit.* p. 562.
43. Papola and Subramanium (1975), p. 113.
44. Piore and Doeringer (1971) in King J.E. (ed.) (1980) *op. cit.* p. 115.
45. Mark Holmstrom (1985), *Industry and Inequality,* Cambridge University Press, Cambridge, p. 38.
46. K.L. Sharma (1995), *Social Inequity in India*, Rawat Publication, Jaipur. He cites Swedish Anthropologist, who worked on stagnant and poor neighbourhood in Kanpur, expressed that everywhere he encountered mobility of entrepreneurial success of caste organisation bargaining effectively with political parties and so forth what he points out that a lot of sociologist while capturing mobility, mobilization, achievements, egalitarianism and kept neglecting growing inequality as well as the process which made this permanently so. pp. 108-109.
47. Williams, Blackstone and Metcalf (1974), *The Academic Labour Market: Economics and Social Aspects of a Profession*, Elsevier Scientific Publishing Company, Netherlands, pp. 10-11.
48. Holmstrom, *op. cit.*, p. 229.
49. Though delicensing and liberalization have led to invigorated competition yet in this study new industry connotes in firms in manufacturing, transport and construction industry.
50. Papola and Subrahmanyam (1975), *op. cit.,* p. 198.
51. Holmstrom (1985), *op. cit.*, p. 53.
52. Frank Conlon (1977), *op. cit.,* p. 138, says that urban values and problems have often stimulated the use of caste as an identifiable focus around which associations and institutions could emerge and prosper too.
53. M.N. Srinivas (1966), *Small Industry and Social Change*, UNESCO Research Centre on Social and Economic Development in Southern Asia, Allied Publisher, Delhi.
54. Derek R. Avery (2003), "Racial Differences in Perceptions of Starting Salaries: How Failing to Discriminate can Perpetuate Discrimination", *Journal of Business and Psychology*, Vol. 17, No. 4, Summer 2003.
55. S.N. Mehrotra (1964), *Labour Problems in India*, S. Chand and Company, Delhi, p. 17.
56. Andre Beteille (1991), "The Reproduction of Inequality", *Contribution to Indian Sociology*, January, Vol. 25, No. 13-28.

5
Power Structure and Resources

The concept or term of Discrimination is notional and abstract but certainly exists in the society, therefore, several studies put efforts to understand various direct and indirect theoretical association of discrimination in different socio-economic setup. Some of them have taken help of qualitative method, while some social scientists claimed that the qualitative methods, are known to be efficient over quantitative methods in places where opinion based survey are needed. Smith[1] says, "An important aim of inquiry must be to capture something of the meaning of life in a particular social setting." Besides interviewing the respondents on the issue of discrimination this study developed five focal questions on the 'likert scale' to know what exactly people think and respond to such straight questions, the questions were further explained to diminish the possibility of confusion and misinterpretation of the questions. In such cases explanations were decoded to know what the interviewee had intended to say. The responses were scaled and 'Oral History'[2] method was adhered to while seeking explanations and extension of the questions and within the 'work history' section of the interview schedule. Authors write "recollection and the reminiscences of living people about the past. As such, oral history is subject to all the vagaries and frailties of human recall." The statement says that 'oral history' method is not foolproof method yet this method informally covered various aspects on their job initiation procedures, methods, views on caste, understanding of discrimination in labour market, impinged inequalities, desire for education and generate well-being on the social parameters.

This study not only has substantial quantitative data with qualitative inputs covering mostly experiences and opinions but also has integrated the employers' views[3] on discrimination. The chapter unfolds some interesting perspectives of the labour relations both as employee and employer. How informal market designs the thoughts of the employer and employee relations and how does this behaviour influence the overall structure of the formal and informal market becomes quite intriguing.

5.1 Employers' Discrimination[4]

Revisiting the definition of employers' discrimination as defined that employer may exercise power to withhold jobs, which may not allow potential employer to apply, disapproved on qualifications ground or straightway dispelled from the opportunity of employment on the grounds of sex, religion, caste or any other irrational discriminating parameter. This section has combined the experience from the first phase of the survey in 1999 and second phase during 2006.

Becker extracted discrimination by means of discrimination coefficient and the difference in the discrimination would predict the intensity in the taste of discrimination of an employer while recruiting people from two different sets of group[5]. Studies on discrimination have opted different *modus operandi* for the detection of discrimination. Fix, Galster and Stuyk suggested 'audit method'; Smith used 'the actor testing'[6] of applicants for the same job one white and another black. Often such methodologies presumed that discrimination existed and due to lack of pure evidences has neither been questioned nor raised to rectify such incidences and other related behaviour. Employer discrimination is generally described as statistical discrimination. Economists often distinguish between two types of discrimination —*animus-based* discrimination and *statistical* discrimination. The former type describes irrational prejudice held by a person against someone of a different race or any other socio-cultural background. By contrast, someone (like an HR screener) can engage in statistical discrimination even if they do not personally harbour hatred towards members of another socio-cultural group. They may engage in discrimination (either negative or positive) based on a statistical view (a stereotype) about the work habits of members of that group, e.g. "I'm going to hire *Brahman* because *Brahmans* are intelligent in this kind of work or I will ask a *Badhai* to do woodwork than a *Luhar* or *Kumhar* as they have job specifications by their caste occupations, or the man should be hired for secretarial job Thus, in one sense, the statistical discriminator is acting "rationally", albeit on the basis of their stereotypes, in order to maximize their profit and avoid an open competition for the job. The thesis did not touch this aspect yet employers discrimination is one of the greatest point of enquiry in understanding discrimination dynamics.

The section on employer's discrimination is an extension of recruitment and selection criteria in the labour market. Both employer and employee face certain limitations because of which many strange phenomena were also reported. What an employer thinks before employing a person or what goes into the mind of a worker is also restricted by some unknown circumstances and have varying degrees of freedom to select a job. The employer may evaluate market conditions, cost and benefit, competition, prestige etc. and an employee tries to compare future prospects along with current economic return. Such freedom/limitations can be due to personal choice, preference and discrimination also. Behaviour of employer with employee produces covert discrimination of employer. An employer may deny his preference to a particular community but his general behaviour, gestures, remarks, work description and payment may express his biasness. This is what the study aimed at when deliberating point of discrimination with the employees; asking them on issues of payment, grievance redress, help in adversities legal or human, promotion, learning experience, job profile etc. The response of employee can be cognitive or affective[7]; depending on the preference of the employer. Behaviour of employee or worker becomes inferential which may or may not be due to discrimination.

Employer's Discrimination and hence becomes cardinal for the discrimination analysis. Though it is different in each society and even at micro level yet result of discrimination remain same everywhere which *divides* society into two factions of power players and power responder. It is different in the Indian Labour Market considering the two interesting features of the employer's discrimination definition, first exploitation by paying less and second by making unjustified demands of physical labour such as taking over time, not recruiting reasonable number of workers, indirect mental harassment which is not acceptable under normal circumstances. That is how an employer gets pecuniary advantage, second by the method of avoidance and filling vacant posts to the socially more acceptable group. Both the situations lead to segregation or isolation of such discriminated group. This belief system generates such disequilibria in the market.

The study randomly selected employers doing small level of trading, workshop garage owners, small level of transporters, owner of sweet shops etc. The experience had been multifaceted and rich with many divergent views since employers engaged in each case are from a different walks of life, for example a housewife having a final authority while employing a housemaid, employer owning a small garage or trading in waste items (*Kabadi*) have different perspective of a potential employee.

5.1.1 Kanpur City

Sarbatilal is from trading caste and a 'chat' vendor of medium capacity, he flatly refused to talk initially saying that these days you cannot trust anyone and he might be reprimanded later, yet after great persuasion and prodding he agreed and just talked on his ambitions and his desires. After revisiting him some more time while developing rapport he gave his opinion on the hypothetical questions on caste and occupational relations. He stated the importance of mentioning ones caste on the signboard to attract customer and asked in reverse in a sarcastic undertone if anyone has seen any board which mentions as "*Charmkar*" or "*Balmiki*". He further legitimized his philosophy that he needs to bring up his children who are supported by the 'caste merit scholarship' founded by the '*Samaj*' (cultural organisation of the caste). Even though scholarship money is not sufficient to bear the overall education expenditure yet the enrolled children may derive extra advantage in future higher studies supported again by the caste welfare organization. He does not want to be left out and bear the brunt of the consequences of going against the caste rules.

Moolchand who owns a roadside *dhaba* adjacent to the slum area caters to the demand of local construction workers generally. He is from the lower caste. He also refrained from answering question which he said were sensitive. But his helper wife could not resist the temptation to tell the platitude of her son who after completing graduation also could not find a decent source of livelihood (convinced that service means only getting a government job) and landed up doing a clerical job in a local newspaper. The salary given to her son was not even sufficient to meet his own expenses. Moolchand later added that overall condition of job market is not good and it is sometimes so difficult to get the a simple '*labourgiri*' on a regular basis (revealed his knowledge due to daily interaction with labourers) let alone to get a good *'sarkari naukri*'. He fiercely thinks that his caste is of respectable origin and up in hierarchy. He is an ardent supporter of Ambedkar and believes in his ideologies too. It was felt later that he has been respected generally by all customers and passerby and maintains a leader like aura. He said that he is a self-educated person and like to mobilize people against such problems in the society. While getting back to the question related to the caste selection in the jobs he remarks that the phenomenon is not upper caste restricted but also can be find in the lower caste segment. He insisted that every business has code of ethics, therefore, person cannot neglect his caste brethren and employ somebody else. There is no uniform way of looking at the potential employee for merits where everybody and anybody can learn the skill within an hour according to him.

Kanpur was no different from Ghaziabad on the question of employing an ex-untouchable person for household chores. Though Sangeeta gave some radical opinion that this lower caste community should be given a fair chance in every sphere of life, yet it boils down to the fact that first of all her family would not appreciate such step; secondly, she herself has to abide certain social norms even though wrong and inhuman for the sake of harmony. She commented on the political support given to the lower caste people that rich and politicians alike have to please this community for political gains.

Shiv Singh, a *thakur* respondent though living in slum area exhibits great pride for his achievements; without loosing any opportunity he boasted about his caste background and expressed contentment in his living standard without having done anything for living (gets some rental from land other places unrevealed).

Munna a contractor (mainly for government work) for construction work is from the intermediate caste and gave very vague answers sometimes supporting caste discrimination and sometimes opposed it when question of his own pride was at stack. He denies the charges of discriminator.

A small electrical equipment workshop owner, Shripat remained quite on the subject but while answering other questions and 'positive discrimination' he showed his displeasure and prolifically debated on the recently emerged elite class of the depressed caste section and the political patronage given to them.

Puranchand a small printing press owner employs two helpers. He is from the upper caste and his helpers are from intermediate caste. He began by saying 'who are we to interfere in the system, which has been existing since time immemorial and is still going strong. He is not ready to take the blame of a Discriminator and said it is because of government policies. (It looked as if he was going through a financial problem) and also said that the small establishments cannot do anything in case of lower wage and other industrial problems.

Gummed Singh, respondent from the upper caste owns a wood and furniture workshop finds that the caste has everlasting effect in the market besides being omnipresent in social sphere. Elaborating the point he says "If I need a worker, I prefer to ask his caste primarily because my business specialized artisan caste and secondly, I do not need to train them. Of course, caste background does not decide my worker's payment. I pay them by piece rate.

Kirat (Upper caste) is opposed to the caste system overall and judging somebody by his background in particular. He owns a small cloth shop and has an assistant. His optimistic philanthropic view and its economic consequences can be gauged by his statement "undeclared competition and war in various strata of society will gradually disappear, if everyone in the society is well fed. The whole issue is not of just the caste system but who will have an edge over whom, how can an individual have more, the equations are endless, violence is a routine of life (he referred a fresh incidence of the caste violence in slum area over the grab of ones shop).

Manoj an intermediate caste restaurant owner says, "the caste system is a cancer of Indian society, which is heading towards the destruction of society." Saying all such good things he still likes to his own caste person on powerful positions but without discriminating others.

Rajan a railway employee (working as a *Khallasi* cleaner) is from an ex-untouchables caste background has no grudge against upper caste and have bohemian relationship with his colleagues. But at present he is a worried father of two unemployed sons who are not getting government job and he is due for retirement in the very next month. While talking to his sons the study could fathom some underlying depressing feelings since they both are willing to work even harder than their father but are not able to get chance to prove their well deserved position to get a job in railways like his father. Expressing on the caste discrimination one of the sons says that he had never experienced such favouritism and he has some very good friends from the upper caste who keep helping him in problems and definitely will help in job search too if asked to. The other son gave diagonally opposite views and said that he could not find a respectable job (he sells pork in the locality) because of the market hegemony of the upper caste and the intermediate caste people.

Nem Singh (leather worker) does varied part-time jobs as well. He is a young, energetic, thoughtful person who wants to achieve big in his life (he said that he wants to learn computer also). He has applied for loan and was keenly interested to start his own workshop for leather cutting. While talking he showed a lot of interest in developing his business plans only and gave placid reply to the caste questions but soon his long nurtured and sometimes experienced views came as an important input. He thought that the caste is important in the Indian Society because it has given source of earning through an inscribed occupation and provides each stratum social security (as a community and he appears to have answered may be because he was granted loan because of his caste background).

Sunil is from the ex-untouchables caste and he does sundry jobs at a time. He works as a sweeper in the morning till noon and in the afternoon he takes up rickshaw-pulling and in the evening he goes to the music parties also (he plays trumpet) whenever there is one or two marriage parties where he is a bandmaster if there is no event then he would practice in the night. He is apparently very shy and especially on the caste issues. After his initial hesitation he told that he does not like if anybody treats him in such degrading manner due to his caste as he firmly believes he works harder than anybody else enjoying better lifestyle. He often felt humiliated because as a regular job he gets jobs as a cleaner without any protection and did not like the treatment of the people also[8].

Bandhuram told that he has recently migrated and does not tell his true caste identity to anybody. He recently managed to get a job as a cook. He does not want to go back to his native village where except his parents no near and dear one is living. He told that he got repeatedly insulted in the village and does not want to go back. He looked extremely agitated and felt that the caste terms should be removed and there is no other option except this.

Saiji does not have any standing job and do any job offered to him in off-season. He is also a *shehnai* (saxophone) player in the band company. His work starts during marriage season, therefore, he does not get any proper regular job which he may like. The people in the *basti* learn flute playing from him that is how he makes both ends meet even during off-season. He is very polite and would not like to interfere in the common functioning of the society and is not interested in to ponder over such small issues such as caste generated discrimination.

5.1.2 Ghaziabad

Anand (32 year old, high caste, diploma holder in computer software) having a humble establishment. He takes computer classes and claims to be above the caste notches but while explaining the recruitment processes he confides two points: first, money matters (lower wage settlement), second is the qualification of the applicant. Selection on the basis of caste is not his idea and it is alien while judging a person but he does give importance to the applicant who has approached through relative, friend or any known source because he thinks that these are the people who helped him in problems and will also support in any adverse situation and therefore, it is important to give due regard to such candidate who can be a safe bate.

Malati, a 45-year old housewife of the intermediate caste, was felt so enraged apropos question of a recruiting a housemaid from untouchable caste affiliation that she restricted the interviewee from entering her house even. Kishan Pratap and his wife (upper caste) though were not averse on the proposition of other lower caste catering to the household needs yet chose to keep mum on the subject of an untouchable entering at least the kitchen. Sudha (upper caste respondent's wife) outrightly said that all cleaning jobs are to be designated to the untouchables and the exterior of the house is the place where an ex-untouchable find work.

'Judging somebody is not difficult by their caste background', an upper caste employer in tea and other beverages trade developed suggests of an attitude difference (such as living style, thinking and knowledge) amongst different caste groups. His belief in the caste behaviour thus indirectly shows the recruitment style in Indian labour market and reflects such biases.

Ram Nayak has small scale of sweet shop and he is from upper caste. He strongly believes that caste does not matter in professional world what matters to him is his exponential scale of earning and not the caste background of his employees. He had three employees—two helpers and one main cook—all were from the intermediate caste.

Ram Sevak has come from M.P. to Ghaziabad in search of living. He is from the lower caste and has been debarred from the *Sabji Mandi* (vegetable market). He is not allowed to be there in the market let alone sell the vegetables. As a result he has to go the colonies even at the risk of being caught by the municipal authorities. To run his business hassle free he needs to feed regularly to the local watchman either by kind or cash.

Sreeram is a harizan worker in a steel rolling mill. He has to do such hard labour that it stretches to eighteen hours continuously (so he claimed). He is very sad at the prevailing job conditions which so high in risk (he does *Garam Kam*; carrying hot iron from the furnace for moulding) that he mentioned a week previous to the interview was conducted a worker got 60 per cent burn injuries due to broken instrument which was to be changed long time back.

5.2 Responses on the Caste Structure and Labour Market

This study aims to bring focus straight to the hard hitting questions of caste as an instrument in the labour market and education as 'items' on a 'likert scale'[9]. Likert Scale developed by Rensis Likert, a sociologist at the University of Michigan. The scale was developed to measure psychological attitude in a scientific way. He thought of a scale which could produce attitude measures that could reasonably be interpreted as measurements on a proper metric scale in the same way as inches or degree Celsius can be measured. It has been frequently used in psychological research nonetheless scientists dispute over the reliability of the 'Likert scale' because the data may be heavily skewed. An individual item may produce a sealing and floor effect, respondents using lowest and highest available options. In such problem scientists have advised to see the normality[10] of the Likert item and mean of the item. But here in this study where normalcy is not captured in each 'Likert item' then item has been further substantiated by open ended queries. Moreover the main aim of 'Likert Item' was to control the response and to know the opinion within the given options. The questions were on the importance of caste in the market, individual preference given to the caste identity, change of opinion after the revelation of caste identity, and experience of discrimination in the job market. It was clarified in the beginning of the section that reservation given by government and government institution should not be considered while answering the question; secondly, question of discrimination is strictly restricted to the market conditions and not applicable in social or other circumstances.

The questions were scaled from strongly disagree (1) to strongly agree (5). This study has tried to know the instances like physical harm, deliberate allotment of accident prone work, long hours for work, duration of payment, compensatory allowances, behaviour of employer etc. were the discussion points which covered as an extension and explanation in the 'likert questions'.

Responses and Non-Responses

Overall responses in Kanpur were hospitable, well thought and generally individualistic than Ghaziabad. A very high non-response for all questions (37.1%) is reported from Ghaziabad except one question which was on change of opinion after revelation of caste identity. The study may give two reasons that there people who lived in slum area had no privacy and there was too much of interference while giving answer this led to group discussion than individual response. The study hence did not ask questions when found many respondents living closely or when they formed group when answering questions based on Likert Scale.

5.2.1 Importance of the Caste in Finding a Job

The question was pertinent to the subject of this study and gave a general lead to ask some more linking questions from the respondent. This question also clarified some more questions (Chapter Four) which were asked indirectly and were essentially focused on the accessibility, approach and recruitment methods in the labour market. Ghaziabad and Kanpur City are categorically different from each other in the response to this question. Non-response was not high in Kanpur and percentage of people agreeing with the statement were also higher in Kanpur (62.5% agree and 24.5% strongly agree) than in Ghaziabad (46.5% agree and 25.4% strongly agree). Ghaziabad clearly shows the influence of modern industrial setup and a growing city in global competitive environment (Table 5.1).

While observing caste-wise it is found that a significant percentage (31.7%) of the respondent from lower and ex-untouchables, 35.4 per cent of the upper caste and 27 per cent of the intermediate caste respondents said that the caste background does not have any influence in the job market in Ghaziabad. The respondents were able to relate the question not only with their own experience but have also told that the caste has a lot of role to play in obtaining a job because people trust there own caste people first. In most of the replies '*Vishwas*' (trust) was repeatedly given as a reason. There were 8.3 per cent of

Table 5.3: Responses to Importance of Caste in Finding a Job

(In per cent)

Scale on	*Upper Castes*	*Intermediate Castes*	*Low and Ex-untouchables*	*All*
		Kanpur City		
Non-response	4.2	7.2	4.7	5.6*(15)
Strongly Disagree	0	0.9	0.9	0.8(2)
Disagree	10.4	7.2	5.6	7.1(19)
Not Sure	10.4	2.7	0.9	3.4(9)
Agree	58.3	52.3	65.4	58.6(155)
Strongly Agree	16.7	29.7	22.4	24.4(65)
All	**100.0(48)**	**100.0(111)**	**100.0(107)**	**100.0(266)**
	χ = 3.77 σ = 0.99	χ = 4.06 σ = 0.95	χ = 4.00 σ = 0.92	χ = 3.9 σ = 0.94
		Ghaziabad		
Non-response	31.2	39.1	33.1	37.5*(96)
Strongly Disagree	4.2	3	0	2.7(7)
Disagree	8.3	9	12.2	9.4(24)
Not Sure	4.2	5.4	2.4	4.7(12)
Agree	35.4	26.9	31.7	29.3(75)
Strongly Agree	16.7	15.6	19.5	16.4(42)
All	**100.0(48)**	**100.0(167)**	**100.0(41)**	**100.0(256)**
	χ = 3.77 σ = 0.99	χ = 4.06 σ = 0.95	χ = 4.00 σ = 0.92	χ = 2.36 σ = 2.02

*Column percent, Numbers in parentheses.

respondents from upper caste, 9.0 per cent from the intermediate caste also disagreed that the caste has any bearing in the labour market.

In Kanpur, however, the respondents who disagreed were less (7.1%) than Ghaziabad (9.4%) and the respondents who agreed with the statement were high (58.6%). Even going by the caste categories, the study did not find much variability and there were no significant percentage in any particular caste group in Kanpur City. Mean and standard deviation in both the cities showing some interesting insight as all caste responses remain in agreement that caste is important in finding jobs (mean is 3.77, 4.06 and 4.00 for the upper caste, intermediate caste and low and ex-untouchables respectively) but it is even more interesting to find that there is high level of deviation in all caste responses. Respondents in Ghaziabad rather do not seem to believe in that the caste would help them fetch a job as the mean and standard deviation have similar numbers for all caste respondents.

5.2.2 Preference to the Caste

This question was formed linking with the first one that caste is important in job search. It was asked to the respondents asking them to assume themselves as an employer. In such situation what could be their response to the people belonging to the other caste group and their own caste brethren.

Table 5.2: Response to 'Preference to own Caste Groups'

(In per cent)

Scale	*Upper Castes*	*Intermediate Castes*	*Low and Ex-touchable*	*All*
		Kanpur City		
Non-response	4.2	7.2	4.7	5.6(15)
Strongly Disagree	0.0	1.8	0.9	1.1(3)
Disagree	22.9	18	18.7	19.2(51)
Not Sure	4.2	2.7	2.8	3(8)
Agree	54.2	43.2	46.7	46.6(124)
Strongly Agree	14.6	27.0	26.2	24.4(65)
All	**100.0(48)**	**100.0(111)**	**100.0(107)**	**100.0(266)**
	χ = 3.56 σ = 1.13	χ = 3.77 σ = 1.17	χ = 3.77 σ = 1.18	χ = 3.73 σ = 1.16
		Ghaziabad		
Non-response	31.2	39.1	33.1	37.5(96)
Strongly Disagree	4.2	0.6	0.0	1.2(3)
Disagree	22.9	15.6	12.2	16.4(42)
Not Sure	4.2	7.8	7.3	7(18)
Agree	29.2	20.4	22	22.3(57)
Strongly Agree	8.3	15.6	24.4	15.6(40)
All	**100.0(48)**	**100.0(167)**	**100.0(41)**	**100.0(256)**
	χ = 2.21 σ = 1.81	χ = 2.14 σ = 1.98	χ = 2.56 σ = 2.07	χ = 2.23 σ = 1.95

*Column per cent, Numbers in parentheses.

To the total respondents, interestingly 7 per cent respondents in Ghaziabad and 3 per cent in Kanpur were not sure whether they will prefer their caste or not, 16.4 per cent in Ghaziabad said that they will not give any preference to their caste group and only 19.7 per cent in Kanpur City. The upper caste (22.9%) and lower and ex-untouchable (18.7%) respondents have the highest percentage within the caste group in Ghaziabad who were ready to select the candidate unbiased in a hypothetical situation yet there were more than 20 per cent of respondents said they will prefer their own caste community (Table 5.2). However, situation reverses in Kanpur City where more than 45 per cent respondents agreed that they will favour their own caste and there is not much change in all caste categories. Overall 19.2 per cent in Kanpur City and 16.4 per cent of the total respondents in Ghaziabad said that they will not prefer own caste persons of which 22.9 per cent of the upper caste, 18.7 per cent of the lower and ex-untouchable respondents disagreed to the preference given to their own caste groups in the selection process. The study assumes that such observation generally gives some respite as people to some extent have started accepting and respecting other caste people in society for fairer deal especially in the modern growing industrial spaces (it is important to see the difference in Ghaziabad where people less stringent on the caste identity).

5.2.3 Caste Identity and Change in Opinion

The next hypothetical situation was given to the respondents where after getting to know the caste identity of other person if their opinion changes. The responses were very well thought because transforming oneself in such situations has varied reactions especially in the labour market.

Table 5.3: Response to the Change of Opinion after Knowing the Caste Identity

	Upper Castes	*Intermediate Castes*	*Low and Ex-touchables*	*All*
		Kanpur City		
Non-response	4.2	7.2	4.7	5.6*(15)
Strongly Disagree	0	0.9	1.9	1.1(3)
Disagree	37.5	42.3	35.5	38.7(103)
Not Sure	18.8	9.9	13.1	12.8(34)
Agree	18.8	9.9	13.1	30.8(82)
Strongly Agree	10.4	10.8	11.2	10.9(29)
All	**100.0 (48)**	**100.0 (111)**	**100.0 (107)**	**100.0 (266)**
	X=3.04 σ=1.15	X=3.07 σ=1.17	X=3.13 σ=1.20	X=3.09 σ=1.17
		Ghaziabad		
Strongly Disagree	2.1	0.6	2.4	1.2(3)
Disagree	33.3	21.6	22	23.8(61)
Not Sure	12.5	15.6	14.6	14.8(38)
Agree	16.7	15.6	12.2	15.2(39)
Strongly Agree	100.0	100.0	100.0	100.0
All	**(48)**	**(167)**	**(41)**	**(256)**
	X=1.94 σ=1.58	X=1.86 σ=1.73	X=2.12 σ=1.85	X=1.93 **σ=1.716**

*Column per cent, Numbers in parentheses.

In Kanpur 38.7 per cent of the total respondents said that their opinion does not change when caste identity is revealed on them of which 37.5 per cent of the upper caste respondents and 35.5 per cent of the lower and ex-untouchables said that the caste identity does not affect their opinion about a person. Nevertheless 40 per cent still agreed (which is higher than Ghaziabad) that the caste identity of a person leaves certain image on a person that is why their opinion changes after knowing the caste identity of a person that was the general reply as an explanation in this response (Table 5.3).

There were 23.8 per cent of the respondents in Ghaziabad who felt that their opinion will hardly get affected after knowing the caste of other person and 14.8 per cent were unsure of the reaction of which the lower and ex-untouchables have the highest percentage share (26.8%; combining both agree and 'strongly agree'). In this response the upper caste respondents tops the list following the intermediate caste and after which the lower and ex-untouchables (Table 5.3).

5.2.4 Experience of Discrimination

The next question was straight asking them about the experience related to discrimination in the labour market. The respondents were briefed about this question before hand. In Ghaziabad there were 27.3 per cent who disagreed and 4.3 per cent strongly disagreed of which 58.6 per cent of the intermediate caste respondents said that they never faced discrimination, 52 per cent of the upper caste respondents reported that they were never discriminated, 45.8 per cent of the intermediate and 46.3 per cent of the lower and ex-untouchables (the lowest of all caste categories) said that they were never discriminated in the labour market, however it leaves one wondering what about the remaining percentage. Quite importantly there were 20.7 per cent of the respondents in Kanpur City and 16 per cent in Ghaziabad who were still (after explanation also) not sure if they have ever been discriminated. In the lower and ex-untouchable respondents (20%) agreed that they were discriminated one or other occasion and 3.7 per cent strongly agreed that they were discriminated while looking for job or on the job in the labour market. Even the upper caste respondents said that they were discriminated (12.5%). While recalling the field experience one of the respondents told to have approached manager of a leather factory where he was appointed as a lath worker which he thought was neither suitable nor according to his qualifications as he was a diploma holder in drawing and design. Another respondent (upper caste) said due to extreme poor condition at home, started vending tea along with egg and some other eatable items in the locality where everyone teased him beyond his tolerance limit for selling egg and tea that he ultimately abandoned the job in the locality and resorted to vending vegetables which was less profitable according to him (Table 5.4).

Table 5.4: Response to the 'Experience of Discrimination'

(In per cent)

	Upper Castes	*Intermediate Castes*	*Low and Ex-untouchables*	*All*
		Kanpur City		
Non-response	4.2	7.2	5.6	6.0*(16)
Strongly Disagree	4.2	0.9	1.9	1.9(5)
Disagree	52.1	58.6	45.8	52.3(139)
Not Sure	27.1	16.2	22.4	20.7(55)
Agree	12.5	13.5	20.6	16.2(43)
Strongly Agree	0.0	3.6	3.7	3.0(8)
All	**100.0(48)**	**100.0(111)**	**100.0(107)**	**100.0(266)**
	χ=2.44 σ=0.85	χ=2.59 σ=0.93	χ=2.67 σ=1.04	χ=2.59 σ=.95
		Ghaziabad		
Non-response	31.2	39.1	33.1	37.5(96)
Strongly Disagree	10.4	3	2.4	4.3(11)
Disagree	25	26.9	31.7	27.3(70)
Not Sure	22.9	15	12.2	16.0(41)
Agree	8.3	12	9.8	10.9(28)
Strongly Agree	2.1	3	9.8	3.9(10)
All	**100.0(48)**	**100.0(167)**	**100.0(41)**	**100.0(256)**
	χ=1.73 σ=1.44	χ=1.65 σ=1.56	χ=1.90 σ=1.69	χ=1.72 σ=1.56

*Column per cent, Numbers in parentheses.

5.2.5 Role of Education in Breaking Caste Barrier in Society

This question was asked as a general statement which in fact, unlike earlier questions, tried to cover all caste generated inequality in our society and hence not restricted to the labour market. The question meant to be the general discussion where the study wanted to gauze respondents' belief and their responsibility as a member of society assuming that the educated society can prove to be the only solution of caste and caste generated complexities of society and to let the society grow in uninhabited manner. It was thought that education generally empowers a person with unbiased and well-informed perspective (Objective and research question of this study) and hence this study has tried to correlate this observation with the level of education of people. There were some kind of vague replies and contravening statements were reported from much educated respondents while people who are less educated gave firm replies.

The question undoubtedly had many supporters and respondents in general agreed that education can democratize society and bring everyone at level playing field but the replies were also loaded with apprehension which were reflected in the 'not sure' group (in Ghaziabad there were 7.4 per cent and 12.4 per cent were in Kanpur City). The percentage of respondents were less in the 'disagree' and 'strongly disagree' category in Ghaziabad while the respondents in these groups were high (15%) in Kanpur City. It appears that the respondents in Kanpur City were not happy overall with the industrial and employment opportunity and their disenchantment is covered in this question (without forgetting that the percentage of educated respondents and unemployed both is higher in Kanpur than Ghaziabad) and therefore, it can be interpreted that the interviewees were educated and unemployed has led to such restless outpour of situation in the labour market.

Table 5.5: Response to the Role of Education in Breaking Caste related Discrimination

(In per cent)

	Upper Castes		*Intermediate Castes*		*Low and Ex-untouchables*		*All*	
			Kanpur City					
Non-response	2.1		0.9		1.9		1.5*(4)	
Disagree	10.4		11.7		15.9		13.2(35)	
Not Sure	4.2		15.3		13.1		12.4(33)	
Agree	72.9		64.9		63.6		65.8(175)	
Strongly Agree	10.4		7.2		5.6		7.1(19)	
All	**100.0(48)**		**100.0(111)**		**100.0(107)**		**100.0(266)**	
	χ= 3.77	σ= 0.93	χ= 3.65	σ= 0.85	χ= 3.53	σ= 0.95	χ= 3.62	σ= 907
			Ghaziabad					
Non-response	31.2		39.1		33.1		37.5(96)	
Strongly Disagree	6.2		1.2		0.0		2.0(5)	
Disagree	6.2		8.4		0.0		6.6(17)	
Not Sure	6.2		7.8		7.3		7.4(19)	
Agree	39.6		29.9		31.7		32(82)	
Strongly Agree	10.4		12.6		26.8		14.5(14.5)	
All	**100.0(48)**		**100.0(167)**		**100.0(41)**		**100.0(256)**	
	χ= 2.48	σ= 1.94	χ= 2.24	σ= 2.00	χ= 2.83	σ= 2.13	χ= 2.40	σ= 2.01

*Column per cent, Numbers in parentheses.

Going by the caste groups this study could not find any noticeable difference and all caste groups favour education as a general panacea of all social evils especially evils like caste discrimination, favouritism, hatred in the society can be removed by the educated enlightened mind. Still the lower and intermediate people were in stronger support of the question. Mean and standard deviation statistics of all scaled question though invariably indicates that Kanpur still follows the traditional heritage of caste identity while Ghaziabad may no longer be following the caste identity as an important support point to chase either the occupation or earning. However, the opinion on Likert scale has certain polarity and does not show the any relationship with other analysis on wages and occupational details.

5.3 Power Axis and Discrimination in the Market

It has been observed for a very long time that the caste power configuration does not change homogenously, but a few leaders take the charge of whole caste power structure in the area. The respondent could not even imagine a casteless society. A study done in Rajasthan village showed, people seriously thought that the caste as a system should be modified but not abolished totally which may lead to a situation of utter chaos in the society[11]. The resource base is the most important to wield power in society. The debate on exercise of power in the labour market especially is based on the number and type of the resources, which the different groups possess. The resource bases and accessibility to resources are the foundation stone of power; other variables are numerical strength and utility or importance of basic functions of society. All elements of earth, which are useful or necessary to man, can be considered as resources. The resources are cultural appraisals rather than absolute assets and are produced, as elements of objective environment, filtered through perception and evolutes as necessary or useful[12].

The most general use of word 'Power' in English is synonymous with the capacity, skill or talent. Hobbs defined it "man's present means to any future apparent good". Russell says "power is the production of intended affect". Wrong modifies Russell's definition by saying "power is the capacity of some persons to produce intended and foreseen effects on others". Wrong also feels that a common approach to evaluate power is to enumerate the bases or resources that make possible its exercise. 'Assets' and values or value bases are terms often used synonymously with resources." David[13] feels that power is an elusive concept and argues that power involves the capacity of a person or group to achieve compliance from others to bring about or resist change. A distinction is often made between institutional bases and power vested in individuals. In former power is attributed to people with access to political parties, business corporations, religious organizations and so on, which have power resources in such forms as wealth, votes or prestige; persons able to employ an institution's power resources are considered to have power. In the latter, the compliance of others is based on the power that an individual can bring to interpersonal relations, such as those between monarch and subject, employer and employee, union leader and member, or consumer and monopoly supplier.

The caste is a social order, which absorbed its strength and hierarchical position through various resource bases. Asceticism, altruism, knowledge are the founding power corners of Hindu social order[14]. Knowledge and political power earned more credence than economic power initially. The strife to occupy the power crest in the caste system took a long time to give authentic source base for the hierarchy of the caste system. The power base thus originated from the occupation, knowledge, and territorial rights. The spoils of these power bases added to manipulation by high caste orders and dissatisfaction to many other lower caste orders, which in turn gave a way for the extension of new social section (Jainism and Buddhism) order free from the traditional caste order.

Romila Thapar[15] says that *vaishya* who were third in position amongst *varna* system, accumulated lots of economic power, yet their economic power was of no match to the knowledge and political power of other higher *varna* occupants (*Brahman, Rajput*), which led to social tension where mercantile caste was unable to construe political power. This whole rigmarole led to the origin of two new religions, Buddhism and Jainism.

No other social system in other parts of the world wielded ritual and political power in such extent as caste system. Economic power intertwining with political power has made much headway at the dawn of democracy. Constitution of India provides equality by law to all citizens of India irrespective of one's background. There is a massive upsurge and political awakening in the depressed caste segment. Gupta[16] who analysed electoral results and alliances in elections found caste affinity has little to do with alliance pattern into elections and this is the most secular way of interpolating the new emergence of caste as a system. He also says that there is interlinkage among ritual, economic and political power in the caste system, whereas economic and political power are the most sought after. Evan[17] has conceptualized the pressure groups formations and politics and stability of caste system in India. He has tried to find out the 'rent seeking' to understand the change in social structure of post-independence India. In his second finding he says that rent seeking opportunities combined with a substantial number of readymade pressure groups that existed in India at independence have stunted the growth of the more traditional groups, such as those found in other parliamentary democracies in the developing world and elsewhere. Defining Pressure groups he says that there is prior common economic interest that causes citizens to unite in order to influence the government. And hence the pressure group needs to combine three aspects one common cause (economic) which leads to mount political pressure. He refers the case of India where post-independence period witnessed already existing social factions whose organizational structure determined by the 'marginal relative transaction costs'. If there are already social groups with a high degree of excludability, then state appears (or, in India's case, after the state structure was substantially changed at independence) and pressure groups may organize along these lines rather than along class or other economic criteria. India's complex, highly identifiable and excludable social structure provided such an opportunity for traditional social groups to dominate, with results that have profoundly influenced India's post-independence experience. India thus is a country in which Becker's "other factors[18]" are worthy particular attention. Evan sited Franklin's study where the efficacy of such voting patterns that is the increasing capacity of members of SCs, STs and OBCs to use voting either alone or in coalition with other groups, to acquire additional reservations at the state and national level. There is an emergence of *Pan Caste* phenomena strongly over a period of time. Evan while quoting Beteille also found that only the very lowest castes are uniformly poor. Theories are week in predicting why caste still remains relevant and growing stronger day by day though presence of strong economic and social reforms? Evan refers Lal who agrees that caste is loosing its importance in finding and defining occupation yet its role as a means of identification is increasing.

But, these three power edifices not necessarily lead to a social control. There are more elements in power definition. Dahl[19] listed other bases for power like "individuals own time, access to money, credit, wealth, control over information, esteem or social standing; the possession of charisma, popularity, legitimacy, legality, solidarity for an advance of political power." Here elements like access to money, credit, control over information, esteem as social standing, solidarity can be considered as for social power too. Dahl[20] further distinguished five constituents: (1) the base of power, provided by economic assets, constitutional prerogatives, military forces, prestige etc., (2) means of power; how influence is exerted through promises, threats, public appeal and so on… (Generally intangibles), (3) the scope of power or the specific action that one person is actually performing, (4) some specific action due to another's use of means of power against him, and (5) extension of power or the set of individuals over whom the power is held. Last four are seen to be the most relevant to understand covert means of discrimination and first may be the outcome practices of discrimination.

Rueschemeyer also concurs with Parsons statement where he says that in determining the power resources where 'breaking out' of primitive stage of social evolution is helped by two developments, first well marked system of stratification and second a system of explicit cultural legitimisation of differentiated functions. These two are crucial as they free economic and political will of dominant groups from the restraints and rigidities of the of kinship. He adds further that these organised economic domination if left free from governance, impose division of labour and allocate people to disagreeable works. Elevation of the caste system in conjunction with political and knowledge power in historical past and now in combination of political and economic power education (knowledge) have drawn new combinations in domination and division of the labour. Thus, there is a new structure emerging in context of the caste in labour market. Caste has become deeply institutionalised in the Indian subcontinent, to the extent that it does not leave even the highest echelons of society. The new combinations of caste in market have greatly influenced the regulations and stretch of power for social contest. Rueschemeyer [21] while pointing out the power steering and production in market gives two valuable points relevant in Indian market:

(1) Market forces; competitive or not strongly affects social interests with varied power resources, it tends to provoke multiple attempts at regulation and power based 'interventions' in the market.

(2) There are not just single rule of supply and demand for the equilibrium in market but another rule is of social contest. Within this parameter gender, religion and region, caste roles churn out on entirely different outcome of local market configuration. Interest in the balancing expansion of power has a special place among them.

Two things emerge from this discussion of power bases in caste system and market forces, first, the people already occupying power positions would do everything to expand their power and second, the resistance to this power will emanate from such situations to reach equilibrium. If those countervailing forces are given a direction, shall lead to more equitable distribution in society.

Power arithmetic is not only visible in the caste system but also in other social or economic hierarchy of other parts of the world too. Sometimes, it is acquired or sometimes it is inherited to achieve respectable status in society.

Conclusively the study interprets employer's point of view and employees in the same way as the thoughts of subjugation controls the very realm of manipulation to their hidden desire to have control on others. These excuses from employer's side are the instances of imputation of power, anticipatory influence and collective power/ solidarity.[22] The Hindi translation of caste '*Jati*' is understood as a 'group of same people from the same stock', Gould[23] says that *Jatis* should be taken: as a naturalized social compartment whose members have especially powerful natural bonds, feeling and obligations because they are somehow the same 'kind' (the same blood), somehow different distinct from, apart from all others. The result is, in the context of modern Indian social life, very highly developed sense of ethnicity which draws its ultimate sustenance from the concept of *Jati*." That is how on this solidarity principle many employers though not necessarily discriminating but favour their own caste group.

The power exhibitions are not only openly experienced rather intertwined with action, words and work methods in the work area. Unorganised work culture is prone and exposed to exploitation then it happens that there is no option left to the unorganised sector labour force but to have a common bondage on caste basis. Giving an example of solidarity Holmstrom[24] finds Naidus favouring their own caste fellow while not discriminating other caste people. But there are instances sighted where employers confided their dislike of

Scheduled Caste people working in the close vicinity. Thurow[25] also confirmed in his study of poverty and discrimination that though white employers would favour fair distribution of economic share yet they oppose competition in a few select jobs. This phenomenon can be seen in the light of Mandal Commission agitation 1992, when unreserved categories openly opposed the idea of revised reservation seats in government jobs, for just not the fear of the impending competition from once lowly placed castes but also for the danger of loosing their monopoly in jobs.

Beteille[26] opines that political power emanates from economic dominance, social status, numerical support or personal qualities of leaderships. His line of thinking agrees with Wrong[27] who also finds that no single axle of power will stay alone for long and needs to be supported by other power variables. Beteille[28] again says that the terminology like 'dominant caste' connotes straight to the power combination resting in single caste.

Beteille and Gupta both argue that the recent political awakening at such a massive scale has generated a strong countervailing force in caste and power relation. Economic power is no more decisive in the overall structure of the distribution of power. Interestingly Boulding[29] has slightly different definition of power, he describes power as a potential change. The term power is also used, however, to describe the ability to achieve common ends for families etc.

But this study gives a different picture altogether. The lowest of lower caste is still under scrutiny in job market more so in informal practices of unorganised sector. It is virtually difficult for them to find a decent dignified occupation. The phenomena do not prove that depressed caste people are not getting well off but the 'distributive justice' is almost negligible in this condition. Kanpur City where respondents were extremely aware of their political rights talked in a superfluous tone about their voting rights, preference for a particular leadership, and chances of a particular leader winning in their area. But they hardly know which leader of their choice may help them in improving their living condition. In the end respondents of employee status felt and expressed that "politicians do not have any caste". Boulding's[30] statement fits here very well; he says "the end means of power corrupting, power tends to corrupt and absolute power corrupts absolutely."

Any type of power nonetheless is irresistible, intoxicating, invigorating and absolutely un-ignorable. Study on Harijan elite identity by Mumtaz Khan[31] proves that education has empowered Scheduled Caste respondents with rationality that dispels the theory regarding high caste people possess high IQ level and low-caste people have low IQ level.

5.4 Resources to Power in the Present Study

In the present study power sources are captured by interpretation of education, employment and earning status in the labour market by the defined caste categories. The study found that these three—education (knowledge), earning (money), employment (occupation) may connote to the labour discrimination (because not only sample size is small but going by simple percentage may not give a clear picture since the differences in earning, occupation and education structure may happen for more than one reason).

5.4.1 Education

The study has adopted Chi-square test to test the hypotheses of the relation between the castes groups and their earning, education and labour status. In this discussion on the power edifices the study would like to say that it has not taken into the consideration the political variable.

Under the null hypothesis education and the castes are two independent variables. The value of the chi-square for both the places (Table 5.6) on education group is higher than the table value thus the null hypothesis is rejected and it can be interpreted that both variables caste and education may find association with each other. The test is important in signifying the number of educated people from the lower caste is highly required to match with the upper caste workers education level and their position in the labour market.

Studies done in American society proved that education is a salient factor in occupational placement; simultaneously social origin affects educational and occupational attainment too[32]. This study conceives that the segmentation in occupational structure has a precursor; education becomes one tool in the hands of a few privileged group of the society. The technical function theory[33] proposes that skill requirements in an industrial society increases due to technological changes (the study apropos to this adage that does it mean, higher the industrial level, higher would be the requirement of the educated/

Table 5.6: Chi[2] of the education and Caste

		Upper Castes	*Intermediate Castes*	*Low and Ex-untouchables*	*All*
		Kanpur City			
Illiterate	Count	3	34	26	63
	Expected Count	11.4	26.3	25.3	63
Up to Primary	Count	11	23	30	64
	Expected Count	11.5	26.7	25.7	64
Up to H. Secondary	Count	24	49	48	121
	Expected Count	21.8	50.5	48.7	121
Up to Graduation	Count	10	5	3	18
	Expected Count	3.2	7.5	7.2	18
All	**Count**	**48**	**111**	**107**	**266**
	Expected Count	**48**	**111**	**107**	**266**
	Value	df	Asymp. Sig. (2-sided)		
Pearson Chi-Square	27.309[a]	6	0		
Likelihood Ratio	25.458	6	0		
		Ghaziabad			
Illiterate	Count	6	61	19	86
	Expected Count	16.1	56.1	13.8	86
Up to Primary	Count	1	9	2	12
	Expected Count	2.2	7.8	1.9	12
Up to Secandary	Count	25	83	18	126
	Expected Count	23.6	82.2	20.2	126
Up to Graduation	Count	16	14	2	32
	Expected Count	6	20.9	5.1	32
All	**Count**	**48**	**167**	**41**	**256**
	Expected Count	**48**	**167**	**41**	**256**
	Value	df	Asymp. Sig. (2-sided)		
Pearson Chi-Square	30.801[a]	6	0		
Likelihood Ratio	28.39	6	0		

technically trained people? or *vice versa*). This theory predicts greater demand of newly trained people or upgradation of the existing skills of the workers. The theory also says that occupational structure thus generated will create demand for particular kind of jobs and education/

training is a way to meet the generated demands. Functional perspective of education says that there is a generally fixed set of positions whose various requirements the labour force must satisfy. Social change thus can be explained by judging the change in the demands according to the modernisation. But this theory has limitation, first, the demands are not fixed and second, on all levels of the education and occupations there are some powerful groups dominating. The author supports this argument by giving example of the mobility data, which summarised that social origin has a direct effect on occupational success.

Conflict theory[34] is governed by the principle of relative power of each group in question or inequality recognized by the groups. It first, finds that 'Status Group' (sharing common culture, sense of same status, religious, language, ritual observations etc.) generally determines the structure of society overall. There is continued struggle for power or prestige, wealth. Education is one of the insignia of the status culture, schools imparting particular set of tests, aesthetic values etc.

The meaning of this comment is very useful in this study the functional theory[35] says that educational requirements depend on the demand of importance of some particular occupation. Thus, social change can be seen with the reference of the shift in such occupation in the society. It is not totally false and this study has seen that as soon industrialisation has set its foothold the change in the occupational structure was remarkably in favour of the upper caste people. This has not changed drastically but some positive changes also cannot be ignored. The conflict theory also proves that countervailing forces are working towards the equilibrium in the Indian society. The status group though have realised that the change cannot be totally overruled but sure can be delayed. This study is optimistic that the process of equilibrium can be hastened by the genuine effort to educate people with consonance of the requirement, which means more importance should be focused on the primary education and vocational training. The study has realised that the people do not want to get just educated but get educated for meaningful purposes.

5.4.2 Earning

Under null hypothesis earning and castes are considered two independent variables. The chi-square value of the contingency table (Table 5.7) is higher than the table value thus null hypothesis is rejected.

The study may consider that the two variables—caste and earning are related to each other.

Money, which is considered to be a symbol of power, has broken boundaries of caste's hierarchy and supremacy of a few. The most aspired change, which education could not usher; money to some extent has succeeded to do so. Beteille[36] also accepts the fact that money is the most significant symbol of power, saying, "Status honour in a caste hierarchy is based partly upon wealth, but not entirely." He further comments on the caste and class structure:

Table 5.7: Chi² of the Earning and Caste

		Upper Castes	Intermediate Castes	Low and ex-un-touchables	All
			Kanpur City		
Below 3000	Count	9	78	75	162
	Expected Count	29.8	70.5	61.7	162
3000-6000	Count	21	25	13	59
	Expected Count	10.9	25.7	22.5	59
Above 6000	Count	14	1	3	18
	Expected Count	3.3	7.8	6.9	18
All	**Count**	**44**	**104**	**91**	**239**
	Expected Count	**44**	**104**	**91**	**239**
	Value	df	Asymp. Sig. (2-sided)		
Pearson Chi-Square	74.270	4	0		
Likelihood Ratio	66.955	4	0		
			Ghaziabad		
500-3000	Count	14	116	33	163
	Expected Count	31.8	104.2	27.1	163
3000-6000	Count	17	27	5	49
	Expected Count	9.6	31.3	8.1	49
>6000	Count	16	11	2	29
	Expected Count	5.7	18.5	4.8	29
All	**Count**	**47**	**154**	**40**	**241**
	Expected Count	**47**	**154**	**40**	**241**
	Value	df	Asymp. Sig. (2-sided)		
Pearson Chi-Square	43.832	4	0		
Likelihood Ratio	40.146	4	0		

"the different classes are not separated into watertight compartments. Individuals belong to one class to another

> in the course of a short period. This tends to impede the development of a consciousness of class, although. The conflict of interest between classes often acute and does sometimes come to the surface. More frequently this conflict tends to be posed in terms other than those of class and to run along cleavage which are more sharply defined in the social structure, such as those of caste."

5.4.3 Employment

This study has considered labour status for the chi-square test and not occupations, knowing that the labour status includes very important factors of vulnerability in the labour market. Third contingency table on (Table 5.7) labour status and caste also repeats the same phenomena. The chi-square value of the contingency is higher than the table value in both cities thus null hypothesis is rejected and the study finds an association between the two variables, i.e. caste and labour status in the market.

Therefore, the study explains its stand that education is not accessible equally to all strata of the society. The fruits of education have been harvested continuously by a few sections of the society. Earning and labour status again are the advantages of the some resourceful section of the Indian society.

5.5 Equality and Social Justice

It is stressed more often that the caste system has intensified inequality in the Indian society. The primordial feature of the caste system is based on the ascription. By this fixed nature of society mobility is also frozen, until there is an induction of modernism[37]. Democracy has played a reverse role where basic claim to the resources (in this study education, money, occupation) has become the prerogatives of a few sections whether low caste or upper caste (basically elite group of the caste strata). Rawl's principle of justice says that these inequalities will be permissible only if inequalities remain the advantage or disadvantage for everyone. He also comments on the caste system where a rational individual would not like a system, which decides a privilege or unprivileged group on the predefined social system. He further feels that a person if asked to select two societies one which is regulated on the caste system and another on open social system, he

Table 5.8: Chi² of the employment and Caste

		Upper Caste	Interme-diate Caste	Low and ex-un-touchables	All
	Kanpur City				
PR (Protected Regular Wage Worker)	Count	17	24	11	52
	Expected Count	9.6	22.6	19.8	52
UR (Unprotected Regular Wage Worker)	Count	4	24	20	48
	Expected Count	8.8	20.9	18.3	48
URST (Unprotected Regular Short Term Wage Worker)	Count	2	8	9	19
	Expected Count	3.5	8.3	7.2	19
UI (Unprotected Irregular Short Term Wage Worker)	Count	0.0	10	18	28
	Expected Count	5.2	12.2	10.7	28
Capital Owning Self-Employed	Count	19	13	13	45
	Expected Count	8.3	19.6	17.1	45
Marginal Self-Employed	Count	0	18	16	34
	Expected Count	6.3	14.8	12.9	34
Independent Wage Worker	Count	2	7	4	13
	Expected Count	2.4	5.7	4.9	13
All	**Count**	**44**	**104**	**91**	**239**
	Expected Count	**44**	**104**	**91**	**239**
	Value	df	Asymp. Sig. (2-sided)		
Pearson Chi-Square	50.018	12	0		
Likelihood Ratio	57.536	12	0		
	Ghaziabad				
PR (Protected Regular Wage Worker)	Count	20	22	7	49
	Expected Count	9.6	31.3	8.1	49
UR (Unprotected Regular Wage Worker)	Count	8	49	11	68
	Expected Count	13.3	43.5	11.3	68
URST (Unprotected Regular Short Term Wage Worker)	Count	1	29	5	35
	Expected Count	6.8	22.4	5.8	35
UIST (Unprotected Irregular Short Term Wage Worker)	Count	0	22	10	32
	Expected Count	6.2	20.4	5.3	32
Capital Owning Self-Employed	Count	12	14	3	29
	Expected Count	5.7	18.5	4.8	29
MSE (Marginal Self-Employed)	Count	0	7	3	10
	Expected Count	2	6.4	1.7	10
Independent Wage Worker	Count	6	11	1	18
	Expected Count	3.5	11.5	3	18
All	**Count**	**47**	**154**	**40**	**241**
	Expected Count	**47**	**154**	**40**	**241**
	Value	df	Asymp. Sig. (2-sided)		
Pearson Chi-Square	49.804	12	0		
Likelihood Ratio	56.094	12	0		

will choose to enter in an open social system. Because on theoretical grounds the caste system will not place talent where it is most needed or encourages talent to make its best contribution[38].

This study has discussed many theoretical aspects and concepts on the inequity, discrimination and inequality. Poverty, prejudice, segregation, crowding, exploitation, status groups etc. are the concepts linking one with another. The study has found that the caste has not only segregated society but also there are many reasons for which people are not able to brake this exit spell for centuries. People fear to go against the caste system because primarily it is an advantage in the labour market and not an obstacle to find jobs in a short run. The lower castes are happy about they get and do not think that it imposes hindrance in going up in the status.

The study concludes whether high caste or lower caste people exert their power either from the political, economic power or with other combination of power parameters to show the importance of functions in the society. Employers want to remain on the other side of the shop to explain, manipulate discriminate for their own betterment. Employees, however, are more subservient lot, and have to accommodate their displeasure many times to earn two square meal only. The instances of 'colleague discrimination' say that how unorganised market is being operated on a thin rope of survival. Holmstrom[39] writes—

> "The people at the casual labourers and the uneducated unemployed—are cut of not only from those more fortunate than them, but from each other. They are the ones most likely to stay in separate closed compartments, jealous of each other but more or less equally miserable and hopeless. They are the most likely to believe that what keeps them in their own little boxes is caste or ethnic discrimination, and sometimes, especially if they are untouchables—they are right."

Keeping above mentioned study as a benchmark, the situation has hardly changed in case of unorganised labour, though this study can also presume that urbanisation or industrialisation has diluted many stringent social boundaries, which were rampant in village India. Lambert[40] in his study says that almost half the workers in his sample believed that belonging to a certain caste group would have helped them in job advancement.

Studies on urban social milieu have different opinions. Frank

Conlon[41] says that historical setting of urban growth predicts the caste impact in the economy and land allocation by quoting Gillion who studied urban growth of Ahmedabad. Urban rise[42] and economic opportunities associated with were given special attention by academia these studies found upcoming urbanism and channelization of caste occupation had link with the economic growth of caste. Given the cause behind the caste existence in Urban India he says that,

> "Urban values and problems have often stimulated the use of caste as an identifiable focus around which associations and institutions could emerge and prosper.... Customary service relationship may survive migration of patient client to the city, but no socially reinforced responsibilities appear to be present. The occupational diversity associated with urbanisation has meant that caste, which was never a strong predictor of employment in the city at anytime in modern history—will matter only if it provides an identity upon which a job seeker may obtain an advantageous entry in the labour market."

This study has consensus with Frank's findings. The opinion by employees and the occupation structure in the chapter on recruitment and labour status have the same conclusion that caste does matter in the urban informal (the study stresses on informal nature of jobs) market to fetch jobs.

The present study delved into many aspects on the discrimination in an urban market. Theoretically, no single theory could explain the phenomena behind the discrimination. However, as this study formulated its assumptions around the institutional approach, the findings confer that the caste as an institution is a carrier of discrimination. The discussion on power and its resources tells the greater the monopolistic characters[43] in the market the higher the chances of discrimination. Control of power by one particular segment would bequeath that section to manoeuvre market regimen according to the whims and fancies of own profit. The chi-square test in this section has also proved that the distributive justice of power resources is not equally distributed and this study believes that the monopsonistic (employer) discrimination may have helped in the compartmentalization of resources to a few privileged section of the society.

The process of discrimination starts at the parental place where opportunities are restricted due to economic and social compulsions. People concentrated in one particular segment remain on the same place for generations. This vicious circle, if broken will provide the bridge to cross into the more fortunate section. Lack of earning puts formidable constraints in this direction. Thus this study strongly feels that equal opportunity[44] (but with a feeling of social responsibility) for growth is the key word for equity in the caste-structured society.

The opinions of the workers though were important yet the study feels that people have become very conscious when discussing the caste issues. The behaviour is covert and implicit. The principles of caste behaviour which have grounded by now, do not operate in isolation unit leaves a lasting impact on the economic outcome in the socity.

But, how far the caste society will survive on these principles is a big question. Or the system of caste will never perish since the caste identity is a resource provider and not abolisher? Will the market forces equalise the discriminatory attitudes of the people? Will competition dilute prejudice or on the contrary it will enforce prejudice? These are the questions, which this study thinks are the key thinking threards as far as the discrimination in the labour market is concerned. Here with most positive wish that the people must get wiser for the overall development of society and hence, caste as a principle of solidarity should not be given a place of importance. The chapter concludes by a statement of Russel[45]:

> "Our institutions rest upon injustice and authority. It is only by closing our heart against truth that we can endure the oppression and unfairness by which we profit....What is necessary, if a society is to grow up, is that our institutions should be so fundamentally changed as to everybody that new respect for the individual and his rights which modern feelings demands."

NOTES

1. S.J. Smith, "*Constructing Social Knowledge*" in Eyles and Smith (ed.) (1988). *Qualitative Methods in Human Geography,* Polity Press, Oxford, p. 19.
2. Sitton, Mahafey and O.L. Davis (1968). *Oral History: A Guide to Teachers and Others,* University Texas Press, Austin, p. 4.
3. This study did not include Employer separately but to know the opinion and

the perception from the other side of the table the study had incorporated and selected some of the self-employed respondents from the sample those were included as Employer though were not covered separately. It is strictly speaking that the employers had regarded their individual opinion and not for generalization yet the study wants to take this opportunity to further extend discrimination studies in this direction while considering labour market discrimination as a stem.

4. Employers' Discrimination though was covered in the second phase of the study yet the selection of the employer was not systematic and generally purposive since here under this heading the study intends to raise the issue of employers' preference which are reflected in ways while analysing the data on the occupation profile in labour market.
5. Becker (1971), *op. cit.,* p. 27.
6. Smith (1979). *Racial Disadvantage in Britain*, Pelican Publications, U.K. pp. 9-20.
7. Johnson and Johnson (1990). (ed.) *op. cit.,* says that the attitude have three types of responses, first 'cognitive' which manifest beliefs and perceptions about the consequences, second 'affective' which may be expressed in positive or negative feelings towards the object in question, 'Cognitive' which are behavioural inclinations, intentions and commitment that involve the attitude.
8. Singh (1984). *Kin, Clan and Land Reforms*, Rawat Publisher, Jaipur. In this study evidences were given when landowner sacked a Harizan who traditionally do the jobs of Rakhwala for no obvious reason and kept a Kurmi as a crop watchman. p. 78.
9. Uebersax, J.S. (2006). Likert Scales: Dispelling the Confusion. Statistical Methods for Rater Agreement. www.ourworld.compuserve.com/homepages. March2006. Dennis L. Clason and Thomas J. Dormody (1965). "Analyzing Data Measured by Individual Likert-Type Items". *Journal of Agriculture Education.* pp. 34-35.
10. Here the study has given standard deviation and mean value of answers. The standard deviation is important as it give us an indication of the average distance from the mean and mean will give us the direction of answer.
11. K.L. Sharma (1969). "Stresses in Caste Stratification: A Study of Six Villages in Rajasthan". *Economic and Political Weekly*, January 18th, Vol. iv, No. 3, p. 219.
12. Dennis Wrong, (1988), *Power: Its Form, Bases and Uses,* Basic Blackwell, New York, pp. 124-125.
13. David Smith (1977). *Human Geography*, Edward Arnold Publisher, London, p. 132.
14. Deepak Lal (1988), *Cultural Stability and Economic Stagnation*, Clarendon, Oxford. p. 23.
15. Romila Thapar (1966). *A History of India*, Vol. I, London, pp. 23-24.
16. Dipankar Gupta (2000). *Interrogating Caste*, Penguin India, New Delhi.

17. Evan Osborne (2001). "Culture, Development and Government: Reservations in India", *Economic Development and Cultural Change,* Vol. 49, pp. 659-85.
18. In Evan Osborne (2001). *Ibid.*
19. Dahl (1951). in David Smith (1977).
20. *Ibid.*
21. Rueschemeyer Dietrich (1986). *Power and the Division of Labour,* Polity Press. London.
22. Wrong, *op. cit.,* p. 336, says that imputation of power and anticipatory power are two main axes in delegation of decision to the subordinates. These power axes empower authority to legitimise their authority and are associated with leaders.
23. Harold Gould (1969). "Toward a 'Jati Model' for Indian Politics", *Economic and Political Weekly*, February 1st, p. 293.
24. Holmstrom (1988), *Op. cit.,* p. 308.
25. Thurow (1969), *Poverty and Discrimination*, Brooking, Washington D.C. pp. 48-57.
26. Beteille (1969). *Caste, Class and Power: Changing patterns of Stratification in a Tanjore Village*, Oxford University Press, Bombay. p. 159.
27. Wrong. *Op. cit.*
28. *Ibid.,* pp. 199-200.
29. K. Boulding (1989), *Three faces of Power*, Sage Publication, California, p. 15.
30. K. Boulding, *op. cit.,* p. 67.
31. Mumtaz Khan, *op. cit.,* pp. 191-192.
32. Collins (1971). "Functional and Conflict Theories of Educational Stratification", *American Sociological Review*, Vol. 36, p. 1002.
33. Clark, 1962, Kerr *et al.* (1960).
34. Collins (1971). *op. cit.,* pp. 1004-1010.
35. Collins (1971). *op. cit*
36. Andre Beteille (1969). *Caste, Class and Power: Changing Patterns Stratification in a Tanjore Village*. Oxford University Press, Bombay, pp. 98 and 99.
37. B. Turner (1986). *Equality,* Ellis Horwood Lmt. and Travistock Publication, UK, p. 18. Author says that in principle modernism is a political egalitarianism and associated with the development of the Nation-State. Political empowerment is the prime focus in the literature of equality. In India we have witnessed the political awakening but mobilisation towards greater equality is missing and the thrust is again for the compartmentalisation on the basis of the caste.
38. John Rawls (1974). *Constitutional Liberty and Social Justice* excerpts published in G. Mahajan (1998). *Democracy, Difference and Social Justice,* Oxford, New Delhi. pp. 290-293.
39. Holmstrom (1988), *op. cit.,* p. 287.
40. Lambert, *op. cit.,* pp. 166-167.

41. Frank Conlon (1977). *Urbanisation and Indian Society: The Aspect of Caste*, pp. 138-139 in Allen G. Noble and Ashok K. Dutt (ed.) (1977). *Indian Urbanisation and Planning Vehicles of Modernization*, Tata McGraw Hills Publication, Delhi.
42. Robert Hardgrave (1969). *Nadars in South Tamil Nadu*, and Owen Lynch (1969). *Jatavs in Agra*.
43. Hutt (1964). *The Economics of the Colour Bar*: The Institution of Economic Affairs Limited, London. He recommends that increased competition would help in cutting down in the discrimination experiences. The prejudiced forces will disappear under the economic liberation since the prejudice is the simply the manifestation of powerful customs. p. 11.
44. Jandhalaya also recommended in his study that discrimination in the labour market can be computed until the basic amenities such as water, housing, sanitation are not efficiently distributed in the weaker section of the society. *op. cit.,* p. 112. This study also agree with the author since this study also found it monumental task to found the sample with equal background such education qualification, residential area etc.
45. Russel (1921). *Principles of Social Reconstruction,* Ruskin House, London. pp. 23, 29.

6
Geography of Discrimination and Development

The present study has dealt with caste discrimination and inequity in two geographical spaces, i.e. Kanpur City and Ghaziabad in earlier chapters where quantitative and qualitative data corroborated the objectives of the study. Besides banking on the field-based information, the study has also extensively researched on the topic of discrimination along with inequity in other geographical areas. The present study, however, still finds a long way to establish discrimination on caste background, yet certainly asserts that the caste plays substantial role even in urban labour market which may vary in operational strength other geographical spaces for different factors. Ghaziabad which is one of the districts in close proximity of Delhi evinces mild influence of caste in labour market but Kanpur industrial set up is very different of that of Ghaziabad and hence higher sense of caste was noticed in Kanpur City.

In this chapter theories are discussed by using the statistical methods by understanding the uniqueness of two geographical areas. The discussion aims to analyse why discrimination still persist even after several efforts to abate discrimination either by lawful means or by enlightening people to refuse to accept injustice and hardships because of their social or economic category. The chapter focuses on the distribution, processes and welfare objectives which aimed to reduce the social distances. The socio-cultural aspects when used for political foliage generate a stagnant economy. Geography may help to identify such conundrum to salvage policy bottlenecks' fruitfully.

6.1 A Probable Model of Development to Eliminate Caste Discrimination

Geography has contributed extraordinarily first to speculate, then explored the speculations and verified them to understand the complexities of human being. Geography provided thus excellent policy ramifications by measuring differences on spatial scales. However, such human phenomena are too complex and intricate to provide readymade one time answers to the consequential socio-economic situations. David[1] mentions the rise and significant contribution of human geography in welfare approach by stating:

> "From the beginning of the 1970s the literature on social problems and what may be loosely termed welfare issues expanded rapidly was published calls for 'Geography of social well-being' have been made...possibility of welfare economics as a point of departure for location theory and the possibility of welfare as a focal point in human geography has already been tentatively explored and Harvey has drawn attention to the question of social justice in spatial context."[2]

Geography as an exploratory science has helped many complex phenomena and converted them in an understandable form which can be evaluated *in situ* and compared for the implementation of policy. David while judging the welfare society and geography by many scholars from various fields said "the more values impinge on scholastic activity, the more discipline is needed." A major task is this to develop intellectual structure to guide the evaluation of alternative spatial arrangement of human affairs in such format which are easily applicable.

Here the author has redenies to rearrange and develop such spatial spread which minimise the local arbitrary policy structure to a more evolved and widely excepted model of development. He also poses the imminent danger of human conflict due to lack of equality (in this study the material gain and human resource). Inequity has given rise to the social dissatisfaction and according to the conflict theory such inequity will enhance chances of human confrontation. When sources of inequity are built into the social system (differences in resources) resulting differences are neither trivial nor discrete such inequities will persist over time and space which may be a case of caste inequity.

Drawing inspiration from the several writings on justice,

inequity, source of power, discrimination, welfare etc. this research work attempts to analyse the discrimination and inequity in urban labour space by enquiring distribution of education as facilitator to enter labour market and occupation as consumption function for need satisfaction. These two models aim to find out first the likely determinants of employment status (market discrimination) in the labour market and second, if the age, background of the workers, caste and locality influence, education attainment as considered pre-market discrimination. According to the research questions the thesis wants to see the relational aspects of parental status of occupational and education attainment.

6.1.2 Labour Market in Uttar Pradesh

The study also captures the labour condition in urban Uttar Pradesh by analysing the quinquennial NSS round on employment and unemployment situation falling in the same period when the present study was conducted in 2004 and 2011.

NSSO data from round 65 and 66 gives adequate evidence on caste based division of labour and establishes a relationship between the social hierarchy and occupation. Like any other state of India, Uttar Pradesh is also a state where caste has displayed oppressive function which has impeded equal development in past. The data also provide base that caste and occupation are linked with each other. Table 6.1 shows the urban labour situation in Uttar Pradesh.

What appears from the table is that the labour situation rather than improving has further deteriorated; Casual workforce has increased in all caste categories especially in the other backward caste (10.53% to 16.70% equivalent of intermediate caste in this study) and for Scheduled Castes (low and ex-untouchables in this study) it increased from 27.3 per cent to 29.21 per cent. Unemployment situation has increased for both the caste categories, i.e. other backward caste and other caste (2.77% to 4.25% and 3.05% to 4.53% respectively) though it has reduced in case of Scheduled Caste from 5.44 per cent to 2.57 per cent.

Regular salaried wage workers have significantly improved (22.07% to 29%) in Scheduled Caste category. It would be, however, interesting to find that in which kind of regular salaried employment they are engaged[4] in. Other interesting observation is that the total

Table 6.1: Principal Usual Status of Urban Workers in Uttar Pradesh 2004 and 2011

	2004				2011			
P. Usual Status of Workers	*Scheduled castes*	*Other backward castes*	*Others*	*Total*	*Scheduled castes*	*Other backward castes*	*Others*	*Total*
Worked in h.h. enterprise (self-employed): own account worker	33.00	41.03	35.69	37.91	25.69	37.67	37.37	35.85
Worked in h.h. enterprise (self-employed): employer	0.05	0.38	1.43	0.75	0.13	0.64	1.34	0.81
Worked as helper in h.h. enterprise (unpaid family worker)	12.13	23.36	16.74	19.32	11.55	19.27	12.06	15.53
Worked as regular salaried/ wage employee	22.07	21.89	37.51	28.06	28.89	21.02	35.62	27.51
Worked as casual wage labour: in public works	0.00	0.03	0.00	0.02	1.96	0.44	0.52	0.68
Casual labour in other types of work	27.31	10.53	5.58	10.74	29.21	16.70	8.56	15.54
Did not work but was seeking and/or available for work	5.44	2.77	3.05	3.21	2.57	4.25	4.53	4.08
Total	100.00	100.00	100.00	100.00	100.00	100.00	100.00	100.00

(NSS 62nd Round)

absence of Scheduled Caste and other caste categories as casual labour in public works in 2004-05 but in 2011 Scheduled Caste category (1.96%) has slightly higher per cent share to other caste categories (other backward caste is represented by 0.44% and other caste by only 0.52%). While giving a good foundation to explore the inequality in the urban labour market in Uttar Pradesh, the data also shows path to investigate the detail of the employment structure in the proposed cities of Uttar Pradesh.

6.1.2 Bivariate Model on Education and Occupation

Bivariate Regression analysis focus on the dependence of one variable, the dependent variable on one or more other variables, the explanatory variables with a view to estimate means or average value of the former in terms of the known fixed values of the later. Bi-variate logistic regression is easier to interpret. In this analysis instead of using logistic regression coefficients, odds ratios are used.

$$\log \frac{p_i}{1-p_i} = b_0 b_1 x_1 + b_2 x_2 + b_3 x_3 ....b_n x_n + e$$

Where:

P_i = Probability of the event occurring

b_0 = Constant term representing the value of log $(P_i/(1-P_i)$ with the base line value of all values x_1 to x_n in the model

x_1 to x_n = independent variables

b_1 to b_n = unknown regression coefficient associated with the independent variables x_1 to x_n. A unit change in the corresponding independent variables produces a change in the log $(P_i/(1-P_i)$

e = error or disturbance term representing unobserved variables that influence dependent variable.

Odds ratios are easier to interpret as the odds is more intuitively meaningful concept than log odds (coefficients) and are more readily understandable as a measure of effect. The original coefficient represents the additive effect of a one unit change in predictor variable

Table 6.2: List of Variables used for the Analysis

Variables	*Name of the Variables*	*Defined statistics*	*Type of Variables*
Independent variables	Age	1- Below 30 2- 31-45 3- Above 45	Categorical
	Education of father	1-Literate 0-Illiterate	Dichotomous
	Occupation of Father	1-Skilled 0-Unskilled	Dichotomous
	Education of mother	1-Literate 0-Illiterate	Dichotomous
	Caste	1- Upper castes 2-Intermediate castes 3- Ex-untouchables	Categorical
	Locality	0-Slum 1-Non slum	Dichotomous
Dependent variables	Education	1-Literate 0-Illiterate	
	Occupation	Skilled-1 Unskilled-0	

on the log odds of response variable. Similarly, the odds ratio represents the multiplicative effect of one unit change in predictor variable on the odds of response variable. Therefore, log model is either additive model or multiplicative model, depending how the response variable is conceptualised. When a log odd is considered as response variable the logit model is additive model. When odds are considered as the response variable, the logit model is multiplicative model, regarding the definition and interpretation of effects. For example, the odds ratio (a) of variable X means that every unit rise in X the odds ratio is increased by $(a - 1) \times 100$ per cent.

Model 1

Test one—Educational attainment is often associated by the parental background and location.

Education (Dependent Variable)

Independent Variable

1. Age
2. Parental Background
   - *Father's education*
   - *Mother's education*
   - *Father's occupation*
3. Locality
4. Caste

Table 6.3: Odds Ratio of Education in Kanpur City

Variables in the Equation					
		B	*S.E.*	*Sig.*	*Exp(B)*
Age	below 30			0.043	
	31-45	1.023	0.478	0.033	2.78
	above 45	1.229	0.506	0.015	3.419
Education	Education of father	1.479	0.421	0	4.389
	Occupation of father	-0.31	0.355	0.382	0.733
	Education of mother	0.957	1.1	0.384	2.603
Loc	Locality	0.414	0.356	0.246	1.512
Caste	Upper caste			0.258	
	Intermediate caste	0.742	0.715	0.299	2.101
	Low-exuntouchables	-0.34	0.341	0.319	0.712
	Constant	-0.577	0.714	0.42	0.562
a. Variable(s) entered on step 1: age.ana, edu.f.R, occu.f.R, edu.m.R, locality.R, caste.new.					

After running the binary logistic regression on the above mentioned variables while keeping the first category as the reference category. In comparison to the younger age group 14-30, the likelihood of the age group (30-40) being literate goes up by 1.23 times in Kanpur but decreases by a factor of 0.54 in Ghaziabad. Odds of a person being literate in the age group of 'above 45' decreases by a factor of 0.36 in Kanpur and by 0.12 in Ghaziabad. In general it has been found that the increasing age has higher factor of being illiterate in both the cities. The odds of a person being literate when father is literate increases by a factor 4.38 in Kanpur but increases by a factor of 2.47 in Ghaziabad. Similarly, when mother is literate the likelihood of a child getting literate increases by a factor of 3.49 in Ghaziabad and by 2.60 in Kanpur City. This shows that education level of parents is a good determinant of a person being literate in both the cities. It is observed that the odds of a person being literate reduces by a factor of 0.733 in Kanpur for those people whose father is in skilled category compared to unskilled category but improves likelihood of being literate in Ghaziabad. The reason behind is that better penetration of schooling in slum areas of Kanpur City. In comparison to the upper caste person the odds of person from intermediate caste reduces by a factor of 0.33 in Kanpur and by 0.229 in Ghaziabad. Same is repeated in case of low and ex-untouchables in both the cities. Locality also matters in educational attainment where the likelihood of a person from non-slum area increases by a factor of 1.51 in Kanpur City and by 2.17 in Ghaziabad (Tables 6.4 and 6.5).

Table 6.4: Odds ratio of Education in Ghaziabad

	Variables	*B*	*S.E.*	*Sig.*	*Exp(B)*
Step 1a	Below 30			0.001	
	31-45	2.066	0.548	0	7.894
	above 45	1.454	0.55	0.008	4.278
	Education of father	0.907	0.347	0.009	2.477
	Occupation of father	0.224	0.542	0.679	1.252
	Education of mother	1.25	0.847	0.14	3.491
	Locality	0.776	0.315	0.014	2.172
	Upper caste			0.04	
	Intermediate caste	1.479	0.609	0.015	4.388
	Low-ex-untouchables	0.273	0.392	0.487	1.313
	Constant	-2.985	0.923	0.001	0.051

a. Variable(s) entered on step 1: age.ana, edu.f.R, ooc.f.R, edu.m.R, laclity. ana, caste.new.

Situation seems to be same in both the cities with different magnitude. Thus the premise that the parental disadvantage or advantage cast shadow on the offspring's future attainment appears to correct in the present study. Also caste, locality, and age have compounding effect on the education status of a person. In a nutshell it can be concluded that the initial inputs or investment in human capital of child's are largely depends on the capacity, willingness of parents where their social background puts an inclusive burden of difficulties.

Model 2

Test two—Does occupation can be influenced by age, parental background, education attainment and caste status?

Occupation (Dependent Variable)
Independent Variable

1. Age
2. Education
3. Parental Background
   Father's education
   Mother's education
   Father's occupation
4. Locality
5. Caste

Table 6.5: Odds ratio of occupation in Kanpur City

	Variables in the Model	*B*	*S.E.*	*Sig.*	*Exp(B)*
Step 1a	Literate	0.349	0.373	0.35	1.417
	below 30			0.361	
	31-45	-0.698	0.49	0.155	1.107
	above 45	-0.596	0.505	0.238	2.009
	Education of father	0.95	0.331	0.004	2.586
	Education of mother	-0.028	0.634	0.965	0.973
	Occupation of father	-0.109	0.331	0.741	0.897
	Locality	-0.106	0.323	0.742	0.899
	Upper caste			0	
	Intermediate caste	2.329	0.507	0	.414
	Low-ex-untouchables	1.447	0.33	0	.097
	Constant	-1.202	0.696	0.084	1.381

a. Variable(s) entered on step 1: edu.R, age.ana, edu.f.R, edu.m.R, occu.f.R, locality.R, caste.new.

The study analyses odds ratio to answer if age, parental background, education and caste has any influence in labour market. The odds of an educated person to be in skilled occupation increases by a factor of 1.41 in Kanpur City and by 1.64 in Ghaziabad. Father being literate also increases likelihood of son being skilled workforce by a factor of 2.58 but decreases by a factor of 0.83 in Ghaziabad. The explanation of this interpretation could be that number of migrants is higher in Ghaziabad and also respondents live in nuclear family. But mother being literate shows a different result in these cities. Mother being educated improves likelihood by a factor of 1.69 in Ghaziabad but decreases by a factor of 0.97 in Kanpur City. Odds of a person belonging to the intermediate caste being in skilled jobs, decreases by a factor of 0.414 in Kanpur City and by a factor of 0.299 in Ghaziabad while likelihood of a low and ex-untouchable persons being in skilled jobs decreases by 0.097 in Kanpur and by a factor of 0.252 in Ghaziabad. Living in slum area also puts constraint to find skilled jobs as odds of a person finding skilled jobs decreases by a factor of 0.899 in Kanpur City but increases by a factor of 2.18 in Ghaziabad. The reason behind this probability in Ghaziabad could be because slum areas occupied by the people working mostly in neighbouring industries (Tables 6.5 and 6.6).

Table 6.6: Odds ratio for Occupation in Ghaziabad

		B	S.E.	Sig.	Exp(B)
Step 1a	Literate	0.495	0.348	0.154	1.641
	below 30			0.2	
	31-45	0.277	0.526	0.598	1.32
	above 45	0.808	0.543	0.137	2.242
	Education of father	-0.182	0.354	0.607	0.833
	Occupation of father	0.96	0.535	0.073	2.612
	Education of mother	0.53	0.69	0.442	1.699
	Locality	0.783	0.344	0.023	2.189
	Upper caste			0.144	
	Intermediate caste	1.379	0.72	0.056	3.97
	Low ex-untouchables	0.171	0.391	0.661	1.187
	Constant	-1.829	0.889	0.04	0.161

a. Variable(s) entered on step 1: edu.R, age.ana, edu.f.R, ooc.f.R, edu.m.R, laclity.ana, caste.new.

Locality, education of mother, father and age do not have higher influence to be in job in Kanpur City but in Ghaziabad these factors show greater importance to be in unskilled jobs.

The study concludes that the concentration of lower caste people in lower end jobs not only puts severe handicap on their current living standards but also jeopardise the future of their offspring's and hence, it is important to provide the lower rung workers concentrated in unorganised labour market to provide them security of jobs, skill enhancement opportunities and also better access to educational facilities to their children.

6.3 Distribution and Discrimination

Geography as a science of spatial distribution leads us to study the relative differences and similarities of spaces and of spatial organisations. From classical period to the current time the study of distribution has never become irrelevant in the discipline. Many Geographers contributed to the theory building of Geography and also brought the topic of spatial distribution but it was Hettner (1905)[5] who systematically studied physical distribution and greatly emphasized on the role of similarity of social structure which he defined as chorological spaces. He gave the theory of distribution by spaces, loci, and place, this encompassed spatial structures featuring all sorts of interaction such as economic, social and political and also scaled up to discuss the mental imagination which changes faster than economic, political or any societal situation.

Though Robert Kates (1962)[6] studied the behavioural human perceptions of environmental hazards while trying to understand the perceived uncertainty and unpredictability in coping mechanism, yet his scheme has wide range of applicability in plotting human behaviour. Kirk (1952)[7] also prepared behavioural models where he said that same information would mean different meaning to different set of people and also, they react differently. He also said that phenomenal (physical surrounding) and behavioural parts uniquely imbibe to create exclusive structures in society. Geography is a dynamic subject not just due to ever increasing interdisciplinary enhancement, but it gives back what it receives from other disciplines in knowledge content.

Some of the concepts of psychology also helped to find relationship between, physical environment, image construct and behaviour of the people in particular social setting. Gestalt psychologists[8] were the first to admit the fact that the way in which an object is perceived is determined by the total environment in which it is rooted. This theory particularly was not well received in its own discipline nevertheless it gave a sound backup to behavioural differences in similar spaces which became quite important induction in Geography since it allowed to find the relationship with spaces. Gestalt theory is associated with essentially two basic assumptions. The first according to Deutch and Krauss (1965)[9] implies a perception of wholes, where 'psychological phenomena should be conceived as occurring in a field ... as part of a system of coexisting and mutually interdependent factors having certain properties as a system that are not deducible from knowledge of the isolated elements of the system'. The second basic assumption is that certain states of the psychological field are more orderly than other fields. Thus, perceptual organization is viewed as an ideal state of order and simplicity rather than a haphazard one. This unifying process according to Allport[10] is termed 'configurationalism' and it is postulated to have a physiological basis within the organism. Perception, therefore, is not learned, but natively inbuilt and passed on, a property of the organising action of the nervous system. Thus, the Gestalt psychology provides a basis to interpret what cultural and growing up of the citizens in Kanpur city and Ghaziabad brought differences in discrimination behaviour in these two spaces.

The present research work has valued such geographical insights which theoretically underpin what Geography explicate physical and behavioural uniqueness to promote development. However, such image construct of spaces and places in Geography lacks the methodological application. To overcome such methodological shortcomings, the research has emphasised on the complete record of the trajectory of the workers in the market. Kanpur city and Ghaziabad presents such perfect setting to not only comprehend and analyses the cities but also to imagine the future of caste in Urban India. The research therefore finds four corners where psychological behaviour, traditional milieu, economy and development factors make all the difference in these two cities and also provide a framework to initiate the dialogue to underplay the caste roles by giving advantage to the people with skills and merits which will reduce the inequity and pace the development in true meaning.

Development is one of the most contested concepts which has been described, defined differently over the years and by social scientists. Whatever the points of elaboration over the years or by social researcher had been, it is no denying that development is closely linked with the social phenomena and hence it becomes innate to peel off the layers of development growth of society. The present research work though not extraordinarily ambitious yet envisaged what geographers have always aimed at to design and contour the social dimensions for promoting human development and achieving an 'equitable equilibrium' to all structures of society in development. The focus of the study has been from the modern geography perspective where caste order became a cause which has impacted the process and ultimately distribution of development also showed the result of such processual differences. Such structural differences have caused disturbances in this equilibrium and led to the conflict, disenchantment, and development chaos. The cause-and-effect relationship is studied in geography with the focus on the distribution basically focussing on where. No event can take place without a cause. Similarly, no cause can remain dormant. This is very well realised in modern geography. Therefore, phenomena of discrimination also carry those distributional differences and thus proposes some solution on the dock itself.

All these geographical thoughts were mutually helpful in understanding individual responses including facial gestures to annotations and put down them into notations to analyse by methods which are convincing to the scientists who want statistical prove and also to the scientists who are less contented if ground realities are not covered in the result interpretations. Thus, from the behavioural modelling to the institutional causes provided by the caste structure, the research work followed a methodological approach in locales of Kanpur city and Ghaziabad.

Processes are becoming an important mechanism to segregate people in the name of caste, region, religion, higher or lower economic order. The task of human geographer is at present to understand the processes for development and to the development and underdevelopment. Process distinguish will help in reducing inequality and mal-distribution of society simultaneously process leading to the development or retarded development can be brought into the focus to rectify the process failure of comparable places. Here in this study Kanpur and Ghaziabad presents two interesting geographical spaces one which is educationally, politically aware society and another ignorant on these fronts, devoid of apparent caste attachments place higher value to earning. Sidanius and Pratto[11] argue that group-based hierarchies are driven and maintained by three processes:

1. aggregated individual discrimination,
2. aggregated institutional discrimination, and
3. behavioural asymmetry.

Aggregated individual discrimination refers to "the simple, daily, and sometimes quite inconspicuous individual acts of discrimination by one individual against another." The aggregated behaviours lead to accumulated effect of the discrimination and overall polarised development results. In other words one isolated example of discrimination may not be of any significant value but thousands of such cases will certainly show inequality in achievements.

As the objective of this study greatly explored the theories of discrimination (mainly Becker and other exponents on discrimination and inequity) soon conceptual understanding of the discrimination brought by the geographical differences on the local leads to focus on the local challenges to address the persisting discrimination and inequity at root level. First it straight followed the analysis *in situ* of the workers from all caste backgrounds, education, background of the respondent and occupation, nature of occupation, recruitment processes and experiences their opinion on the subject matter. Though the present study has tried to cover many untouched concerns of the discipline but many other parameters which are important from the point of view of occupational mobility could not be analysed due to limitation in scope, time and to avoid deviance from the main objective. The study nonetheless, has tried to analyse the impact of discrimination or biasness in the labour market analysis from different caste category. In this section an attempt has been made to build the model first by regressing education and earning on the variables which have been identified has the main source of discrimination.

Distribution becomes extremely important form of welfare function. Marx writes on the structure of production in a society—

> One man is superior to another physically or mentally and so supplies more labour in the same time, or can labour for a longer time; and labour to, serve as measure, must be defined by its duration or intensity, otherwise it ceases to be standard of measurement. This equal right is an unequal right for unequal labour. It recognises no class differences because everyone is only a worker like everyone else; but it tacitly recognises unequal individual endowment and thus productive capacity

> as natural privileges. It is, therefore, a right of inequality in its contents, like every right.[12]

The stagnant situation of the Indian labour market can be very well linked with the mall distributive justice where people from the poor background and lack of skill endowment accessibility get trapped in the lower part of the labour market. The data show that labour situation have not improved and continue to grim because of distributive efforts are polarised in the society. There is another study[13] where author develops policy suggestions by developing model on social distributive justice as propounded many theorists on justice in society comparing US and India. Distributive model may fail in such conditions where the rich and powerful few run the economy. India is one classic case where expenditure on public welfare is generated through taxes but eventually do not ascertain the rightful distribution. Smith[14] proposes greater stress to the egalitarianism (as a method) for better distributive justice. He says—

> "otherwise powerful members of society with most to lose from the egalitarianism, often have the capacity to publicise their view and to try to persuade others, especially in these days of expensive mass media; it would not, therefore, be surprising if arguments for an equal or more equal distribution were muted in everyday discourse."

Here Geography plays role of an active egalitarian selector for need assessment and distribution method to justly reach the people who need the most. This study has experienced several unhealthy practices which severely affect the nuances of education, skill, earning, saving and overall investment in life. People live in bizarre expectations from the government and government run institutions.

6.3.1 Geography of Discrimination: Inequity, Social Order and Welfare

What are the ways to formulate policy which may address the social equitable upliftment of the people? David[15] says that welfare is not something directly observable condition but we can judge whether it has increased or decreased or even remained same from time to time and from place to place. Here the study observed and put forth the evidences of extremely tardy penetration of development efforts which has several layers of absorption from top to bottom.

Dugan[16] says that the root cause of inequity could be prejudice on the level of individual and political imbalance on the social level. But in this study it is found that old industrial relations in Kanpur have given firm political backing to the socially deprived section and respondent in general are found to be politically enlightened though not socially. She also says that what is unarguable that when prejudice produces discriminatory behaviour and power imbalance reify individual behaviour into structural difference in access and treatment, gross social, political and economic inequality.[17] Discrimination can lead to unexpected and pernicious forms of inequity. Even in the cities where caste is observable through networks leading to dangerous stagnation of the labour force, hidden dissatisfaction and conflicts. David[18] warns that one of the greatest dangers in the present situation of development inequality is its potential for human conflict.

Dilemma of welfare gives confonding factors of dovlopment variables to the academicians to judge the right method of welfare approach but planners have also been in the maze of pros and cons while substituting worse with better and better with of course worse. Graaff (1957) puts the former position as follows—the job... is not to try to reach welfare conclusions for others, but rather to make available the positive knowledge—the information and the understanding—on the basis of which even a laymen can pass the judgement[19].

Vast expansion of heavy industry and transportation and communication devices made momentous change in the structure of the capitalist economies. Centralisation of capital made giant strides and large scale enterprises moved into the centre stage displacing and absorbing the small firms sheltering the competitive mechanism which regulated the economic scene. Western penetration of backward colonial areas led to ruthless oppression and exploitation of the subjugated nations. Unleashing on the economists who are only theoretically inclined Baron[20] says that they do not give reasonable palatable theory of economic and social change. They propose problems as they 'do not know enough', sometimes obstacles to industrialisation steaming from the character of the labour force or scarcity of managerial talent. Welfare economists try to appraise that social order and its so called efficiency and its contribution to human welfare by criteria that it has evolved itself. Paul Baron––Recalling the contribution made by the classical, neoclassical and communist economists in political economists developing keen observation of society in which they lived and how much they faired in economic development and other progress made in their society. Political economist (classical) predicted thinking progress upon removal of outdated political social and economic institution upon creation of fair competition under which individual enterprise and indusrialisation would have given ample opportunity for unhampered performance.

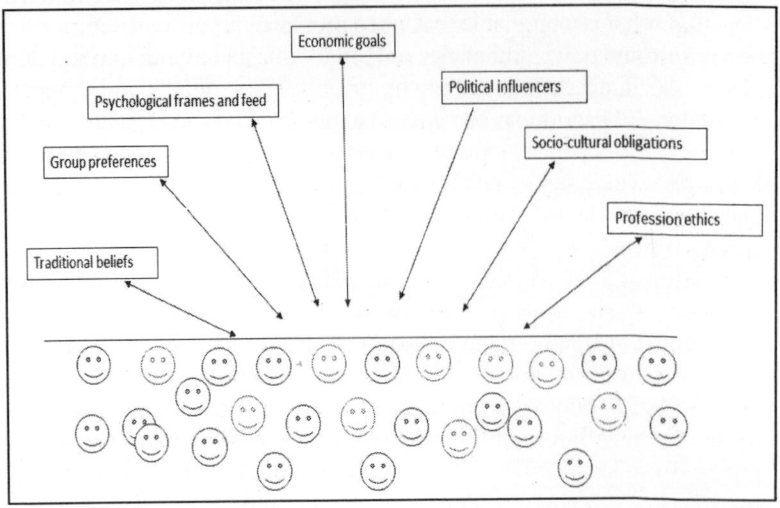

Fig. 6.1: Interaction coordinates and controls of individuals in market

Fig. 6.1 shows different interaction points of politico- psychological aspects which influence choice of an individual and also many socialised traditional values of social cultural norms interspersed with individual preferences, weighed with economic compulsions and family needs lead to set ultimate selection of work.

So far all theoretical assumptions fail to explain the labour situation in India. Since, globalisation impact on labour structure has complicated whole scenario in India where higher level of urbanisation and shrinking opportunities in villages has tremendously influenced entire labour market. Fair competition though is evidently proliferated yet left labours in much more insecure grades of work. Rate of unemployment high in educated group leading to unaccountable waste of human skill and resource creation is cause of concern. Some of the issues which are identified by the study are the lack of information channel and circulation of information though informal channel has also led to segmentation and stagnation of labour force. Study by Sasi

Kumar and Karan[21] also finds some of the similar causes of waste of human resources which this study also found are—(a) weak labour market information, (b) mismatch in demand and supply, and (c) disliking about the nature of available jobs.

6.4 A Complex World of Labour Market Interaction/Network and Social Paraphrase of Development

6.4.1 Social Identity and Access to Job Market

Social Identity plays a certificate to find a job in the market even if the job in non-secure, lowly paid and does not give any skill enhancement. People heavily bank on the relatives to find job especially in unorganized market. There is little confusion while seeking job when labour is unskilled or lowly skilled as they either learn after joining the job or there is no need to learn as the job is of unskilled category which has little capital requirement.

6.4.2 Role of Education and Preference in Labour Market

How and when people change their opinion as soon as asked whether education can help mitigating the social rigid construct. The responses were vehemently agreed with the option but switched the tune after they were asked if they would give preference to their own circle of relatives and caste people. The question meant to be the general discussion where the aim was to gauze the belief of labourers and their responsibility as a member of society if educated society can prove to be the only solution of caste and caste generated complexities of society and to let the society grow as a natural bio-mass. These two contradictory answer actually leads to the *status quo* in labour market where own caste worker is given upper hand over the more genuinely skilled person?

6.4.3 Where and How Economic End Meets the Social Reality

Truly extremely difficult finding was where and how occupation takes over the social identity and *vice versa*. In most general case only remuneration remain the ultimate motive to fetch a job but Caste as a sailing identity gives the social security too and hence more often in typical cases labour is not able to move out of the boundaries marked by their social origin.

6.4.4 Politics of Social Origin

It is a slogan in India which emerges to be the most favourite of all – "Caste is Dead Long live the Caste!" All want to write the obituary to caste but cannot do so since it has survived through other means especially due to political patronage. Osborne[22] predicts the future of caste on the basis of political sympathies it has garnered over the time. He also says that the caste system to be inconsistence with the modernization in general and urbanisation in particular according to other theorists but according to the Osborne[23] caste will continue to be politically important and hence important as a cultural phenomenon as long as members are readily identifiable. Even if urbanization and modernization eliminate the link between *jati* and occupation, which seems a reasonable, reservation based on caste will continue to be major feature of Indian politics as long as the eligibility of beneficiaries can be readily determined and the government is in a position to dispense valuable rents to various pressure groups. Thus incentive to maintain caste identity is thus quite powerful. Sheela Rai[24] also precisely points out the politicization of caste phenomena and the spread of such linkages all over India. She doubts the national feeling of such leaders and parties and says that these leaders are openly practicing politics of Group interest. She also says that land reforms have led many OB castes to better off conditions yet the conditions of *Dalits* have not improved so far. She questions the criteria of just distribution in the society if it should be on the basis of rights, or need. Barooah, A. Dubey[25] *et al*. also in the analysis on job reservation and occupational status of people from various social background conclude that though reservation has benefited many, socially depressed castes of the Indian society yet the benefit from reservation has not been equally spread through the section. Job reservation as such has not given direct benefit to the deserving section and attributes related to the job would have certainly helped them to enhance the reservation. An important aspect of the caste system that it facilitates the formation of pressure groups on a government that has many rents to dispense and many factionalized citizens eager to seek them. Perhaps the most remarkable feature of reservation based rent seeking in India is that it has occurred primarily through the most ordinary (cheap means) means, i.e. voting. Pre-existing factions often obtain rents through the government simply by using political strength to ensure that their groups are listed as ST, SC, OBC. Osborne sites that Becker made free rider problem a central element of his theory, voting is usually sufficiently low cost that organizing factions along caste lines is a simple task. Such rent seeking behaviour in rural Uttar Pradesh has been given attention for political gains and addressed by Amiya Baghchi in his article on rent seeking[26]. He writes that the concept of rent seeking is a direct by product of the new political economy, which started out as a development of the 'old' interest group or elite theory of politics associated with Robert Michels, Gaetano Mosca and Vilfrade Pareto. The assertion of the dominated section in the rural area through the political support has evolved now fully as Bagchi states that dominated section use methods of control often appears to be themselves and to the people they control only as an extension of traditional power exercised through caste dominance and caste solidarity as against other subordinate castes.

Summing up

The society which has been functioning for ages on such social construct is need to think beyond the caste or development will remain the distant dream for the labour in lowest rungs of market. The phenomena which cannot be easily decoded but complex system has provided some answers first the system which works on the behaviour which delicately balance the harmony of society and hence political guidance and democratic selection of occupation, enhancement in work skill will only give to more rational picture of labour market which at present is infested with ignorance and subject to too many social contract rather than getting opportunity in pursuit of human value inputs for long run economic gains. The chapter thus is able to identify that processes and distribution if understood in better detail can furnish a better model for holistic development in all spaces. David[27] says that Geography must stand or fall by its demonstrated capacity to enhance human well-being and not by virtue of its convenient to the existing organisation of society or academia.

NOTES

1. David M. Smith (1977). *Op. cit.,* p. 5.
2. *Ibid.*
3. A study by Noor Mohammad, *Dynamics of Caste and Occupation in the Saryapar Plain In India*, [in Noble, Thakur *et al.* (2000). "Geographic and

Planning Research Themes for the New Millennium", Vikas Publishing House New Delhi]. His study in Sarayupar Plain in Uttar Pradesh concludes that high prestige jobs (crop farming, service jobs) are done by the high caste people while Ahirs are largely engages in Dairy farming while low caste people grow coarse grains.

4. The study has found that the workers in the ex-untouchables category are generally engaged in regular salaried jobs in the municipal corporation and other organizations.
5. Richard Hartshorne (1939) "Geography as the Science of Distributions", *Annals of the Association of American Geographers*, 29:3, 127-129, DOI: 10.1080/00045603909357289 accessed on 20th June 2014
6. Kates, R.W. (1962) *Hazard and Choice Perception in Flood Plain Management*, Department of Geography Research Paper no. 78, University of Chicago Press.
7. Kirk, W., (1952). "Historical Geography and the concept of the behavioural environment". *Indian Geography Journal*, Silver Jubilee Issue, 152-60.
8. Paul M. Koroscil (1971) The Behavioural Environmental Approach, The Royal Geographical Society (with the Institute of British Geographers), Vol. 3, No. 2, pp. 96-99, https://www.jstor.org/stable/20000543 accessed on 20th June 2014.
9. Deutsch, M., and Krauss, R. M.(1965), *Theories in Social Psychology*. Basic Books, New York. In Paul M. Koroscil (1971) ibid.
10. Allport, F. H. (1955), *Theories of-Perception and the concept of Structure*. John Wiley and Sons Inc., New York. In Paul M. Koroscil (1971) ibid
11. Sidaneus, Jim and Felicia Pratto (1999). *Social Dominance: An Intergroup Theory of Social Hierarchy and Oppression*. Cambridge: Cambridge University Press, p. 38.
12. David Smith (1977). p. 138.
13. Sheela Rai, (2002). "Social and Conceptual Background to the Policy of Reservation", *EPW*, October 19.
14. David Smith (1994). *Geography and Social Justice*, Blackwell, Oxford, UK.
15. David Smith (1977). *ibid*. p. 8.
16. Maire A. Dugan. http://www.intractableconflict.org/author.jsp
17. *Ibid.,* p. 3.
18. David Smith (1977). p. 18.
19. David Smith, *op. cit.,* p. 364.
20. Paul Baron (1957). *The Political Economy of Growth,* Monthly Review Press, New York.
21. Sasi Kumar and Karan, (2010) "Skill Mapping in Indian Labour Market", *Labour and Development*, Vol. 16-17, June, p. 30.

22. Evan Osborne (2001). "Culture, Development and Government", *Economic Development and Cultural Change*, Vol. 49, pp. 659-85.
23. Evan Osborne (2001). *ibid.*
24. Sheela Rai (2002). "Social and Conceptual Background to the Policy of Reservation", *Economic and Political Weekly*, October 19.
25. Vani K. Borooah, Dubey, Sriya Iyer *et al.* (2007) "Has Job Reservations in India Been Effective? Caste, Religion, and Economic Status" (with), *Development and Change*, Vol. 38, No. 3, pp. 423-445.
26. Amiya Kumar Bagchi (1993) "'Rent Seeking', New Political Economy and Negation of Politics", *Economic and Political Weekly,* August 21, 28 (34), p. 1734.
27. David, *op. cit.*, p. 368.

7
Conclusion

This study has explored aspects related to discrimination and inequity in the urban labour market on the grounds of caste. The study inquires into change and unchanged aspects of the caste as an institution. There is mammoth literature available on the changed and unchanged image of the caste in urban India by the academicians and freelancers[1]. The caste becomes a centre point of discussion in all the studies with reference to urban behaviour. Some studies are positive, some are critically negative and a few studies have examined both sides of the coin. Gupta[2] sees urbanization as one of the major factor to divert people's mindset from traditionalism to modernism, yet he also joins the group of researchers who finds caste as never fading social fact even in urban India. He writes and feels:

> "there is no escaping the fact that the mode of relations among people in our country is still not modern. Family connections, privileges of caste and status....characterise our relations deeply...and further defining modernity (which in real sense is non-existent in Indian Society *per se*). Modernity is an attitude which represents universailistic norms where dignity of an individual as a citizen is inviolable and where one's achievement counts for more than family background and connections."

Gupta's comment has more than one coterie; one of them is Madan[3] who scathingly criticize Myrdal's understanding of caste. Myrdal in his famous book titled *Asian Drama* describes negative caste phenomena in the rural and urban India. Madan points out on the analysis of caste done by Myrdal that it lacks ethnographic citations; author has deliberately ignored the change in the caste system and he keeps his notion on the caste as degenerating system.

Keeping focus on the objective of this study, the preset study has also made an effort to assimilate the details on 'Changed and unchanged aspects' facets of caste as a pivot Indian social system. The study has become all the more important in the aftermath of the 'World Conference against Racism' (Durban, 2000) where delegates from different countries brought into focus discrimination in their society and Indian delegates also went there to ensure that the caste generated discrimination at least get some attention if not incorporated full-fledged in the conference agenda by legitimizing their demand saying that "caste and caste based discrimination have a similar impact to that of race and racial discrimination."[4]

Summary of Findings

The present study puts forth findings which sometimes reinforce the already existing phenomena and some are new in the discrimination parlance. The study scrutinises the caste as a key factor of employment provider/discarder in the urban labour market or it acts as screen in the labour market along with other essential qualifications.

1. In the beginning it was assumed that the parental background like parent's education, occupation, leads people to pursue career in the same field. The study found this assumption right. The parental (especially father's education and occupation) background has influenced the worker's education and occupational potential.
2. According to the Dual-Market theory there are two segments in the labour market first primary which has white-collar jobs and secondary market which constitutes dead end jobs, exactly saying that the secondary market is over represented with lower caste respondents. This secondary market in the present context has all the characteristics of unorganized sector. This finding also confirms that occupational discrimination does exist *per se* but it could be because of segmentation and preference over other community and caste[5].
3. Both the cities have shown that people in this sector heavily bank upon the information's provided by the relatives,

neighbours and natives. This indirectly confirms that the system of recruitment may be the harbinger of caste discrimination or segregation in the urban labour market.

4. Studies on discrimination have indicated that nature of job is very important to know the scale of discrimination. In absence of this scale the study had divided occupation according to the prestige, incentives, skill essentials and job environment. Though nature of job may give the actual anatomy of occupational discrimination yet due to fragmentation and small size of sample this analysis could not be achieved. However, the descriptive and interview schedule did throw light on the nature of job which though statistically could not be validated but successfully decoded through the qualitative interview and further probed under 'Likert items'. The findings are very important from the discrimination point of view. Workers in both the cities from lower caste groups are found to be working in lower hierarchical positions in industries. There were examples which refute this claim yet the number of such respondents was comparatively low in both the cities. The study can say that the respondents from lower caste have been living in segregation in Ghaziabad (interaction 'points' were minimal here with the upper caste) whereas the cases of discrimination were high in Kanpur because of interaction 'points' was high.
5. Disguised wage discrimination found to exist in both the cities. The upper caste respondents not only occupied more remunerative jobs but also are better paid for occupations on the same level in some cases, people from lower caste and ex-untouchable respondents even if got same wage the unidentified returns (behavioural) or perks were less and were into less competitive terms with their counterparts. The reason could be lower level of education (immaterial in such unorganized jobs, no training or experience in their work area, lack of capital (in case of own account and self-employed respondents) lack of network of customer and non-availability of approachable market space, opportunity to work in extended hours etc. The age factor is also important which affects earning. The study has found that younger age groups till (20-35) have earned the highest in general in both the cities. The reason could be that the younger respondents

have better awareness and bargaining power plus invigorant (which are important in unorganized and contractual jobs). Secondly, industrial differences in the study may have left a shadow effect on the earning. Third possibility of based and inflated response cannot be ignored.

6. This research study has given many insights to the phenomena of discrimination in India and the study can generalize that there is a constant stigma towards the Balmikis, though the leather workers (*Charmkar*) have successfully created a passage through the discrimination by virtue of traditional skills, gained educational qualification, acquired monetary and political power and recent promotion to enhance the entrepreneurship in this community. *Badhai* (carpenter), *Luhar* (blacksmith) and *Kumhar* (potter) were the main artisan community present in good strength in both the cities. These caste respondents were proud to have inherited skills and feel that the lack of opportunity (related to their caste occupations) in the market has enabled them with a vocation to become independent in their own field. They also assert that in case of competition the competitors are also of their own community members.
7. The intermediate caste group has demanded and shown that the different caste community should live with benevolence and tolerance towards each other. The upper caste, however, has mixed response. Some of the workers from the upper caste were highly idealists. A few of them favour as interactive mode in their household and outside world too[6]. The lower and ex-untouchables respondents easily revealed the caste related discrimination if ever felt. It was observed that even if they were discriminated still the sense of integration and acceptance in neighbouring areas has increased.
8. To an extent Urbanisation and Urbanism[7] has emerged as a boon for the ostracized community in the Urban Labour market. The caste does cast its shadow but in a very subservient manner. The harshness and starkness of the 'Casteism' like in rural India is not openly visible in the Urban Centres; even in the city like Kanpur where caste historically played an important role has become more political relevant and less for economic gains. Ghaziabad interestingly has more cosmopolitan features than Kanpur City, people have started believing in the class (livelihood is superior to their social

category) than the caste. This study, therefore, construes from the field analysis that it is important to spread across the value of 'urbanism'.

9. Though, it was not the objective of the study yet finding indicates that there is a demarcation of residential pattern according to the caste groups. The equation is very complex yet simplifying this study admits that percentage of migrants is high from the lower caste rungs. They may have migrated with or without pre-existing contact yet largely they settle down in the unorganized camps and earn livelihood from the unorganized work. Consequently, the residential area also have same story to tell that the people from the lower level lives in the lowest and cheapest available shelter and people who have slightly better earning live in the better houses and finally, the people from the organized sector occupy the legal organized housing colonies. The caste groups also follow the pattern of residence in the locality. In academic circle it is known as residential discrimination.[8] Accessibility and employment have been evaluated by David[9] shows the advantageous city plan for the overall development of the city and finds there is negative or positive accessibility (cost of transportation) to the parts of the city which may vary the development of the area. He writes—the roots of the inner city poverty thus go deeper into the social and economic fabric of society than simply the spatial disposition of homes and jobs.
10. The upbringing of a child makes a very important mark to build a good future. The study profoundly discussed and analysed the data on the intergenerational mobility, influence of parental education and economic status. It is found that once the pressure of earning develops in early years of life there is hardly any scope left to devote time for formal education or skill enhancement. People get trapped in the same kind of situation. What they require, opportunities and facilities which shall pave way for a better future. Thorat[10] argues that the Indian private sector which works under monopolistic and oligopolistic markets provides conditions favourable to discrimination and hence reservation in private sector is necessary for fair and non-discriminatory access. But, if applied such policies cannot reap full benefit in a situation where labour force is unskilled.

Suggestions

The present work have tenuously worked to decipher the meaning of discrimination in the Indian Society and it intends to catch the vision of policy makers concerning caste and labour trapped in the unorganized sector the study proposes some suggestions. As David[11] also said that welfare is not something like weather which can be observed directly but it can be judged if it has increased or decreased with a change in society from time to time if appropriate assumptions are made. He further says that normative and value judgements are the two ways of deciding the overall social policy and to continue doing positive work by these norms may alone be satisfactory for the society. But converging the scope of human geography has some positive actions and some are bound by the principles of value judgement of bad and worse rationalizing the implementation part. He feels that the normative analysis especially becomes extremely difficult because geography is concerned with the distribution in space, i.e. among group of people identified by area of residence and it is difficult to use geography as entirely positive analysis and positive action. He stresses because the more values impinge on scholastic activity, the more discipline is needed to control policy measures especially drew on the group norms. A major task is this to develop intellectual structure to guide the evaluation of alternative spatial arrangements of human affairs in such a way that the arbitrary value content of any policy recommendations is minimized. The purpose is to ensure that judgements among alternative geographical states are made on the basis of reasoned analysis. The job human geographer is like any other scientist is to provide means whereby the full power of human intellect may be applied to the solution of problems. The thesis truly believed that in Indian society where norms play larger role than the law enforcement activities and thus while suggesting policy will not be easy where abundance of evidence of the prevailing policy *versus* norms are in astounding numbers.

Identification of the caste beneficiaries should be the prime importance of various departments. Galanter[12] has advocated "vociferously that the mismatched placed by the law on compensatory privilege thought it open a new vista to opportunities, yet did not provide the corresponding weapon."

The finding of the study suggests that this corresponding weapon (education and economic security) is not equally spread along the caste groups. There is a need of an urgent attention to enhance the quantity but more so the quality to ensure the educational accessibility targeting lower strata of the Indian Society.

Social Security for unorganized sector has been raised from time to time. It becomes more important since casualisation of labour is increasing[13]. It is even more disheartening that instead of protecting the casual labour, Government Bill[14] to amend the Contract Labour (Abolition and Regulation) Act which seeks to delete the provision under which any contract employment may be prohibited. Though trade unions[15] protested the bill and asked the Labour Minister to consider changes only after detailed research and of the recommendations of the Second National Commission to look into the matter of social security in unorganized sector.

Affordable migrant oriented housing policy can break this vicious circle of migration and poverty. The study found that in the wake of costlier houses migrants generally land up squatting along the railway tracks, footpaths, under construction or legal vacant spaces and open drains. Szelenyi[16] provides an approach to this type of problem in persistent in the Hungarian cities "to break that vicious circle. It may be necessary among other things to provide more housing...what kind of houses are to be built and who gets them...A housing policy deserves the name only if it goes beyond questions of construction to ensure that the housing system as a whole does not contribute to the accumulation of social advantages or reduce social mobility.

It is not always necessary to look at the policy makers or the government to guarantee the well-being in the society; what is important to know is the social responsibility of an individual, knowledge (especially it is imperative to tell people about caste system in the past and present context). May be the 'born identity' should not be given too much emphasis.

Picking up from the theoretical chapter (chapter two) and discussion on the discrimination and social equity (chapter six) this study would once again like to reiterate a few things. Along with the criticism of various theories the study realized that there is always sameness in the theories, i.e. the caste phenomena is a vicious circle if cannot be destroyed entirely but can be changed for betterment. Each theory stresses on something important for life and addresses that specific issue. The distributive justice should remain the main area where planner should concentrate. According to the Rawl's theory of justice there are three principles which should be the focus of constitution frame—(i) interpretation of the principle justice so that they define a consistent and complete conception of justice, (ii) to explore the possibilities of the arrangements of the institutions of a constitutional democracy so that these principles are satisfied, and (iii) the foundation of distributive justice comply with the general notion of justice[17]. Thus justice can be defined where each person gets his/her due according to the effort one invests in. There is a need to construct and need to detect the instances of injustice and then method to redress and proper follow up[18]. Though it is very difficult due to escaping routs provided by the caste system are more than one and secondly, market forces are too many and third is that the emergence, of these kinds of situation of the discriminations are rare because this study has found the segregation and not the integration. Jandhalaya also said that discrimination in labour market could not be completed until basic amenities such as water, housing, sanitation are efficiently distributed in the weaker section of society[19]. There is so much variation in the society, which is the greatest impediment in the discrimination studies in Indian Society.

The strategy[20] should be adopted where social awakening mobilisation should not only be appealed in the lower caste groups but the upper caste groups simultaneously juxtaposed in this social revolution by shaking their conscience. As a peroration quoting Sen and Dreze[21]:

> "Public Action is not ....just a question of public delivery and the state initiative. It is also a ...matter of participation by the public in the process of social change. It studies not merely what is done for the public by the state, but also what is done by the public for itself."

Hence, it required to organize the unorganized through participation, mobilization and sensitization of the issues like discrimination on any background.

Future of the Study

This study which has faced many ups and downs and commenced with much difficulty and apprehensions while taking its very step has finally made some headway in the right direction with more of mind reading and interpreting the 'brain waves' besides taking quantitative parameters as well. The study strongly feel if the employers' version of discrimination can be included as a main focus of the study then the conclusion on discrimination can be made with a lot of certainty.

The caste feelings do exist at every step but how these notions affect the economic structure of the society still remains amorphous and the danger of biasness and personal influence too cannot be ignored. Yet the study would like to suggest if employers' side is given more importance with viable questions then perhaps discrimination study may contribute even more significantly. Secondly, if mode of induction, education and age of the workers in formal labour market (which is not difficult to approach) *vis-à-vis* the caste background can be cross-checked with the perspective of formal sector which may give even broader perspective and understanding to the discrimination in the formal organized sector. The third challenge which discrimination study may have is the interpersonal relations in the mix of professions (Middle, lower middle and below lower middle level).

This study believes and hopes for an equitable society and a future for all where there is no prejudice and discrimination. The study ends with a quote by Brian Barry[22]:

> "Though contact with other societies, people come to realize that social arrangements are not natural phenomena but human creation. And what made by human beings can be changed by human being....For a theory of social justice a theory about the kind of social arrangements that can be defended."

This body of research would like to emphasise the role of Geography in providing a distinct dispensation of theory and methods for developmental distributive justice to all citizens by imagining a society less prejudiced and more based on humanitarian principles.

> Prof.James Fairgrieve[23] (1926) expressing his thoughts on the basic values and function of geography principles that "the function of geography is to train future citizens to imagine accurately the conditions of the great world stage and so to help than to think sanely about political and social problems in the world around."

He accurately reposed the future of geography which guides us to build a society on cooperation and coexistence.

NOTES

1. Louise Dumont (1998). (Rev. Ed.) *Homo Heirarchichus: The Caste System and Its Implications*, Oxford India Paper Back, New Delhi. In this revised edition, he mentions Ghurye who notices changing faces of rituals and behavioural parts concerning purity-pollution in towns but the caste groups naturally coalescences manifests the sentiments the solidarity and caste 'conciousness' in his words 'caste patriotism'. Study of Shah in Baroda, where university graduates exposed to high level of modernity, overall do not like to challenge the traditional values of the society. Sachin Chaturvedi says in his findings of urban India that life in town often remained rural in context and spirit. pp. 221-225.
2. Dipankar Gupta (2000). *Interrogating Caste: Understanding Hierarchy and Difference in Indian Society*. Peguine India, New Delhi. p. x.
3. T.N. Madan (1969). "Caste and Development", Book Review, *Economic and Political Weekly*, Vol. IV, No. 5, February, p. 287.
4. Shiv Visvanathan (2001). "The Race for Caste: Prolegomena to the Durban Conference", *Economic and Political Weekly*, Vol. XXXVI, No. 27, July, p. 2531.
5. Papola writes that discrimination is observed less now as compared to 30-40 years back. T.S. Papola: "Social Exclusion and Discrimination in the Labour Market" Working Paper No. 2012/4, Institute for Studies in Industrial Development. http://isidev.nic.in/pdf/WP1204.pdf
6. D.N. Trivedi, *Modernisation of the Caste System in Urbanising India*, author says that the upper caste posed to be more progressive which is a welcome change for a developing and changing social interactions. In Allen G. Noble and Ashok K. Dutt (1977). (ed.) *Indian Urbanisation and Planning: Vehicles of Modernisation*. A Hill Publishing House, Delhi, pp. 148-149.
7. Studies sited in this study have agreed upon that Urbanisation and Urbanism have at least successfully dissociated the caste (social background) and the type of job a person do. The problem of integrating the lower strata of society can be achieved by contexualisation of Urban space. Contexualism (historical, physical, social and mass cultural) which is the main feature of Postmodern Urbanism has successfully bonded well with the past unlike Modern Urbanism. In India urban growth has been mainly focused on the accommodation of the migration and *in situ* while not considering the historical importance of the city. Whether it is Kanpur or Ghaziabad there is little or no importance given to the Contexualism. If given it can certainly check the haywire growth of the city and provide people a dignified space to live in a more integrated way and may subsequently relive the phenomena of residential discrimination

too. Nan Allen (1996), *Post-Modern Urbanism*, Blackwell Publishers. Oxford, UK, pp. 160-161.

8. There are proofs of residential segregation in Western societies. Initial studies were done to find out the pattern of residential segregation in Western societies. This study also found though by default that the pattern of housing is also a reflection of physical segregation of castes in urban areas too yet the percentage may vary from area to area.
9. David Smith (1977), *Human Geography*, p. 318.
10. Thorat (2005). "Reservation and Efficiency: Myth and Reality", *Economic and Political Weekly*, Vol. 40, Issue 9. February 26.
11. Lavid Smith, *op. cit.* pp. 8, 15-16.
12. Marc Galanter (1986). *Competing Equalities: Law and the Backward Classes in British Rule*, Oxford University Press. New Delhi, p. 21.
13. Ramesh C. Dutta (1991), "Public Action, Social Security and Unorganised Sector: Mathadi Labour Market in Maharashtra", *Economic and Political Weekly*, Vol. XXXIII, May 30-June 5th, p. L-2.
14. See *Hindustan Times*, March 7th, 2001, Wednesday, p. 8.
15. 37th Session of The Indian Labour Conference, Hind Majdoor Sabha Publication, New Delhi, p. 22.
16. Ivan Szelenyi (1983), *Urban Inequalities Under State Socialism*, Oxford University Press, Oxford, p. 28.
17. John Rawls (1967), "Distributive Justice", excerpts published in G. Mahajan (1998). *Democracy, Difference and Social Justice*, Oxford, New Delhi.
18. B. Turner (1986). *Equality*, Ellis Horwood Lmt. and Travistock Publication, UK. p. 43.
19. J. Tilak (1980). "Education and Labour Market Discrimination", *Indian Journal of Industrial Relations*, Vol. 16, No. 1 July. p. 112.
20. Bipan Chandra (1994), "Gandhi and Ambedkar: Attitudes towards Caste System" *The Times of India*, editorial 30th September, 1994, p. 6.
21. In Ramesh C. Dutta (1991), p. L-4, *op. cit.*
22. Brian Barry (1989), *Theories of Justice*, Harvester-wheatsheaf, London.
23. W. Wallace (1956) Geography in further education, The Vocational Aspect of Secondary and Further Education, 8: 16, 40-46, DOI: 10.1080/03057875680000061

Bibliography

Books

A.U.P. Ranga Rao (1989), *Urbanization, Occupational Mobility and Social Integration: A Study of Scheduled Castes*, Deep and Deep Publication, New Delhi.

Aijaz Ahmed (1993) (ed.), *Social Structure and Regional Development*, Rawat Publications, New Delhi.

Albert J Reiss. (1961) *Occupation and Social Status*, The Free Press, New York.

Allen G Noble, A S Mukherjee, Baleshwar Thakur and Frank J Costa et al. (2000) *Geogeraphic and Planning Researh Themes for the New Millennium*, Vikas Publishing House, New Delhi.

Allen G. Noble and Ashok K Dutt (ed.) (1977) *Indian Urbanisation and Planning Vehicles of Modernization*, Tata McGraw Hill Publication, Delhi.

Andre Beteille (1974), *Agrarian Social Structure*, Oxford University Press, Delhi.

Andre Betille (1969), *Caste, Class and Power: Changing Patterns of Stratification in a Tanjor Village*, Oxford University Press, Bombay.

Anil Bhatt (1989), *Development and Social Justice: Micro Action by Weaker Sections*, Sage Publication, New Delhi.

Ashenfelter and Rees (1973), *Discrimination in Labour Market*, Princeton University Press, New Jersey.

Aziz Abdul (1984), *Urban Poor and Urban Informal Sector*, Ashish Publishing House, New Delhi.

Baljit Singh (1961), *Next Step in Village India*, Asia Publishing House, Bombay.

Berremann (1979), *Caste and Other Inequalities*, Folklore Institute, Meerut.

Boulding K. (1989), *Three Faces of Power*, Sage Publication, California.

Bourdieu Pierre (1977), *Outline of Theory of Practice*, Cambridge University Press, Cambridge.

Bradley R. Schiller (1980), *The Economics of Poverty and Discrimination*, Prentice Hall, New Jersey.

Breman Jan (1979), *Patronage and Exploitation*, Manohar Publications, New Delhi.

Brian Barry (1989), *Theories of Justice*, Harvester-wheatsheaf, London.

Bruce Lyons, Martin Hollis, and Shaun Hargreaves Heap (1992), *The Theory of Choice: A Critical Guide*, Blackwell, Oxford, UK.

Bryan Turner (1986), *Equality*, Horwood Limited and Chichester Tavistock Publications, London and New York.

Cadene and Holmstrom (1998) (ed.), *Decentralized Production in India*, French Institute of Pondichery and Sage Publications, Delhi.

Cecil Pigou (1952), *Essays in Economics*, Mcmillan, London.

Coleman James (1999), *Foundation of Social Theory*, Cambridge University & Press.

Darity Williams Jr. (1995) (ed.) *Economics and Discrimination*, An Elgar Reference Collection, U.K.

David J. Smith (1979), *Racial Disadvantage in Britain*, Pelican Publications, U.K.

David M. Smith (1994), *Geography and Social Justice*, Blackwell, Oxford, UK

David M. Smith (1977), *Human Geography*, Hodder and Stoughton Education, UK

Deepa Narayan et al. (1997), *Voices of the Poor: Poverty and Social Capital in Tanzania*, World Bank, Washington DC, USA.

Deepak Lal (1988), *Cultural Stability and Economic Stagnation*, Clarendon Press, Oxford.

Deepak Lal (1989), *Aspects of Indian Labour*, Clarendon Press, Oxford.

Dennis Wrong (1988), *Power: Its Form, Bases and Uses*, Basic Blackwell, NY.

Dietrich Rueschemeyer (1986), *Power and the Division of Labour*, Polity Press.

Dipankar Gupta (2000), *Mistaken Modernity: India Between Worlds*, Harper Collins Publication.

Dumont Louise (1998) (Rev. Ed.), *Homo Heirarchichus: The Caste System and Its Implications*, Oxford India Paper Back, New Delhi.

Dwaipayan et al. (ed.) (2004), *Interrogating Social Capital: The Indian Experience*, Sage Publication, New Delhi.

Elster and Hylland (1986) (ed.), *Foundation of Social Choice Theory*, Cambridge University Press, Cambridge.

Eyle and Smith (1988) (ed.), *Qualitative Methods in Human Geography*, Oxford.

Frykensberg (1979), *Land Control and Social Structure in Indian History*, Manohar Publications, New Delhi.

G. Myrdal (1944), *The American Dilemma: The Negro Problem and Modern Democracy*, Harper and Row, New York.

Gerry Becker (1971), (Sec. Ed.), *Economics of Discrimination*, Chicago University Press, Chicago.

Gurpreet Mahahajan (1998), *Democracy, Difference and Social Justice*, Oxford, New Delhi.

Harriss, Kannan, Rodgers (1990), *Urban Labour Market Structure and Job Access in India*, ILO Research Series, 92.

Hodgson, Samulson and Tool (1994) (ed), *Institution and Evolutionary Economics*, Edward Elgar Publishing Company, Vermont.

Huw Johnes (1990), *Population Geography*, West View; Boulder and London.

Ivan Szelenyi (1983), *Urban Inequalities Under State Socialism*, Oxford University Press, Oxford.

J.E. King (1980), *Readings in Labour Economics*, Oxford University Press, London.

K.S. Singh (1992), *People of India*, Oxford University Press, Vol. I and II, New Delhi.

Lester Thurow (1969), *Poverty and Discrimination*, The Brooking, Washington D.C.

Lester Thurow (1975), *Generating Inequality*, Basic Books Inc. Publishing, New York.

Lundahl and Wadensjo (1984), *Unequal Treatment: A Study in the Neo-Classical Theory of Discrimination*, New York University Press, New York.

M.N. Srinivas (1987), *The Dominant Caste and Other Essays*, Oxford University Press, Delhi.

Mancur Olson (1982), *The Rise and Decline of Nations*, Yale University Press, New Haven.

Marc Galanter (1986), *Competing Equalities: Law and The Backward Classes in British Rule*, Oxford University Press, New Delhi.

Mark Holmstrom (1985), *Industry and Inequality*, Cambridge University Press, Cambridge.

Max Weber; A M Henderson, Talcott Parsons (3rd edition) (1996), *Theory of Social and Economic Organisations*, Oxford University Press, N.Y.

McDonough Katze, Reich (ed.) (1994), *Social Structure of Accumulation*, Cambridge University Press, Cambridge.

Mehafey Sitton, and O.L. Davis (1968), *Oral History: A Guide to Teachers and Others*, University of Texas Press, Austin.

Mumtaz Ali Khan (1994), *Identity Formation and Self Identity Among Harizan Elite*, Uppal Publishing House, New Delhi.

P. Rossi (1955), *Why Families Move: A Study in the Social Psychology of Urban Residential Mobility*, Free Press, Glencoe.

Papola and Rodgers (1992), *Labour Institutions and Economic Development in India*, ILO Research Series, 97.

Paranjape (1970), *Caste and Social Change*, National Institute of Community Development, Hyderabad.

Parry, Bremann, Kapadia (ed.) (1999), *The Worlds of Indian Industrial Labour*, Sage Publications, New Delhi.

Pascal (ed.), *Racial Discrimination in Economic Life*, Lexington, Mass, D.C.

Paul Baron (1957), *The Political Economy of Growth* , Monthly Review Press, New York.

Quigeley Declan (1993), *The Interpretation of Caste*, Clarendon Press, Oxford.

R. Jayaraman (1981), *Caste and Class*, Hindustan Publishing Corporation, Delhi.

R.A.P. Singh (1984), *Kin, Clan and Land Reforms*, Rawat Publisher, Jaipur.

R.C. Sarikwal (1978), *Sociology of Growing Town*, Ajanta Publication, New Delhi.

R.L. Johnson and G.V. Johnson (ed.) (1990), *Economic Valuation of Natural Resources: Issues, Theory and Applications,* Westview Press, Boulder, USA.

R.S. Tiwari (1990), *Role of Informal Sector in Urban Communities: A Study of Kanpur*, Giri Institute of Development Studies. Lucknow.

Rajesh Gill (1994) *Slums as Urban Villages*, Rawat Publications, Jaipur.

Ray Marshall and Perlman R. (1972), *Anthology of Labour Economics: Readings and Commentary*, Wiley, New York.

Reynolds and Lloyd (1995) *The Structure of Labour Market: Wage and Labour Mobility in Theory and Practice*, Green Wood Press Publishers. Connecticut.

Reynolds, Masters and Mosers (1987), *Economics of Labour*, Prentice Hall, New Jersey.

Richard D. Lambert (1963), *Workers, Factories and Social Changes*, Princeton University Press, Bombay.

Russel (1921), *Principles of Social Reconstruction*, Ruskin House, London.

S.N. Mehrotra (1964), *Labour Problems in India*, S. Chand and Company, Delhi.

Satish Sabarwal (1978), *Process and Institution in Urban India*, Vikas Publishing House, New Delhi.

Satish Saberwal (1990) (Sec. Rev. Ed.), *Mobile Men: Limits to Social Change in Urban Punjab,* Indian Institute of Advanced Study, Shimla in Association with Manohar Publications, New Delhi.

Shah and Desai (1988), *Division and Hierarchy*, Hindustan Publication House, Delhi.

Shitla Prasad Saxena (1937), *Wages and Labour Conditions in Cawnpore,* Superintendent, Printing and Stationary, United Province, Allahabad.

Sidney and Webb (1891), *The Wages of Men and Women: Should They be Equal*, Fabian Society.

Solaun and Krounus Sidney (1973), *Discrimination Without Violence*, Interscience Publications, Wiley.

Sukhatme and Sukhatme (1997) *Sampling Theory of Surveys with Applications*, Piyush Publications, Delhi.

T.R. Venkata Subramanyam (1973), *Group Prejudice in India*, Shree Ram Center for Industrial Relations and Human Resources, New Delhi.

V.C. Subramanyam (1973), *Group Prejudice in India*, Shree Ram Centre for Industrial Relations and Human Resources, New Delhi.

W. Wallace (1956), *Geography in further education, The Vocational Aspect of Secondary and Further Education*, 8:16, 40-46, DOI: 10.1080/03057875680000061

William Harold Hutt (1964), *The Economics of the Colour Bar*, The Institution of Economic Affairs Limited, London.

Yogesh Atal (1968), *The Changing Frontiers of Caste*, National Publication, New Delhi.

Journals

A.C Akerlof. (1980), "A Theory of Social Custom of Which Unemployment may be one Consequence", *Quarterly Journal of Economics*,Vol.102.

A.C. Akerlof (1976) "The Economics of Caste and of the Rat Race and other Woeful Tales", *Quarterly Journal of Economics*,Vol.90.

Alexis Marcus (1973), "A Theory of Labour Market Discrimination with Independent Utilities", *American Economic Review*, Vol. 45.

Amiya Kumar Bagchi (1993), 'Rent Seeking', New Political Economy and Negation of Politics", *Economic and Political Weekly*, Aug. 21, 1993, Vol No.p

Andre Bettielle (1991), "The Reproduction of Inequality", *Contribution to Indian Sociology*, January, Vol. 25 No. 13-28

Avery Derek R (2003), "Racial Differences in Perceptions of Starting Salaries: How Failing to Discriminate can Perpetuate Discrimination", *Journal of Business and Psychology*, Vol. 17, No. 4 Summer.

Avtar Singh Dhesi and A.K. Gumbar (1983), "Earning Determination, Earning Differential and settlement Behaviour of Migrant Industrial Workers: Amritsar City", *Artha Vijnana*, 1983, Vol. 25, N.1.

Avtar Singh Dhesi and Harbans Singh (1995) "Education, Labour Market Distortions and Relative Earning of Different Religion Caste Categories in India: A Case Study of Delhi, *Canadian Journal for Development Studies,* December.

Banerjee and Knight (1985), "Caste Discrimination in the Indian Urban Labour Market", *Journal of Development Economics*,Vol.17.

Beach and Finnie (1988), "Family Background in an Extended Earning-Generation Model: Further Evidence", *Eastern Economic Journal*, Vol. XIV, No. 1, Jan-March 1988.

Becker and Chiswick (1966), "Education and Distribution of Earning", *American Economic Review*, Vol VI.

Dennis L. Clason & Thomas J. Dormody (1965), "Analyzing Data Measured by Individual Likert-Type Items", *Journal of Agriculture Education*, issue 3.

E. Rathbone (1977), "The Remuneration of Women's Services", *Economic Journal*, Vol 45.

Elaine Sorensen (1990), "The Crowding Hypothesis and Comparable Worth", *Journal for Human Resource*, Vol 25, No. 1.

Evan Osborne (2001), "Culture, Development and Government: Reservations in India", *Economic Development and Cultural Change*, Vol. 49.

F. Edgeworth (1922), "Equal Pay to Men and Women for Equal Work" *Economic Journal*, vol. 32.

George Borjas (1992), "Ethnic Capital and Intergenerational Mobility", *Quarterly Journal of Economics*, Vol.107, No. 1.

Glen G Cain (1966), "The Challenges of Segmented Labor Market to the Orthodox Theory: A Survey", *Journal of Economic Literature*. December.

Graham Hobbs (2000), "What is Social Capital? A Brief Literature Overview", *Economic and Research Foundation* June.

Glen G. Cain (1975), "The Challenge of Dual and Radical Theories of the Labour market to Orthodox Theory", *American Economic Association*, Vol 65, No. 2. May.

H.R. Collins (1971), "Functional and Conflict Theories of Educational Stratification", *American Sociological Review*, Vol. 36.

Harold Gould (1969), "Toward a 'Jati Model' for Indian Politics", *Economic and Political Weekly*, Feb 1st, 1969.

Haworth, Gwartney and Howarth (1975), "Earning, Productivity and Changes in Employment: Discrimination During the 1960's", *The American Economic Review*, March, Vol. 65, No.1.

J.B.G. Tilak (1980), "Education and Labour Market Discrimination", *Indian Journal of Industrial Relations*, Vol. 16, No.1, July.

J.E. Stiglitz (1973), 'Approaches to the Economics of Discrimination', *American Economic Review*, vol. 63, No. 2.

James J. Heckman (2000), "Policies to Foster Human Capital", *Research in Economics*, No. 54.

Jan Bremman (1976), "A Dualistic Labour System? A Critique of the Informal Sector- III", *Economic and Political Weekly*, Vol. XI, No. 50, Dec, 11 1976.

K. Gannicott (1985), "Women, Wages and Discrimination: Some Evidences from Taiwan", *Economic Development and Cultural Change*. Vol. 34, No.4.

K.L. Sharma (1969), "Stresses in Caste Stratification: A Study of Six Villages in Rajasthan", *Economic and Political Weekly*. Jan 18th 1969, Vol. iv, No.3.

Karla Hoff and Priyanka Pandey (2005), 'Opportunity is not Everything', *Economic Transition*, Vol. 13 (3).

Kates, R.W. (1962), *Hazard and Choice Perception in Flood Plain Management*, Department of Geography Research Paper no. 78, University of Chicago Press.

Kirk, W., (1952), "Historical Geography and the concept of the behavioural environment". *Indian Geography Journal*, Silver Jubilee Issue, 152-60.

Knight and Sobot (1982), "Labour Market Discrimination in a Poor Urban Economy", *Journal of Development Studies*.

Mark Holmstorm (1972), "Caste and Status in an Indian City", *Economic and Political Weekly*, Vol. VII, No. 15.

Mark Holmstrom (1993), "Flexible Specialization in India?" *Economic and Political Weekly*, Aug. 28th, vol.XXVIII, no. 35.

Milicent Fawcet (1918), "Equal Pay for Equal Work", *Economic Journal*, Vol. 28.

Narang (2001), "World Conference Against Racism: Prospects and Challenges", *Economic and Political Weekly*, July 7th, Vol.xxxvi, No. 27.

Olof Aslund & Dan Olof Rooth (2004), "Shifts in Attitudes and Labour Market Discrimination: Swedish Experiences after 9-11

Paul M. Koroscil (1971), The Behavioural Environmental Approach, The Royal Geographical Society (with the Institute of British Geographers), Vol. 3, No. 2, pp. 96-99, https://www.jstor.org/stable/20000543 accessed on 20th June 2014.

R.E. Freeman (1973), "Decline of Labour Market Discrimination and Economic Analysis", *American Economic Review*, Vol 63, No.2.

Ramesh C. Dutta (1991) "Public Action, Social Security and Unorganised Sector: Mathadi Labour Market in Maharshtra", *Economic and Political Weekly*, Vol. XXXIII, May 30-June 5th, 1991.

Ray Marshall (1972), "The Economics of Discrimination", *Journal of Economic Literature*, Vol. 12.

Rees (1966), "Information Networks in Labour Markets", *American Economic Review*.

Richard Hartshorne (1939), "Geography as the Science of Distributions", *Annals of the Association of American Geographers*, 29:3, 127-129, DOI: 10.1080/00045603909357289 accessed on 20th June 2014

S.K. Thorat (2005), "Reservation and Efficiency: Myth and Reality", *Economic and Political Weekly*, Vol 40, Issue 9, Feb 26.

S.K. Thorat (2001), "Caste and Economic Discrimination: Theory and Evidence on Rural Labour Market", *Artha Vijnana*, Vol XLIII, Nos 1-2, March June 2001.

S.K. Sasikumar and Anup K. Karen (2010), "Skill Mapping in Indian Labour market: Supply Side Potential and emerging Demand Scenario", *Labour and Development*, Vol. 16-17, June 2010

Sargant Florence (1931) "A statistical contribution to the theory Women's Wages", *Economic Journal*, Vol 41.

Sarita Agarwal (1993), "Gender Discrimination in Labour market: A Review of Literature", *The Indian Journal of Economics*, Vol.36, No. 2.

Sheela Rai (2002), "Social and Conceptual Background to the Policy of Reservation", *Economic and Political Weekly*, Oct. 19, 2002

Shiv Visvanathan (2001), "The Race for Caste: Prolegomena to the Durban Conference", *Economic and Political Weekly*, Vol. XXXVI, No. 27, July 2001.

Steele and Aronson (1995), Stereotype Threat and the Intellectual Test Performance of African Americans, *Journal of Pers Social Psychology*, 69(5)

T.N. Madan (1969) "Caste and Development", Book Review, *Economic and Political Weekly*, Vol. IV, No. 5, Feb.

Vani K. Borooah, A. Dubey, Sriya Iyer et al. (2007), "Has Job Reservations in India Been Effective? Caste, Religion, and Economic Status" (with), *Development and Change*, Vol. 38, No. 3

Documents and Government Publication

Bipan Chandra (1994) "Gandhi and Ambedkar: Attitudes towards Caste System," *The Times of India*, editorial 30th September, 1994.

37th Session of The Indian Labour Conference, Hind Majdoor Sabha Publication, New Delhi.

Small Industry and Social Change (1966), UNESCO Research Center on Social and Economic Development in Southern Asia, Allied Publisher, Delhi.

World Labour Report 3 (1988)

World Development Report (2006), Co-published by the World Bank and Oxford University Press, New York.

Hindustan Times, March 7th 2001 Wednesday.

Brochure on reservation for Scheduled Castes and Scheduled Tribes (1987), (7th ed.) Govt. of India, Ministry of Personal and Public Grievances.

Report of the Committee on the Unorganised Sector Statistics: National Statistical Commission, GOI February 2012

Web References of Articles

1. Charles and Guryan (2007)http://www.nber.org/papers/w13661 pdf
2. http://www.arthapedia.in/index.php?title=Worker_(Census_Definition)
3. http://www.livemint.com/2010/06/14212328/The-business-of-caste-in-India.html
4. http://www.scmp.com/comment/insight-opinion/article/1307072/indias-bias-against-women-workplace-saps-economic-growth
5. http://www.igidr.ac.in/pdf/publication/WP-20120017.pdf
6. http://faculty.arts.ubc.ca/alahiri/intergenration_4.pdf
7. www.ourworld.compuserve.com/homepages.March2006

Index